From Reform to Revolution

From Reform to Revolution

The Demise of Communism in China and the Soviet Union

Minxin Pei

Harvard University Press
Cambridge, Massachusetts, and London, England

First Harvard University Press paperback edition, 1998

Library of Congress Cataloging-in-Publication Data

Pei, Minxin.
   From reform to revolution : the demise of communism
in China and the Soviet Union / Minxin Pei.
      p. cm.
   Includes index.
   ISBN 0–674–32563–X (cloth)
   ISBN 0–674–32564–8 (pbk.)
   1. Communism—China. 2. Communism— Soviet Union.
3. China—Economic conditions—1976–. 4. Soviet Union—
Economic conditions—1985–1991. 5. Mass media—China.
6. Mass media—Soviet Union. I. Title.
HX418.5.P43 1994
321.9′2′0947—dc 20   93–50948

For Meizhou

Contents

From Reform to Revolution

Introduction

The most important political change of the late 1980s was the ending of the Cold War. This change originated primarily in the wave of reforms and revolutions that swept over all the established communist systems between 1979 and 1991, excluding only North Korea and Cuba.[1] Reforms took place in the less developed communist systems of China, Albania, and Vietnam, as well as in the more developed states of Hungary, Poland, and the Soviet Union. They were launched by communist regimes that had come into power via indigenous revolutions (China, the Soviet Union, Yugoslavia, Albania, and Vietnam) and by those installed and maintained by the Soviet military power (Hungary, Poland, and Bulgaria). Reforms were undertaken both in countries that had experienced similar changes, albeit inconsistently and briefly, between the mid-1960s and early 1970s, and in countries for which the same processes were a novel phenomenon (China, Vietnam, Mongolia, and Albania). In communist states that initially resisted reforms, such as East Germany, Czechoslovakia, Romania, and Bulgaria, the old regimes were eventually overthrown by popular uprisings—peacefully in East Germany, Bulgaria, and Czechoslovakia, and violently in Romania. In the most powerful communist country in the world, the Soviet Union, reform led to revolution and the eventual disintegration of the regime in 1991.

This late-twentieth-century wave of reforms and revolutions poses immense challenges to three communities: the nations in which these changes have occurred and are still unfolding, the international community that is absorbing the revolutionary impact of these events, and the academic community that has been studying them since the late 1970s.

For the 1.6 billion people—nearly one-third of the world's population—in a dozen countries previously ruled by communist dictatorships, this surge of reforms and revolutions has reshaped the political, economic, and social institutions of their states, redirected the future of their societies, and expanded their freedom. For the international community, the changes of the

1980s have put an end to the Cold War, reset the global balance of power, and brought more than twenty newly independent states into the international system. For the academic community in general, and social scientists in particular, the radical transformations of the 1980s raise new questions about their disciplines, especially given the sobering fact that neither students of comparative communism nor social science theories had forecast these developments.[2]

This wave of reforms and revolutions continues into the 1990s. The collapse of communist dictatorships in Eastern and Central Europe and the former Soviet Union has not led to the creation of genuine democracies or functioning market economies. At the beginning of the 1990s, most ex-communist societies were mired in severe economic and political crises. The pervasive corrosion of communist rule by market forces in China and Vietnam had not yet caused the downfall of the authoritarian regimes in Beijing and Hanoi. Although most political scientists share a broad agreement as to what the political systems in these countries were changed *from*, they are less clear about what these former communist regimes have been changed *into*. Indeed, the patterns of political change in the communist world in the 1980s and early 1990s, as summarized in Table I.1, vary significantly among individual countries, indicating the complexities, unpredictability, and ambiguities of regime change from communism.

One striking feature of these patterns, however, is that, between 1979 and 1993, various attempts at transitions from communism resulted in only a handful of successful regime changes in which semiconsolidated democratic institutions began to function. One may include in this category the Czech Republic, Hungary, Slovenia, and Poland.

Certain postcommunist political systems, including Serbia, Romania, the former Soviet Central Asian republics, and Mongolia, where ex-communist leaders won the first open elections and maintained power, defy easy classifications. In parts of the former Soviet Union and Yugoslavia, the breakdown of the old political order was followed by the collapse of interethnic peace, the fracturing of the multiethnic state, and the eruption of civil war between former republics.

In China and Vietnam, the Communist Party formally remained in power despite enormous market-oriented economic changes and periodic challenges from emerging opposition movements. The institutional, economic, and ideological foundations of orthodox communist rule had been so seriously undermined, however, that by the early 1990s "communism" no longer accurately described the autocracies in these countries. The three pillars of orthodox communism in China and Vietnam—the party-state, a planned economy, and communist ideology—have been made hollow by (1) the increasing technocratization of the state at the expense of the Communist Party; (2) the rapid transformation of a planned economy into an increasingly marketized one; and (3) the dramatic retreat of communist ideology from a revolutionary-utopian doctrine to a set of conservative-defensive dogmas that serve principally to legitimize the continual rule of the autocratic regime.[3]

Despite the variations in regime transition in established communist states, two salient historical-structural factors universally influenced the patterns of transition: the political origin of the old regime and the country's level of economic development.[4] As a group, Soviet-installed communist regimes tended to experience fewer complications, and were replaced by new regimes in a shorter period of time, during transition than those created by internal revolutions. By contrast, some homegrown communist regimes experienced total collapse, as was the case in the former Soviet Union, Yugoslavia, and Albania, following a period of regime-initiated reforms and ensuing political turmoil. In the postcommunist former Soviet republics, Russia being the most representative, democratic consolidation encountered severe complications arising from deep division within society and extreme political polarization. Other homegrown communist regimes, for example, China, Vietnam, and Cuba, managed to resist the global tide of democratization.

The level of economic development was also a key variable affecting the outcome of regime transition. All communist regimes that have made the transition to democratic forms of government were located in the "transition zone"—a "middle economic stratum" between $1,000 and $6,000 in annual per capita Gross National Product (GNP).[5] Conversely, communist states at lower levels of development and with large rural populations remained authoritarian, an exception being Albania, whose opposition was finally able to defeat the communists in March 1992 after the country virtually collapsed into civil disorder.

The breakdown of communist regimes in the late 1980s will engage students of comparative politics for years to come. But the present study focuses on two central issues: the paths of change and variations in transitional experiences, and the revolutionary dynamics of transition—Why did initially limited reforms in the two most powerful communist states, China and the former Soviet Union, turn into revolutions or assume a revolutionary character?

In Chapters 1 and 2 I will develop two interrelated analytical frameworks to make two key arguments: first, regime transition from communism is qualitatively distinct from transition from authoritarianism, because it involves the dual process of democratization and marketization. The sequencing of the twin process generates three possible routes of transition. Although elite perception of policy alternatives and subsequent choice were important factors, patterns of transition in former communist states were

Table 1.1 Patterns of transition in established communist regimes, 1979–1992

	More developed communist states	Moderately developed communist states	Less developed communist states
Soviet-installed regimes	Democratization via elections or peaceful revolutions, with the opposition in control of the government immediately: Poland (1988–1989) Hungary (1988–1989) Czechoslovakia (1989–1990)[a] East Germany (1989–1990)	Democratization via elections, with the opposition unable to maintain control of the government: Bulgaria (1989–1992)	Democratization via elections, with ex-communists in control of the government: Mongolia (1989–1992)
		Transition via violent revolution, with ex-communists in control of the government: Romania (1989–1992)	No transition: North Korea

Homegrown communist regimes	Democratization leading to national disintegration and the collapse of the old regimes, resulting in mixed regime types, civil war, and ethnic violence: Soviet Union (1985–1991)[b] Yugoslavia (1989–1991)[b]	Democratization via elections, with the opposition in control of the government after two elections: Albania (1990–1992)
	No transition: Cuba	Ongoing transition to a market economy without democratization: China (1978–1992) Vietnam (1986–1992)

a. Czechoslovakia split into two countries, the Czech Republic and Slovakia, in January 1993.
b. Both the Soviet Union and Yugoslavia disintegrated in 1991.

profoundly influenced by the political origins of the old regime, the social structures and levels of economic development of these countries, and certain initial advantages upon the inception of transition, such as past popular resistance to the old regime, prior experience of government-sponsored partial economic reforms, and the reach of the state.

Second, in transitions from communism, limited reforms tend to become revolutions when the balance of power between the state and society precipitously shifts in favor of the latter. This occurs as a result of both the accelerated institutional decay of the state and the rapid mobilization of previously excluded social groups, leading to swift resource gains by these groups, which thus provide them with the means to radicalize reform.

In testing this proposition, I will briefly summarize and compare the radicalization of economic reform in China (1979–1992) and political reform in the Soviet Union (1985–1991) in Chapter 2. In addition, to generate comparative insights into the microprocesses of regime transition, I will present two detailed case studies (Chapters 3 and 4) that will focus on the emergence of the private sector in China and the Soviet Union. In the other two case studies (Chapters 5 and 6) I will investigate the process of democratization as reflected in the liberalization of the mass media in the two countries.

The choice of the four case studies reflects our basic understanding of regime transition as a restructuring of state-society relations. The definition of a political "regime" here centers on the institutional (formal) and substantive arrangements of power, since such arrangements determine who gains access to power and how that power is exercised.[6] Thus defined, political regimes may be divided into sub-categories according to their institutional arrangements, such as one-party, multiparty, military, or sultanistic regimes. Because the arrangement of power in any polity sets the boundaries between the state and society, the regime becomes the *nexus* between the two.

Analytically, a regime is distinct from the state, which is a Weberian conception narrowly defined here as administrative, law-enforcement, and security-military organizations under the centralized control of a supreme authority.[7] Empirically, the two often overlap and are, fundamentally, symbiotic. A regime uses the instruments of the state to maintain itself and advance its goals. And the state, largely through the power arrangement formalized by the regime, extracts resources from society to keep itself in existence.[8] Changes in the regime type inescapably affect the structure and capacity of the state and vice versa. Indeed, any regime change or transition entails more than changes in the formal institutions of the polity.

More important, regime change leads to a *significant* and *qualitative* restructuring of state-society relations through the redistribution of power between the various political entities collectively known as "the state" and the innumerable social, cultural, and economic organs aggregately called "society." Regime change also has a profound impact on the state's and society's respective autonomy and capacities. It may *expand* or *reduce* the scope of political and economic freedom for society, *increase* or *diminish* its political capacities. In the case of a democratizing regime transition, such freedom and capacities, primarily political liberty and power, are expanded.

The most ambiguous form of regime transition discussed here is that from a communist regime to a postcommunist authoritarian one, as exemplified in the ongoing transitions in China and Vietnam. In these instances, the expansion of political rights, liberty, and political capacities of societal groups is insignificant, but the expansion of economic and civic freedom and private economic resources is substantial. This is typically the case after postcommunist authoritarian regimes introduce market forces to reform planned economies and subsequently are compelled to cede to society a high degree of economic and civic freedom, as well as material resources. The transition from a communist to a postcommunist authoritarian regime should thus be considered a significant and positive development in the strengthening and expansion of the autonomy and political capacities of society.

Conversely, the autonomy and political capacities of society are reduced in cases of *reverse* regime transition; that is, the replacement of democracies by authoritarian or totalitarian regimes, as in the first and second reverse waves of democratization in 1922–1942 and 1958–1975,[9] or in the replacement of authoritarian regimes by totalitarian ones, as was the case following the communist revolutions in Russia, Albania, China, Vietnam, and Cuba.

In examining the restructuring of state-society relations in communist countries in the 1980s and early 1990s, we must pay special attention to the mass media and the development of the private economic sector for three reasons. First, these two sectors are *arenas* where societal actors and the agents of the state compete for control. Second, they are *power-producing sectors* that generate political and economic resources coveted by both autonomy-minded societal actors and control-hungry agents of the state. A society without much control of the mass media is too weak to resist the power of the state in influencing public opinion, and a society deprived of private economic resources is also devoid of the means of defending and expanding its freedom and capacity.

Conversely, a state with dwindling control over public opinion and economic activities will inevitably see its ability to dominate society diminish. Lastly, changes in the degree of the liberalization of the mass media and the rise of the private sector are the two important *indicators* of the progress of regime transition from communism—one in terms of political liberalization (a key sub-process of democratization) and the other in terms of marketization.

Although the reforms in China and the Soviet Union have aroused enormous intellectual curiosity and attracted wide scholarly attention in recent years,[10] few students of comparative communism or specialists on the two nations have attempted to approach regime transition in the two countries by apply-ing an integrated analytical framework. Part of this problem may be caused by the following important differences between China and the Soviet Union at the time of transition:

Level of economic development. China was a predominantly agrarian society at a low level of development, whereas the Soviet Union was an in-dustrialized society at a moderate-to-high level of development, though with significant regional and sectoral disparities.

Sociological characteristics. China had a low urbanization rate (18.9 percent in 1979) and a high illiteracy rate (23.7 percent in 1982) in the late 1970s and early 1980s; by comparison, the Soviet Union was highly urban-ized (65.7 percent in 1986) and had a negligible illiteracy rate. Although both were multinational empires, China had a higher ethnic homogeneity, with Han Chinese accounting for 87 percent of the population. In the Soviet Union, non-Russians accounted for nearly 50 percent of the population in the late 1980s.

Sequences of reform. Chinese reform started in the economy, whereas Soviet reform was led by political liberalization after a brief, abortive at-tempt at economic reform between 1985 and 1986.

Generational differences of the ruling elites. China was ruled by the first-generation revolutionaries who founded the People's Republic.[11] These elites tended to be more committed to the maintenance of the Communist Party's monopoly of power than were third- or fourth-generation elites. After all, who would expect Lenin to reform a Leninist state or Stalin to dismantle totalitarianism? By comparison, the post-Brezhnev ruling elites in the Soviet Union represented by Mikhail Gorbachev were fourth-generation, post-totalitarian rulers thrice-removed from the communist revolutionary experi-ence and state-building process. Their personal commitment to the ideology and institutions of communism lacked the intensity exhibited by their Chi-nese (or Cuban and Vietnamese) counterparts.

Despite such differences, China and the Soviet Union shared important *political-institutional* characteristics. Prior to reform, both countries were ruled by a communist regime with a monist party-state, a planned economy, and a Marxist-Leninist ideology as its legitimating principle. Reforms in each country, moreover, were triggered by intraelite power struggles during the succession crisis—China in 1976–1978 and the USSR in 1983–1985. Both were homegrown Marxist-Leninist regimes that came to power through communist-led revolutions. These similarities suggest that the two countries should experience analogous *process dynamics* during regime transition, making a comparative project feasible and rewarding.

There are two additional compelling justifications for undertaking this comparative study. From a geopolitical perspective, political and economic changes in China and the former Soviet Union affect the international balance of power. The long-term global impact of the collapse of the Soviet empire in Eastern Europe in 1989 and the disintegration of the Soviet Union itself in 1991 cannot be truly measured for years to come. The changes in China since the late 1970s will also reshape the international system in the coming decades.

From an academic perspective, the collapse of the Soviet Union rekindled scholarly debates about the viability and strategy of reforming communism. Similarly, the demise of communist regimes in the former Soviet Union and Eastern Europe led scholars to question the durability of the "communist" regime in China and elsewhere and to rethink Gorbachev's failed experiment.[12] Should he have adopted a different strategy? Does China's prosperity and tranquility in the early 1990s vindicate its "neoauthoritarian" model, that is, economic liberalization without democratization? Does the catastrophic outcome of *glasnost* and *perestroika* negate the democratization-first reform approach? Answers to these and other important questions are impossible without undertaking a comparative project which reexamines the dynamics of regime change in China and the former Soviet Union.

Regime Transition in Communist States

I

t is tempting to treat the process of regime transition from communism as identical to the regime transitions from authoritarianism that occurred between the mid-1970s and mid-1980s in southern Europe, Latin America, and East Asia.[1] Unlike regime transition from other forms of authoritarian rule, however, transition from communist rule must be considered a distinctive *dual transition*.[2] Compared with pretransition communist regimes, pretransition authoritarian regimes of varying types—such as a strong one-party dictatorship (Taiwan), military juntas and dictatorships (Greece, Argentina, Chile, Brazil, and South Korea), and personal dictatorships (Francisco Franco's Spain, Antonio Salazar's Portugal, Alfredo Stroessner's Paraguay, and Ferdinand Marcos's Philippines)—obviously lacked the institutional capacity and means to control society that characterized established communist regimes.

For one thing, none of the authoritarian regimes possessed a tightly organized ruling party that had penetrated all the institutions of the state to the same extent that the Communist Party had through its *nomenklatura* system and army of *apparatchiki*. Second, the scope of civil society, measured in terms of autonomous civic, labor, religious, professional, and business associations, was substantially broader in authoritarian than in communist states. These preexisting organs of civil society, as case studies of transitions from authoritarianism to democracy have noted, acted as coalition partners of the opposition and facilitated the transition process.[3]

The third and perhaps most important difference between authoritarianism and communism was that all the authoritarian regimes had market economies with relatively well defined private property rights, whereas none of the established communist regimes had a market economy or legally protected private assets of production before transition. This singular institutional difference vastly complicates the transformation of a dual-closed system (a communist dictatorship and a state-dominated planned economy) into a dual-open system (a market economy polyarchy). In transitions from communism, the inauguration of competitive political processes and the establishment and consolidation of democratic institutions must occur, either simultaneously or sequentially, with the creation of a market-based economic system and the destruction of the planned economy.

In market economy authoritarian systems in the developing world, the state also wields a considerable influence in managing the economy through large public sectors. However, the intervention of such governments in economic activities is dwarfed by the monopolistic role of the state in established communist systems in running prereform planned economies both quantitatively and qualitatively, as depicted in Table 1.1.

In pretransition communist systems, the state owned and directly managed nearly all productive assets, the most important being the land. Private property was confined to household belongings and savings. Private ownership of productive assets was either banned or limited to insignificant quantities. The state also monopolized the distribution of all producer goods and an overwhelming majority of consumer goods. Most members of the work force were employed in state or quasi-state sectors. Thus, the economic institutions of state-socialist economies not only performed purely economic functions, but also acted as mechanisms of social control and political mobilization for the state.

This all-embracing institutional framework of direct state ownership and management of the economy was unmatched, as Table 1.1 shows, by any of the noncommunist authoritarian regimes in the developing world. In these authoritarian systems, direct state ownership of productive assets and the size of the public sector were substantial—and often excessively large—by Western (chiefly American) standards. Compared with prereform communist regimes, their level of state control of the economy was low. In most of these authoritarian systems, some of which have undergone democratization since the early 1980s, the state sector contributed between 10 and 30 percent of the gross industrial output.[4] It is thus more precise to treat regime transition from noncommunist authoritarian rule as one-dimensional, or *democratizing,* regime change.

The complex interaction between economic reform and regime transition has received serious attention in recent scholarship.[5] Recognizing the qualitative difference in economic systems between authoritarian and communist regimes, Adam Przeworski argued that, despite some similarities between the macroeconomic crises in Eastern Europe after the collapse of communism and those that afflicted most Latin American countries on the eve of transition, the economic structure of the Eastern European countries was "harder to transform . . . economic reforms in Latin America are a matter of, at most, 'structural adjustment,' while in Eastern Europe they call for a transition from system to system, from socialism to capitalism."[6]

In the present analytical framework, the term "democratization" incorporates the two dimensions of polyarchy—contestation and inclusion—first proposed by Robert Dahl. Regime change from communist systems, as we will see later in Figure 1, must thus be viewed as dual transition involving both *democratization* (liberalization and inclusion) and *marketization* (the creation of a market economy). Figure 1 differs from Dahl's model of democratization in that it compresses liberalization and inclusion into one dimension while adding the economic dimension of transition, which Dahl treated as a given and overlooked in his analysis of democratization. Figure 1 also differs from the regime transition model proposed by O'Donnell and Schmitter, who defined the two dimensions of regime transition in authoritarian regimes as "liberalization" and "democratization." Like Dahl, O'Donnell and Schmitter did not take into account the connection between change in the economic system and the political system during regime transition.[7]

Crisis of Communism and the Initiation of Reform

Crisis and Elite Perception

Why did established communist regimes initiate reforms? What were the specific factors that motivated the governing elites of communist states to make the critical choice of changing their political and economic systems in the 1980s?

Historically, nearly all reforms initiated by authoritarian regimes were triggered by systemic crises and undertaken as a self-preserving response by these regimes.[8] More recently, political and economic crises also led to regime transitions in a large number of authoritarian systems.[9] Typically, such crises included military defeat, external threats, succession power struggles, economic collapse, the breakdown of key political institutions, and a sudden intensification of popular demands for social justice and political participation.

Similarly, communist regimes that opted for reform in the late 1970s and mid-1980s were faced with acute political and economic crises that the top leaders of these regimes perceived as serious threats to the survival of communist systems. Deng Xiaoping's remark on the urgency of reform was an apt description of crisis as a catalyst of reform. "If we again fail to implement reform," Deng said in December 1978, "our modernization program and socialist cause will be doomed."[10] In Vietnam, the popular slogan *doi moi hay la chet* (renewal or death) captured the severity of the crisis of communism and the hope placed in reform. Shortly after assuming office in December 1986, the new general secretary of the Communist Party of Vietnam,

Table 1.1   Different degrees of state intervention in the economy: communist systems vs. other political systems

	Share of state-owned enterprises in total output[a] (in percentages)	Share of state-owned enterprises in total nonagricultural employment (in percentages)
Pretransition communist systems		
Bulgaria (1970)[b]	99.7	—
Czechoslovakia (1986)[c]	97.0	—
East Germany (1982)[c]	96.5	94.2
Soviet Union (1985)[d]	96.0	95.9
Cuba (1988)[b]	95.9	—
Romania (1980)[b]	95.5	—
Poland (1980)[c]	83.4	73.4
China (1978)[e]	77.6	78.4
Hungary (1975)[c]	73.3	70.9
Vietnam (1987)[b]	71.4	—
Selected authoritarian regimes[f]		
Tunisia (1982)[g]	56.0	55.0
Brazil (1982)[g]	31.0	14.0
Pakistan (1982)[g]	26.0	22.0
Singapore (1983)[c]	25.0	—
Chile (1981)[h]	24.0	5.0
Egypt (1980)[i]	22.0	17.2
Mexico (1985)[j]	15.5	5.2
Taiwan (1978–1980)[c]	13.5	—
South Korea (1981–1983)[c]	9.0	7.0
Selected less developed democracies		
India (1982)[g]	35.0	23.0
Venezuela (1978–1980)[c]	27.5	—
Turkey (1985)[c]	11.2	20.0
Selected industrial democracies		
Israel (1982)[g]	33.0	13.0
Sweden (1982)[g]	26.0	17.0
France (1982)[c]	16.5	14.6
Italy (1982)[c]	14.0	15.0
United Kingdom (1978)[c]	11.1	8.2
West Germany (1982)[c]	10.7	7.8

Table 1.1   (continued)

	Share of state-owned enterprises in total output[a] (in percentages)	Share of state-owned enterprises in total nonagricultural employment (in percentages)
Australia (1978–1979)[c]	9.4	4.0
Netherlands (1971–1973)[c]	3.6	8.0
United States (1983)[c]	1.3	1.8

a. Unless otherwise noted, output here includes only state-owned enterprises in industrial/commercial activities; it excludes government-provided services.

b. Share of the public sector. Janos Kornai, *The Socialist System: The Political Economy of Communism* (Princeton: Princeton University Press, 1992), p. 72.

c. From Branko Milanovic, *Liberalization and Entrepreneurship: Dynamics of Reform in Socialism and Capitalism* (Armonk, New York: M. E. Sharpe, 1989), pp. 15–20.

d. The employment figure is for 1988. D. J. Peterson, "New Data Published on Employment and Unemployment in the USSR," *Radio Liberty: Report on the USSR,* January 5, 1990, p. 4.

e. Gross value of industrial output. *Statistical Yearbook of China, 1989,* pp. 101 and 267.

f. Democratization has occurred in Brazil, Chile, South Korea, and Taiwan since the above data were collected.

g. Share of industrial GDP and industrial employment, World Bank staff estimates. Mahmood Ali Ayub and Sven Olaf Hegstad, *Public Industrial Enterprises: Determinants of Performance* (Washington, D.C.: The World Bank, 1986), p. 77.

h. The employment figure is obtained from the *Economist*, "Business in Eastern Europe," September 21, 1991, p. 10.

i. Value-added. Alan Richards and John Waterbury, *A Political Economy of the Middle East* (Boulder, Colo.: Westview Press, 1990), p. 197; *Statistical Yearbook of China, 1988,* p. 919.

j. Public enterprises' share of total GDP and employment. Oscar Humberto Vera Ferrer, "The Political Economy of Privatization in Mexico," in *Privatization of Public Enterprises in Latin America,* ed. William Glade (San Francisco: The International Center for Economic Growth, 1991), p. 41.

Nguyen Van Linh, warned that his nation had reached a point where it would move toward either a better life or disaster.[11]

Before becoming general secretary of the Communist Party of the Soviet Union (CPSU) in 1985, Gorbachev had been aware of the economic and social crises besetting the Soviet Union, and he frequently relayed his concerns to his friend Eduard Shevardnadze, whom he appointed foreign minister in 1985. Both men concluded, long before *perestroika,* that the Soviet Union "couldn't go on like this." Shevardnadze used apocalyptical language in describing the extent of the crises and the urgency for change in the Soviet

Union. "Everything's rotten. It has to be changed."[12] In his autobiography, *Against the Grain,* Boris Yeltsin recalled a similar sense of despair in the mid-1980s. "The system was clearly beginning to fail . . . it seemed we had stretched ourselves to the utmost . . . Our stock of ideas and methods had been exhausted."[13]

The top elites' perception of the system-threatening crises was itself not sufficient to act as a catalyst of reform. As Aristotle noted of forces initiating political change in oligarchies, one of the "most obvious methods by which changes are brought about . . . is the unjust treatment of the masses by the government. Any leader is then an adequate champion, especially when it so happens that the leader comes from the ranks of the governing class itself."[14] The experience of reform in the communist world during the 1980s validated this insight. A necessary condition for the initiation of reform was the ascendance of reform-minded elites to the *supreme* leadership positions of the regime, either through the normal succession mechanism, as exemplified by Linh in Vietnam in December 1986, or, more typically, through an internal power struggle such as the one that brought Deng to power in China in 1978, Gorbachev in the USSR in 1985, and the post-Kadar leadership in Hungary in 1987.

Economic Crises and Mass Perception

Public perception of political and economic crises often leads to a serious erosion of the legitimacy of the regime and makes change even more imperative and urgent. For the masses, one of the most basic criteria in evaluating the performance of their governments is economic growth and material prosperity. By the end of the 1970s and mid-1980s, there were unmistakable signs, outlined in Table 1.2, that the economies in established communist systems were failing.

Students of communist regimes have noted the connection between the economic failures of the communist systems and the erosion of their political legitimacy.[15] Available public opinion polling data in Poland in the 1980s confirmed this link. One official study showed that, in December 1986, 50 percent of Poles were dissatisfied with the economic performance of the regime.[16] Widespread public discontent with poor economic conditions was reflected in the Poles' declining belief in key communist values and institutions. A survey among Polish youth in 1977 found that 78 percent supported the idea that "the world ought to develop in the direction of socialism"; only 43 percent agreed with the same view in a similar survey in 1983. In a survey in December 1988, more than 60 percent of the respondents said that the political system "had to be overhauled totally." At the same time, a different poll showed that only 22.7 percent supported the Polish United Workers' Party.[17]

The causes of the deterioration of the planned economy throughout the

Table 1.2 Average annual percentage growth of GNP, 1961–1988

Country	1961–1970	1971–1980	1981–1985	1986	1987	1988
Albania[a]	7.4	4.6	1.7	—	—	—
Eastern Europe[b]	3.8	3.4	1.3	2.5	−0.1	1.5
Soviet Union[c]	4.9	2.4	1.8	4.1	1.3	2.2
Vietnam	1.0	1.0	—	3.4	2.6	5.8
Yugoslavia	—	5.0	1.3	3.9	−0.6	0.1
LDCs (less developed countries)	5.2	5.5	2.6	3.7	4.5	4.3
OECD[d]	4.9	3.2	2.6	2.9	3.6	4.4

Source: The Central Intelligence Agency, *Handbook of Economic Statistics, 1990* (Washington, D.C., 1991), p. 39.

   a. Net material product (NMP) estimates are for 1981–1988. Per Sandstrom and Orjan Sjoberg, "Albanian Economic Performance: Stagnation in the 1980s," *Soviet Studies,* vol. 43, no. 5 (1991), p. 937.

   b. Including Bulgaria, Czechoslovakia, East Germany, Hungary, Poland, and Romania.

   c. At factor cost.

   d. GDP growth for OECD countries.

communist world are complex and lie beyond the scope of this study. Briefly, apart from institutional-structural efficiency-reducing factors, such as the soft-budget constraint, overcentralization, and chronic shortages, built into the planned economy,[18] economic crisis in many communist states was caused by policy-related factors, including political chaos during the Cultural Revolution in China; Vietnam's costly invasion of Cambodia; the Soviet Union's high defense expenditures (15–17 percent of its GNP), and its ill-fated invasion of Afghanistan (at a cost of 60 billion rubles).[19] The deepening economic crisis of communism also manifested itself in several forms—hyperinflation (Poland and Vietnam), wild fluctuation and instability (China in the decade of the Cultural Revolution), heavy foreign debt (Hungary, Poland, and East Germany), and persistent low growth (the Soviet Union and the Eastern bloc as a whole).

Crises and Mass Political Activation

Deteriorating economic conditions alone, however, did not always provide sufficient motives for top elites to undertake reform, even though they typically constituted a necessary condition for change. The communist rulers in North Korea and Cuba, the only two hold-out communist states, managed to resist change despite spectacular economic failures. Before popular uprisings, hardline communist regimes in East Germany, Czechoslovakia, Romania, and Bulgaria also rejected reforms. What made undertaking change more imperative during the 1980s (and the late 1970s for China) was the combination of internal division at the top levels of the communist regimes and pressure for change from major social groups. As noted, in several key communist states, namely, China, Vietnam, the Soviet Union, and Hungary, the ascendance of proreform leaders (Deng, Linh, and Gorbachev, respectively) and groups (Hungary) within the Communist Party preceded and precipitated the launching of more systematic programs of reform; in others, including Poland, Czechoslovakia, and East Germany, political reform was preceded by the massive activation of the opposition.

In communist states where reformers failed to emerge from within the ruling elites, the situation approximated another revolutionary scenario described by Aristotle. "In all these oligarchies those who had no share in office continued to cause disturbance till some share was finally given [to them]."[20] In Eastern Europe, coalitions of industrial workers, anti-Soviet nationalists, religious groups, and dissident intellectuals gained strength and eventually grew into powerful political opposition movements: the Polish Solidarity, the East German New Forum, the Czech Civic Forum and Public against Violence. These groups, clear indications of the political crises of communism in most Eastern European countries in the late 1980s, were instrumental in driving the communist governments from power in 1989.

In Czechoslovakia, while the membership of the Communist Party was declining, that of opposition groups was increasing even before the "velvet revolution." The number of independent political opposition groups, including Charter 77, the Czechoslovak Helsinki Committee, the Movement for Civil Liberties, the Czechoslovak Democratic Initiative (the precursor of the Civic Forum), and other new groups, reached close to forty in October 1988 and included tens of thousands of activists and supporters. All were operating openly.[21] Proliferation of opposition forces and activities also occurred in Hungary, East Germany, and Poland before the collapse of the old regimes. In Hungary, opposition parties were organized before the government lifted its ban on such groups. The Democratic Forum was founded in September 1987; it won the March 1990 elections and formed Hungary's first democratic government. Several other major political parties were formed in 1988, and political groups mushroomed in early 1989 following the government's lifting of the ban on political organization.[22]

Routes of Transition from Communism

There are only three routes of transition from communism, as shown in Figure 1: (1) the *evolutionary authoritarian route*; (2) the *revolutionary double-breakthrough route*; and (3) the *simultaneous single-breakthrough route*.

Precise measurement of the degree of democratization is difficult. But the

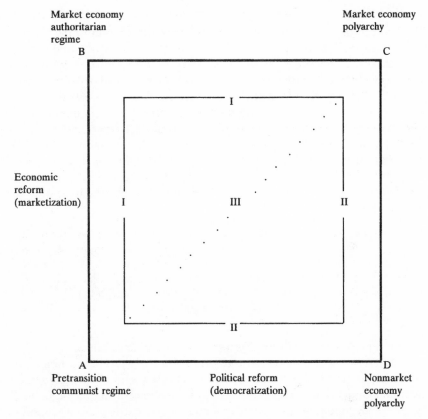

Figure 1 Routes of dual transition in communist systems. Route I: A–B–(?)C—the evolutionary authoritarian route; Route II: A–D–C—the revolutionary double-breakthrough route; Route III: A–C—the simultaneous single-breakthrough route

determination of whether substantive democratization has occurred in a communist system can be made by applying a general rule—the inauguration of the democratic process starts with the holding of the first open and free elections. The political liberalization that normally precedes the formal transition to democratic rule is more difficult to measure. Typical indicators of substantive political liberalization may include the scope of the freedom of press, association, religion, and public gathering.

Measuring the degree of marketization is equally problematic. In this study, marketization will be measured by the size of the private sector, determined by its share of GNP, and the dominant modes of resource allocation. This criterion combines the two key steps in transforming a planned economy into a market economy: liberalization and privatization.

Route I: The Evolutionary Authoritarian Route

The first option of transition, the evolutionary authoritarian route, involves the transformation of a politically and economically closed communist regime into an authoritarian regime based on a market economy. Reforms in this case are limited to economic reforms implemented to transform a planned economy into a market economy, with the regime making no significant move toward democratization. Indeed, reformers pursuing this option view democratization as an obstacle to marketization and economic development. They point to the lack of favorable preconditions in their countries for instituting democratic politics and deeply fear that the potential political instability resulting from democratization will jeopardize their economic reform programs. Deng Xiaoping's view on this issue was the most representative:

> The conditions are now immature in a huge country like ours, where the population is so large, interregional differences so enormous, and nationalities so numerous. First, our cultural development is not good enough . . . We cannot afford to have a Western two-house system; we cannot afford to have a Western multiparty system . . . Even public opinion in the West agrees that, in a large country like China, many things will be impossible without a center to lead the nation.[23]

Deng's preference for the authoritarian route and its intellectual rationale was shared by the Vietnamese top reformist leader Nguyen Van Linh, who said in September 1989: "Democratization is now essentially directed at the economic domain. It is not our policy to hasten renovation of the political system while preparations are still inadequate. Neither is it our intention to effect limitless democratization. Any adventurous step in this direction would certainly lead to political instability."[24]

The political and economic logic underlying the strategy of reform in this model is that of a new type of authoritarianism prominently featured in the developmental success of Newly Industrializing Countries (NICs), located, almost exclusively, in East and Southeast Asia (South Korea, Taiwan, Singapore, Indonesia, Thailand, and Malaysia) since the 1960s. Rejecting both the development strategy of state-socialism *and* the neoliberal orthodoxy, this model assigns an important role to the state, ruled by a technocratic-authoritarian regime, in achieving rapid economic development.[25] For China and Vietnam, both of which pursued this route of transition, the most critical first step was to change the basis of the government's legitimacy from orthodox communist ideology to an economic performance-based *neoauthoritarian developmental ideology*.[26] In the case of China, which had implicitly followed this route since the late 1970s, such a change was explicitly articulated in the open debate about neoauthoritarianism in the late 1980s.[27]

The economic reform strategy of the communist regimes in China and Vietnam shared three striking characteristics: gradualism; an agriculture-first approach; and integration into the world economy. This strategy resulted in remarkable economic growth records for both countries. China's Gross Domestic Product (GDP) grew at an annual rate of 8.8 percent between 1979 and 1990, while Vietnam's GDP growth averaged about 7 percent between 1989 and 1992.[28] Such high levels of economic performance produced a *cushion effect* that countered the erosion of the political legitimacy of these postcommunist neoauthoritarian regimes. Unlike their counterparts in Eastern Europe and the former Soviet Union, which had failed miserably with their economic reform attempts and possessed no alternative source of legitimacy, China and Vietnam managed to survive the political shock wave of the collapse of communism through the establishment of neoauthoritarian regimes.

Despite the best efforts of such regimes to limit political participation, market-oriented economic reforms produce *spillover effects,* which weaken the governments' capacity to control society when the pluralizing effects inherent in market forces penetrate the political process and transfer economic resources away from the state to society. This does not mean, however, that increasing marketization is a functional equivalent of rising contestation in the political arena; rather, marketization merely provides a more favorable condition for various social forces to acquire critical resources in developing countervailing capabilities against the state and raising the costs of regime-sponsored repression.[29]

Moreover, as economic reforms encounter political resistance from conservatives and become stagnant, top reformers, managerial elites, and the liberal intelligentsia may be tempted to form a temporary coalition to implement certain instrumentalist political reforms to overcome such resistance. This was nearly the case in China during the summer of 1986, when Deng thought about addressing political reform as a means of speeding up his economic reform. Although he observed that "the reform of the economic system is difficult to implement without reforming the political system," his own ambivalence about democratization and pressures from the hardliners quickly ended this brief flirtation with political reform.[30] It can also be argued that Gorbachev's shift from his initial program of economic acceleration in 1985 to *glasnost* in 1986 was prompted by the same set of motivations,[31] although in his case, limited political reforms progressed to revolution.

Finally, because this type of regime is often compelled to moderate its internal repression and loosen its social control to facilitate economic activities, cracks inevitably appear and grow in the institutional apparatus set up to prevent the rise of social and political movements, creating opportunities for opposition groups to emerge, operate, and eventually pressure the regimes to move toward more political openness—a phenomenon that may be called "queue-jumping" in that it disrupts the macroreform sequence. The emergence of such groups, their political mobilization and demands for democratizing reforms, force the postcommunist neoauthoritarian regimes to confront democratization as part of the reform. In any case, available examples of change in communist states, primarily those from China and Vietnam, show that, owing to the spillover effects and queue-jumping, it is virtually impossible for a regime to implement market-oriented reforms without also allowing for some movement toward political liberalization by default.

In China, queue-jumping was led by the liberal intelligentsia and took the form of three prodemocracy movements between 1978 and 1989, with each assuming a larger scale and higher intensity. In Vietnam, despite the absence of an organized dissident movement or antigovernment demonstrations, the intelligentsia also became more vocal and critical of the communist regime during reform, while the mass media showed many signs of political decontrol.[32]

Queue-jumping by the urban intelligentsia is certainly not the only complication that arises along the evolutionary authoritarian route from communism. Another crucial problem is how to overcome hardliners' opposition to reform. Two solutions are available. The first and more obvious one is to rely on a high degree of elite consensus on, and commitment to, marketization and the coalition-building skills of the supreme leader in defeating conservative resistance. However, given the unpredictability of the level of commitment of top decision-makers to market-oriented reforms, the fluctuation in the distribution of power among various factions at the top level of government, and the varying skills of coalition-building, this solution promises, at best, uncertain results.

The second and more subtle solution is to undermine hardliners' opposition, not from the top down, but from the bottom up; not through overt political means (purge and electoral defeat), but through covert economic means (self-enrichment opportunities and material incentives that a marketization process generates). Thus, in communist states undergoing marketization, ex-*apparatchiki* may profitably exit politics and enter the private sector. This exit option not only buys off lower-level elites' opposition to marketization, but often—ironically—turns the same elites into some of the more staunch defenders of the newly emerging market through a process of embourgeoisement. Over time, this solution can be expected to create a powerful grassroots-level coalition composed of genuine private entrepreneurs and ex-*apparatchiki*. However, this exit option is problematic in two interrelated respects, one socioeconomic and the other political.

In socioeconomic terms, the embourgeoisement of the ex-*apparatchiki* is highly inequitable in the short-run since it transforms, through various economic incentives, a politically powerful group under the old regime into an economically privileged group in the new system. In the long-run, however, because it is more difficult to monopolize economic power than political power, the expansion of market forces is bound to create more opportunities for ordinary private entrepreneurs, thus balancing out the initial advantages enjoyed by the ex-*apparatchiki*.[33]

In political terms, because of the inequity built into this process—and with it, the deep disdain of the public for the *apparatchiki*—the exit option is possible only when the level of mass political mobilization and open public opposition is relatively low. Once these *apparatchiki* become high-profile targets of newly activated political groups and their self-enrichment activities are subject to press scrutiny and populist attacks, the commercial exit may be closed off. It also remains uncertain whether, after the completion of embourgeoisement, the ex-*apparatchiki* will be receptive to or supportive of the democratization phase of the transition from a market economy authoritarian regime to a market economy polyarchy. Many factors, including insecurity about the protection of the rights of their ill-gotten private wealth, binding interest in maintaining a cozy relationship with the political oligarchy that caters to their interests, and antidemocratic political beliefs, may motivate the *apparatchiki*-turned-capitalists to obstruct the democratization of these postcommunist regimes.

In the event that a prereform communist regime is able to complete the first phase of the transition—from communism to a market economy authoritarian regime—the dynamics of the subsequent regime transition to a full market economy polyarchy may resemble those from authoritarianism to democracy. The most applicable example may be the democratization experience of Taiwan, where a one-party authoritarian system was gradually and peacefully democratized in the 1980s. But what will be the likely forces and factors triggering this process in communist states in transition?

Theoretical works on democratizing noncommunist authoritarian regimes and experiences of democratization in such regimes in the late twentieth century suggest that three factors are likely to be instrumental in initiating this movement. First, certain favorable preconditions to democratization tend to emerge in the marketization process. In addition to generating sustained high economic growth, as in China and Vietnam after reform began, successful marketization can be expected to foster a more pluralist and autonomous society. With access to expanding economic resources, cells of civil society will emerge and grow; social groups, especially the intelligentsia, urban bourgeoisie, and business groups, may gain sufficient strength and form coalitions to pressure the postcommunist neoauthoritarian regimes to democratize.

Second, as economic performance replaces communist ideology as the basis of political legitimacy, the search for a more secure and permanent source of legitimation presents a constant challenge to these regimes. Fear of a legitimation crisis set off by faltering economic performance may motivate the governments to undertake democratizing reforms.

Finally, the postcommunist neoauthoritarian regimes may relax from within. New ruling elites, most likely third- or fourth-generation rulers, may show less aversion to the idea of democratization and put up less resistance to democratizing pressures from below. It should thus be expected that the elites who come to power in China and Vietnam in the early part of the twenty-first century will be instrumental in initiating genuine democratizing reforms.

The above scenario is, of course, an optimistic one, especially when applied to China, whose size and enormous regional and ethnic diversities will complicate the democratization process and increase its unpredictability.

Route II: The Revolutionary Double-Breakthrough Route

Route II—political reform preceding economic reform—appears to be the most commonly followed route of regime transition in more developed communist states. In the more successful cases in Eastern Europe, including Poland, Hungary, Czechoslovakia, and East Germany, the length of the first phase of this transition varied from a few weeks in Czechoslovakia and East Germany to a year in Poland and nearly two years in Hungary. In the Soviet Union, completion of the first phase took seven years (1985–1991).

Given the rapidity and radical nature of transition in Eastern Europe and the Soviet Union in the late 1980s and early 1990s, this route can be characterized as a revolutionary double-breakthrough route for two reasons. First, the democratization phase was accomplished in a dazzling breakthrough, with the driving forces originating in society. Second, an equally revolutionary program of instantly transforming the planned economy into a market economy (the "shock therapy" approach) was immediately launched following the democratic breakthrough. Despite the differences in the actual processes of transition during the first phase, the dynamics of political change along Route II can be characterized by three clear patterns:

(1) All Soviet-installed communist regimes with weak homegrown legitimacy experienced instant collapse as soon as it became clear, both to the opposition forces and to the ruling elites of the old regimes, that the Soviet Union would no longer support these systems with force.

(2) In ex-communist states where the old regimes were replaced, the first breakthrough did not always lead to the immediate establishment of postcommunist democratic governments. A factor significantly influencing whether genuine democratic forces could quickly seize power through the critical first open elections after the collapse of the old regime was the pres-

ence of reasonably well organized, mass antisystem coalitions or opposition forces prior to—or, as in the case of the Soviet Union, during—the collapse. In countries where such coalitions existed, including Poland, East Germany, Hungary, Czechoslovakia, and parts of the Soviet Union (Leningrad, Moscow, and the Baltics), democratic forces all won, by large margins, the critical, initial open elections; in countries where such opposition coalitions were weak or nonexistent (Bulgaria, Albania, and Romania), communists or ex-communists were able to defeat hastily formed democratic forces and win the first open elections, although they eventually proved to be incapable of governing a multiparty system and handling urban-based opposition. This was demonstrated by the persistent political instability in Romania, as well as by the fall of the governments dominated by ex-communists in Bulgaria and Albania after their defeat in the second open elections in 1991 and early 1992, respectively. (In Bulgaria the defeated ex-communists did manage a comeback in 1992 after forming a coalition with a Turkish minority party.)

(3) In homegrown communist regimes, the actual breakdown was more prolonged, as we have seen in the Soviet Union, and produced traumatic consequences, including civil war in Yugoslavia, general social chaos in Albania, and a failed coup, national disintegration, interethnic violence, mini–civil wars, and economic collapse in the Soviet Union. The first breakthrough in this group of ex-communist states also tended to produce mixed results and regime types. In Yugoslavia, the first elections in late 1990 yielded ambiguous outcomes. Ex-communists won in Serbia and Montenegro on nationalist platforms, whereas opposition forces won in Croatia, Slovenia, Bosnia-Herzegovina, and Macedonia. The interethnic armed conflicts that broke out in July 1991 further clouded the prospects for democracy in the former Yugoslavia.

The most important case here is, without doubt, the transition in the Soviet Union, where reform launched by Gorbachev in 1985 turned into a revolution that eventually toppled the communist regime and dismantled the multinational Soviet empire. The combination of the nationalist and democratic forces gave rise to a wide array of ambiguous transitional regimes in the former Soviet Union. While nationalist-democratic forces might be said to have come to power in the Baltics, the Russian Federation, and Ukraine, authoritarian nationalist forces appeared to have replaced the communist-imperialist rule in most republics after the breakup of the Soviet Union. The ambiguity of the first breakthrough in the Soviet Union was most poignantly illustrated by the posttransition trauma in Georgia, where the ardent nationalist and former political prisoner Zviad Gamsakhurdia captured the presidency with 87 percent of the popular vote in May 1991, turned himself into a dictator within months, and was overthrown by a popular uprising in January 1992.

What most distinguishes Route II type transition from Route I is that in the former the first breakthrough usually leads to the establishment of a curious regime type: nonmarket economy polyarchy. In this transitional regime, democratic political processes and institutions operate in a nonmarket economy which is neither capable of sustaining, nor compatible with, new democratic politics. Thus, the complications and difficulties typical of Route II type transition are the product of the unique historical circumstances, that is, rapid breakdown of the old regimes, accompanying the births of these new polyarchical or quasi-polyarchical regimes. In contrast with the evolutionary process of marketization under postcommunist neoauthoritarian rule, these governments face the daunting task of consolidating democracy and transforming a planned economy into a market economy amid the deepening economic crisis that the new democratic governments inherited from the old regimes.

Although the dual-regime transition model in Figure 1 does not specify, *a priori,* an approach to the second phase of the transition, a rare combination of situational factors—the escalating economic crises, the influence of Western economic ideas, the intellectual bankruptcy of market socialism, public euphoria following the fall of the old regimes, and the popular mandate given to the new democratic governments swept into power by the democratic breakthrough—led to the adoption of the radical strategy of shock therapy in most of the ex-communist states in Eastern Europe and Russia.

Because this process of marketization was still unfolding in the early 1990s, it is too early to judge its effectiveness, costs, and likelihood of success. Much skepticism was raised about the wisdom of adopting a grand strategy—which had an uneven record in reforming the economies of less developed countries—in curing economic problems that had accumulated and become entrenched through decades of communist rule.[34] Moreover, criticisms of shock therapy were bolstered by unanticipated difficulties in its implementation (especially the privatization of state-owned enterprises) and high social costs, such as falling production, runaway inflation, rising unemployment, and declining standards of living in former communist states. For example, the cumulative fall of industrial output between 1990 and 1992 was 54 percent for Romania and Bulgaria, 40 percent for Czechoslovakia, and 32 percent for Poland and Hungary.[35] Gross industrial output fell by 18.8 percent in Russia in 1992, while inflation shot up 2,539 percent.[36] The decline in real industrial wages between 1990 and October 1992 totaled 108 percent in Bulgaria, 59.5 percent in Poland, 38.9 percent in Czechoslovakia, and 9.9 percent in Hungary.[37]

In the case of Russia, the introduction of shock therapy in January 1992 led to near hyperinflation and the impoverishment of the Russian people through the loss of their life-savings (caused by high inflation, a huge fall in gross output, and bankruptcy of most state-owned enterprises). By the end of 1993, it was evident that shock therapy had failed, with the ruble having collapsed, the monthly inflation rate hovering around 20 percent, wages having fallen 40 percent from the 1990 level, and industrial output down 30 percent from its December 1991 level.[38]

However controversial the economic logic of shock therapy, which is centered on a belief in the efficiency of the market, the political logic of the adoption of this radicalized neoliberal approach to economic restructuring is based on three assumptions. The first can be traced to Machiavelli's "injury-benefit rule," which advises that "injuries should be done all together, so that being less tasted, they will give less offense. Benefits should be granted little by little, so that they may be better enjoyed."[39] This assumption becomes compelling if one believes that, because a gradualist approach may entail the administration of constant pain and run higher political risks, political stability can be maintained by having the people absorb most of the social costs of the economic transition immediately after the inauguration of democratic politics.

The second assumption is based on the "honeymoon effects" of new democracies. Shock therapists expect to counterbalance the up-front high political costs of the implementation of orthodox economic policies with what Albert Hirschman termed "asset of trust and hope"—"a special reserve of goodwill and trust as a result of the political liberties and human rights that [the new democracies] have restored or established."[40] Third, the adoption of shock therapy is justified by the belief that a nonmarket economy polyarchy would be an unsustainable form of democracy; the direct control of the economy by the state would inevitably lead to the erosion of democratic rule.

In retrospect, however, this political logic did not work in all cases of transition along this second route from communism. Despite the absence of massive social upheavals, high short-term social costs caused numerous economic reformers (for instance, Poland's Jan Krzysztof Bielecki and Russia's Yegor Gaidar) and the first noncommunist governments (in Poland, Bulgaria, and Lithuania) to fall from power—to be replaced by former communists. In the latter three cases, reconstituted former communist parties and their allies were returned to power. In Russia, popular frustration over two years of fruitless but painful shock therapy was a major cause of the popular rejection of the reformist Russia's Choice Party headed by Gaidar and of the unexpectedly strong performance of the ultranationalists and communists in the December 1993 elections for the new Russian State Duma. In Hungary, the ruling center-right Democratic Forum also found its popularity plummeting after four years of economic restructuring and recession, albeit without shock therapy. The Democratic Forum faced a strong challenge from the Hungarian Socialist Party (the former communists) in the parliamentary elections scheduled for 1994.

In varying degrees, the new nonmarket economy polyarchies in the former Soviet bloc were confronted with similar political difficulties, chief among them being the disintegration of the antiregime alliances, the ensuing political rivalry among these erstwhile partners, the fragmentation of the weak party systems, the splintering of the new electorate along both traditional and new socioeconomic lines, the formation of weak multiparty coalition governments, and a rising level of posttransition, mass political disillusionment and discontent.

In Poland, the liberal intelligentsia and industrial workers split when Lech Walesa defeated Mazowiecki in the presidential election of 1990. The breakup eventually resulted in a fragmented political landscape by the end of 1991—when more than 100 parties participated in the first postcommunist elections for the Polish Sejm, with 29 parties splitting the 460 seats and no party winning more than 13 percent of the votes.[41] This outcome lay behind much of Poland's governmental instability in the 2 years following the elections. It immediately forced the resignation of the promarket prime minister, Jan Krzysztof Bielecki, who called the results "a vote against the market economy."[42] President Walesa then reluctantly nominated Jan Olszewski, who campaigned on a populist platform of easing the pains of economic transition, to form a new minority government.[43] Olszewski's government lasted a mere five months. After an unsuccessful attempt to form a new government to be led by Waldemar Pawlak, the leader of a minor peasant party, a political outsider, Hanna Suchocka, formed Poland's fifth postcommunist government in June 1992. Despite her personal popularity and the economic progress achieved by her government when the Polish economy registered a small rebound in 1992, Suchocka's government fell in May 1993 as a result of a Solidarity-led campaign demanding high wages for state-sector workers.

The most unexpected setback for the postcommunist transition in Poland was the electoral victory won by the Left Alliance, a reconstituted party of the former communists, and its rural ally, the Peasants Party, in the country's parliamentary elections in September 1993. Together, the two parties received about 36 percent of the popular vote, but captured roughly two-thirds of the seats in the Sejm. Although the stunning comeback of the former communists four years after the collapse of the old regime was not expected to threaten the process of democratic consolidation in Poland, this event was widely viewed as a popular rejection of the shock therapy reform program that had entailed extremely high social costs.

Rifts also appeared in early 1991 in the Bulgarian opposition coalition, headed by the Union of Democratic Forces (UDF), because of disputes over specific policy issues and its lack of organizational cohesion. In Czechoslovakia, the Civic Forum and the Public against Violence, the two political coalitions credited with organizing the 1989 "velvet revolution," both disintegrated into rival groups in 1991.[44]

In the former Soviet Union, internal strains caused the disintegration of the main democratic alliance, the Democratic Russia Movement, which helped Yeltsin win a landslide victory in the presidential election for the Russian Federation in June 1991. Composed of several political parties and groups, Democratic Russia was dealt a deathblow in November 1991 when several major partners in the alliance announced their plan to form a separate alliance to be called the Coalition of Democratic Forces of Russia.[45] The vice-president of Russia, Alexander Rutskoi (a key leader of the movement), allied himself with Yeltsin's opponents and openly attacked the president's shock therapy economic reform program. Yeltsin responded by curbing much of Rutskoi's power.[46] Meanwhile, the Civic Union, which splintered from the Democratic Russia alliance, became a potent political force in June 1992; for about a year, it prominently opposed Yeltsin's reforms, but suffered an internal fracture in mid-1993 after Yeltsin's victory in the April referendum. In many ways, the political landscape of Russia after the dissolution of the former Soviet Union was a much-fragmented one, dotted with a multitude of weak organizations, political parties, and groups that shared little common ground and had no mass following. The political costs of disunity among progressive forces could be high, as was the case in the outcome of the parliamentary elections in Russia in December 1993, when the reformers were split into three competing parties—Russia's Choice, the Yavlinsky Bloc, and the Russian Unity and Accord Party. Together, they polled only about a quarter of the popular vote.

Dire warnings about postcommunist populism notwithstanding, these transitional problems were not uncommon in the consolidation phase of new democratic regimes. Such complications were an integral part of the political evolutionary process. Newly established democratic institutional procedures might be ineffective; long-accumulated socioeconomic crises endemic to these societies might persist and even worsen, regardless of the types of regimes in power. However, mass disillusionment following the rise of new democracies in southern Europe and Latin America in the 1970s and 1980s did not translate itself into antidemocratic, extremist mass movements and seldom led to the quick overthrow of new democracies—even though individual incumbents routinely suffered electoral setbacks.[47]

In this respect, studies of whether new democracies were less capable than either "old" democracies or authoritarian regimes of consistently pursuing macroeconomic stabilization programs and other orthodox economic reform policies have yielded mixed results and offered little theoretical assistance in predicting the likelihood of success of the radical reforms adopted by the postcommunist regimes pursuing the double-breakthrough strategy.[48]

This political shift toward the left-of-center forces in Eastern Europe in the early 1990s—exemplified by the political comeback of the former communists in Poland, who promised to ease transitional economic pains, and the rising popular support for the Hungarian Socialist Party—raises questions about the feasibility of this strategy. In the case of Russia, such an ambitious approach is politically unviable, as indicated by the results of the Russian parliamentary elections in December 1993, when twelve of the thirteen parties competing in the elections attacked the shock therapy program and about 80 percent of the voters cast their ballots against the government.

Moreover, in the case of ex-communist systems, the posttransition political difficulties described above are structured into the dual-regime transition process when rapid democratization precedes marketization. There are four main difficulties here: the difficulties inherent in the movements' transition from their protest-orientations to governance-orientations and in their low level of institutionalization; the problem of maintaining oversized coalitions;[49] the competitive institutional dynamics present in any democratic process; and the peculiar social structure of the postcommunist nonmarket polyarchies that was created by the pretransition developmental policies of the old regimes.

Despite their political courage, antiregime forces such as the Polish Solidarity and Democratic Russia incorporated diverse and conflicting social and political interests that could be unified only when there was a common enemy to oppose. Once the object of their opposition was overthrown, such protest-oriented organizations quickly lost their purpose, and a breakup became inevitable. Moreover, given the rapidity of the first phase of the transition, these opposition forces lacked the time to acquire the institutional cohesiveness, adaptability, and complexity necessary to sustain themselves as viable political groups during the second phase of transition. That these relatively simple and, in many cases, disorganized forces were able to seize resources from the decaying party-state, radicalize the reform, or even force out the old regimes during the democratization phase was more of a testimony to the institutional decrepitude of the old regimes than a demonstration of the organizational fortitude of the opposition forces. As studies of Poland's transition indicate, even the Polish Solidarity, arguably the most formidable and best-organized opposition coalition, was long fraught with internal tensions before its disintegration in 1990.[50]

Finally, the breakup of the precollapse opposition alliances caused by divergent socioeconomic interests often led to open rivalry between the emerging political forces representing these interests in the new democratic process. In new democracies, this creates an impression of political gridlock. In the case of Eastern European countries after 1989, the predominance of parliamentarian systems with a combination of weak executive branches and proportional representation institutionally fostered the fragmentation of, and competition among, these forces, with the predictable result of decision-making paralysis, manifested most clearly by the inability of Poland's postcommunist governments to pursue a consistent austerity program during the first two years of shock therapy.[51]

Legislative deadlock raised the temptation for the executive branch to concentrate power on the grounds of necessity. Polish president Walesa attempted, but failed, to assume the position of prime minister in late 1991, when the elections produced a fractious parliament. In Estonia, Prime Minister Edgar Savisaar resigned in frustration after his request for special powers was rejected by the Estonian Supreme Council in January 1992. In Czechoslovakia, playwright-turned-president Vaclav Havel, handicapped by the lack of real executive power of his office despite his widespread popularity, proposed constitutional amendments in March 1991 to broaden presidential powers.[52]

In Russia, President Yeltsin, when challenged by a fractious legislature, publicly attacked the inefficient democratic decision-making process and emphasized the need for the temporary concentration of presidential power. Calling a parliamentary republic with a decorative presidency "suicide," Yeltsin said, "Permanent interparliamentary struggle against the background of unfavorable social and economic developments [would mean] endless talks and political games with pseudodemocratic rituals . . . When the multiparty system in Russia is an embryo and a deep crisis is taking place, the transition to a parliamentary form of rule would be extremely difficult, undesirable, and, I believe, inadmissible."[53]

This high-stake power struggle between Yeltsin's executive branch and the legislature, which was composed of many of his opponents, spiraled into a full-blown constitutional crisis. The clash between Yeltsin and the Congress of People's Deputies first came to a head in March 1993, when the frustrated Russian president threatened to abolish the Congress and impose direct rule. Last-minute compromise enabled the two sides to seek a temporary truce through a referendum, which Yeltsin won in April. The bitter rivalry resumed in the summer and culminated in Yeltsin's decree to dismantle the Congress in late September—a confrontation that ended with the October Moscow revolt led by anti-Yeltsin forces and the subsequent storming of the Russian Parliament by the military units acting under Yeltsin's orders. Although the forcible abolition of the Congress allowed Yeltsin to concentrate power in his hands and remove the political obstacles to his economic reforms, the haunting image of the burning Russian Parliament raised doubts about the political direction of the Russian transition. Specifically, several post-crisis measures taken by Yeltsin—banning several opposition parties and newspapers, dismissing dissident regional leaders, disabling the Constitutional Court, forcing the passage of a new constitution that would give the president overwhelming political power over the other branches of the government, and withdrawing his promise to run for reelection in June 1994—seemed to suggest that Yeltsin was gradually moving toward a "soft authoritarian" transitional model: maintaining a democratic institutional framework at a significantly reduced level of political competition.

The most worrisome aspect of nonmarket polyarchies is their unique social structure, characterized by the predominance of the industrial proletariat and the absence of a commercial middle class. This has resulted from the old regimes' development strategy, which gave the state the exclusive role in economic modernization, suppressed private entrepreneurship, favored large industrial organizations, and discriminated against the service sector. Market-oriented reforms require massive privatization of state-owned enterprises, the internationalization of these economies, the introduction of structural adjustment measures, and the reduction of subsidies to urban residents and industrial labor—measures that force the new leaders to adopt policies that victimize their former allies, supporters, and sympathizers. The hardest hit are the industrial laborers, a social group which had been sheltered from international competition and protected by a state-socialist welfare system under communist rule.

In an evolutionary transition to a market economy, the new commercial middle class that is gradually created supplies much of the entrepreneurial skills and leadership. In the rapid transition toward a market economy attempted in Eastern Europe and Russia in the second phase of the dual transition, however, the instant creation of such a class was problematic. Janos Kornai, aware of the importance of a commercial middle class as the bulwark of democracy and the driving force of marketization, cautioned that "the private sector develops step-by-step. It is impossible to institute private property by cavalry attack. Embourgeoisement is a lengthy historical process."[54]

The absence of a commercial middle class presented two challenges for new nonmarket polyarchies. First, it gave the elites in the old regime an initial advantage in seeking opportunities for self-enrichment through the utilization of their previous connections and managerial expertise. In Eastern Europe and the former Soviet Union, this phenomenon, known as "spontaneous privatization," became a divisive issue, politicizing and complicating state-sponsored privatization programs.[55]

Second, in the absence of a commercial middle class, the democratic state assumes, by default, the leading role in the creation of a market economy, the ultimate goal of which is, paradoxically, to get the state out of the marketplace. Using the power of the state—especially that of a new democracy—to intervene in economic activities involves two risks, the first of which is overloading the fledgling democratic state with additional responsibilities for managing the disintegrating economy. These new democratic governments lack the time, experience, loyal administrative personnel, and resources to intervene effectively. The same overloading of the state also creates ample opportunities for official corruption, damaging the credibility of new democracies.

The other danger is allowing groups whose interests will be hurt by the marketization process to gain access to political influence, through electoral means, to defend their interests at the expense of reform. This occurred in Poland in the October 1991 parliamentary elections, which resulted in the defeat of the proreform Bielecki government and the formation of a five-party coalition government whose members campaigned on populist anti-market platforms. (Its quick fall did, however, prevent it from carrying out its promises.)

The predominance of the industrial proletariat in the ex-communist societies, in this context, presents an especially difficult political problem. Detailed comparative data presented in Table 1.3 show a striking contrast between the structure of the labor force in the West and that in the former Soviet bloc countries in the late 1980s. These figures accentuate the structural characteristics of the employed labor force in the former Soviet bloc: oversized agrarian and industrial sectors and an underdeveloped service sector.

If, as Barrington Moore argued in *Social Origins of Dictatorship and Democracy,* the existence of a large peasantry prior to the development of modern capitalism obstructed democracy and formed the social basis of commu-

Table 1.3   The structure of the labor force in the G-7 countries, Eastern Europe and the Soviet Union, in 1988 (weighted percentage)[a]

	Agriculture	Industry	Trade	Transportation, construction, and communication	Other
G-7 countries[a]	4.99	23.63	20.58	13.36	37.44
Eastern Europe and the Soviet Union[b]	19.46	30.91	8.46	17.91	23.26

Sources: Calculated from data provided by the International Labor Organization, *Yearbook of Labor Statistics, 1989–1990,* reprinted in *Statistical Yearbook of China, 1991,* p. 823.

a. Data for Great Britain are 1987 figures.

b. Data for the Soviet Union and Bulgaria are 1987 figures; data for Romania are 1985 figures. The Eastern European countries here include East Germany, Czechoslovakia, Poland, Hungary, Romania, and Bulgaria.

nist dictatorships in China and Russia,[56] the predominance of the industrial labor force employed in state-owned enterprises as a social group and a potent political force may have two major negative implications for the transition to market economies in the more developed ex-communist societies for the following reasons.

First, higher employment in the poor-performing industrial sector reflects high labor redundancy and inefficiency. In Poland, two years after shock therapy, the state sector had between 30 and 50 percent more employees than needed in 1991.[57] In Russia, a survey of 500 state-owned enterprises conducted by the International Labor Organization in early 1992 showed that 25 percent of the work force was redundant.[58] Marketization must drastically downsize this sector and risk high unemployment.

Second, the socialist welfare state fostered an institutionalized dependency on the state among industrial workers and other state employees. This dependency lay behind the fear these groups had of market forces, as indicated by the numerous opinion polls from the Soviet Union and Eastern Europe. A poll of state-sector employees in Poland conducted at the beginning of 1990 found that 70 percent were either unenthusiastic or horrified by the prospect of increased unemployment caused by transition to a market economy. Another poll in April 1990 showed that 58 percent of Poles thought that "it would be possible to do without privatization if enterprises employed the right directors." A poll of 2,675 Bulgarians conducted in January 1990 also indicated the public's general preference for socialism and aversion to a capitalist market economy (58.8 percent disapproved of unemployment and 70.3 percent believed that the existence of rich and poor would be unacceptable).[59] In Czechoslovakia, two separate polls of Czechs and Slovaks in November 1991 found that more than half the respondents were opposed to privatization of all state enterprises.[60] Data from the Soviet Union similarly revealed that workers tended to be less supportive than other groups of making the transition to a market economy.[61]

Such dedication to the socialist welfare state may change very slowly, even after the introduction of shock therapy. In two separate surveys conducted in October 1991 and January 1992, most Poles supported retaining the core features of the socialist welfare state even though they rejected a planned economy. Nearly 90 percent supported retaining the state welfare system, 82 percent wanted to keep full employment, 80 percent called for subsidized housing, and 46 percent wished to see the state maintain ownership of industries and services.[62]

The creation of a market is thus a political rather than a purely economic challenge. The most difficult issue is how to deal with a large industrial labor force that possessed a significant organizing capacity and defended its interests fiercely. Besides their traditional means of protest, such as strikes by Polish railway workers in May 1990 and riots by Romanian miners in September 1991, the industrial laborers greatly enhanced their political power through access to the ballot box after the inauguration of the democratic process.

For those in power, a politically mobilized industrial labor force was clearly a threat to their ability to govern and carry out austerity programs. At the risk of losing its aid package from the International Monetary Fund (IMF) in the spring of 1992, Boris Yeltsin's government was forced to provide 22 billion rubles in wage increases and other subsidies to Russia's coal miners.[63] For free-market economists, such demands presented a more immediate threat to the viability of economic reforms and prompted Kornai to suggest that the transition to a market economy in Eastern Europe requires a strong government which must respond with an "iron hand" to pressures from industrial workers for wage increases.[64]

These problems will most likely require a modification of reform programs according to the specific conditions of each ex-communist society to lower the social costs and secure the necessary political support from its people and the groups adversely affected by the economic transition. The result of these measures may be a slowdown of the transition and the lengthening of the second phase. The rapid breakthrough to a market economy will probably take more time than anticipated.

Route III: The Single-Breakthrough Short Cut

This route, incorporating simultaneous democratizing and marketizing reforms, appears to be the most attractive way to transform communist regimes. It promises to make progress toward the two interdependent goals—a market economy and polyarchy—simultaneously. In practice, however, such a transition has not yet occurred in any communist state. Perhaps the post-Kadar regime in Hungary between 1988 and 1989 might qualify as a close exception, but it was replaced by a democratic regime before it could manage such a transition. Students of regime transitions in noncommunist authoritarian systems also observed a striking absence of successful simultaneous democratic and market-oriented reforms (even allowing for the relatively low degree of state control of the economy in noncommunist authoritarian systems), the high level of political instability accompanying simultaneous reforms, and reversal of movement on both dimensions of reform along this route.[65] Several factors may help explain the absence of a successful single-breakthrough transition from communism to a market economy polyarchy.

A critical variable in making any significant breakthrough along either the "authoritarian" or the "democratic" route is the reformer's ability to forge a powerful single-purpose alliance. In China and Vietnam, such an alliance initially encompassed supreme leaders personally committed to market-oriented reforms (Deng and Linh), moderate technocrats, the liberal intelligentsia, and the peasantry. In the Soviet Union, the democratizing alliance forged under Gorbachev after 1987 included the liberal intelligentsia, nationalist forces, reformers inside the establishment, segments of the urban population, and industrial laborers. In most Eastern European countries, a similar democratizing alliance that included parts of the industrial labor force, the intelligentsia, religious groups, and moderate reformers spearheaded the democratic transition.

Empirical cases of transition showed that such a broad-based alliance seldom endured along Route I and Route II. The alliance that worked in one phase of the transition tended to dissolve in another phase, as in all postcommunist Eastern European countries and the former Soviet Union in their drive toward a market economy. Even in China, the initial grand reform alliance broke apart after 1986 over the issue of political liberalization. Gorbachev's grand alliance cracked first with Yeltsin's defection in 1987 and then collapsed altogether after massive defection by the liberals in 1990. The difficulty in maintaining a sustainable alliance committed to both democratization and marketization lies in the fact that groups that must be included in such an alliance will have conflicting interests that can rarely be reconciled satisfactorily.

The success or failure of such a transition depends largely on a stable balance of power among the diverse groups and coalition partners. A sudden shift of power balance weakens some groups' positions while strengthening others' and helping to radicalize their demands. In a previously closed system undergoing a simultaneous transition, however, political and economic resources are being constantly shifted from one group to another. Even under the most ideal circumstances, the gains by different groups from the reform tend to be unequal, making it impossible to maintain a balance of power among the diverse partners in the coalition.

Finally, a simultaneous transition calls for cooperation and compromise between the forces within the regime and those opposing it. It demands from both sides a basic consensus upon reform, its goals, and the pace with which it should be undertaken. Here lies a cruel dilemma for simultaneous reformers: the short cut is least practical where it is most promising. In Soviet-imposed communist systems, the conservative forces were relatively weak, while the ruling elites suffered from a permanent legitimation deficit and might be tempted to embark on such a gradual simultaneous transition to enhance their political legitimacy. But the governments' moderate reform projects were quickly replaced with the opposition's radical revolutionary projects. The fundamental weakness of the regime was only accentuated by its moderately paced reform along both dimensions. The opposition thus had little incentive to accommodate the regime. In virtually every instance in which the communist governments tentatively tried such a simultaneous approach, they were swept from power once the Soviet military support for their regimes was withdrawn. Instead of waiting for the governments to carry out a simultaneous transition, the opposition seized power, completed the takeover phase of the transition instantly, and launched radical economic reforms.

In contrast, in homegrown communist systems where the conservative forces were stronger, the hardline ruling elites, who might tolerate moderate market-oriented reforms, tended to reject democratizing initiatives; their refusal to implement moderate democratizing reforms then helped radicalize the opposition. In this case, the short cut was neither practical nor promising.

Regime transition from communism along Routes I and II falls into Hirschman's category of "sequential problem solving," which also includes Huntington's "Fabian strategy," Dahl's liberalization-before-inclusion sequence, and Rustow's four-step sequence of democratization.[66] Route III may be called "simultaneous problem solving." However, progress along the two dimensions of the dual transition is by no means assured. As demonstrated by the sporadic reversals and stalemates that both the Chinese and the Soviet reforms experienced in the 1980s, "sequential problem solving brings with it the risk of getting stuck."[67] Similar signs of stagnation also emerged in many ex-communist states and republics of the former Soviet Union.

In the transitions following the authoritarian route, structural factors favoring democratization are not sufficient for its inauguration. The initiation of the second phase of transition may be delayed by the ruling elites' resistance to democratization, the institutionalization of a progovernment, patronage-client system capable of mobilizing grassroots conservative support against prodemocratic forces, and the opposition's poor coalition-building skills.

In those Eastern European countries and parts of the former Soviet Union where the transition to formal democratic institutions was completed along the democratic breakthrough route, the drive toward a market economy might get stuck because of the short-term economic difficulties and structural complexities of transforming a planned economy. Some former communist countries may simply collapse into political chaos and anarchy, as Albania did after the fall of its communist rulers in 1991. Several newly independent states, such as Serbia, Bosnia-Herzegovina, Croatia, Georgia, Moldova, Armenia, and Azerbaijan, were engulfed by ethnic conflicts.

Finally, reversals are likely, especially in those countries where regime transition was only cosmetic. The new postcommunist governments in these states were controlled by the ruling elites of the old regimes, who were likely to practice authoritarian politics behind the democratic institutional facade, as in Romania, Serbia, Georgia under Gamsakhurdia, Uzbekistan, Tajikistan, and Turkmenistan. In some cases, the new ruling elites may be tempted to reverse the democratic process to centralize power in the development of a market economy. Such a move—from a nonmarket economy polyarchy to a market-economy-based authoritarian regime—would approximate the neoauthoritarian model pursued by China and Vietnam.

For instance, in September 1991 the president of Uzbekistan reportedly told Western journalists that his country would follow the Chinese model of economic reform under authoritarian rule because it was "not ready for full democracy or a market economy."[68] In late 1992 the Chinese model also appealed to the anti-Yeltsin forces in the Russian Parliament and the Civic Union.[69] After his visit to China, even Yeltsin was impressed by the country's economic progress and, while rejecting a wholesale borrowing of the Chinese model, praised its reform sequence.[70] Indeed, one may argue that the strong measures taken by Yeltsin after he forcibly vanquished his political foes in October 1993 amounted to a significant reversal of the democratization of the Russian polity and modified its sequence in a direction closer to the authoritarian model (although of a variety much softer than the Chinese or Vietnamese version).

These patterns of dual transition in ex-communist systems were emerging clearly in the early 1990s. As measured by the achieved levels of marketization and democratization as of 1993, states where transition away from communism had been in progress since the late 1980s can be divided into five groups.

China and Vietnam.   Measured by the structural-institutional changes in the marketization dimension, China and Vietnam had, by the early 1990s, moved rapidly toward a market economy. In Vietnam, the agrarian-based private sector accounted for some 65 percent of GDP in 1992.[71] In China, the combined share of the private and quasi-private sectors, similarly based in the rural areas, was about 59 percent of its Gross Social Product (GSP) in 1992.[72] Despite the absence of democratic reforms in these two countries, a significant degree of *civic* and *economic* freedom had been obtained as a result of the spillover effects from economic reforms. The movement toward a market economy in China and Vietnam was irreversible, but the prospects for democratization were dim in the short-run.

Hungary, Poland, Slovenia, and the Czech Republic.   Democratic consolidation and the breakthrough to a market economy had made significant gains in this group and reached the point of irreversibility. The new democratic governments in these states had survived serious political crises, including Slovenia's war with Serbia, the fall of five governments in Poland, the expulsion of extremists from Hungary's coalition government in 1993, and the separation between the Czech Republic and Slovakia. Economic reforms had advanced rapidly. The private sector in Poland and Hungary accounted for 40 percent of GDP in 1992 and was growing at a rate of 15–25 percent a year. Although the Czech private sector, nonexistent on the eve of transition, contributed only 15 percent of GDP in 1992, the anticipated mass privatization of state-owned enterprises and the growth of the private sector were expected to raise the share of the private sector significantly in the 1990s.[73]

Slovakia, Estonia, Latvia, Lithuania, Russia, and Ukraine. Democratic consolidation and economic reform in this group of countries lagged behind the countries in the last group, as a result of their late start, the severity of the macroeconomic crises and external shocks (the collapse of the previous trading system inside the Soviet bloc and within the former Soviet Union), and the high concentration of the military-industrial complex in their economies, excluding the three Baltic states. There was variation even within this group. Slovakia, Estonia, Latvia, and Lithuania made greater progress than Russia and Ukraine toward democratic consolidation and marketization (despite the defeat of the Sajudis by the Lithuanian Democratic Labor Party, composed of former communists). Russia also achieved greater progress in the same two dimensions than Ukraine, which was especially lagging in economic reforms and hurtling toward total economic collapse in late 1993. Given the smaller size and certain initial advantages (such as a vigorous private sector) of the Baltic states and Slovakia, the viability of democratic consolidation and economic reforms seemed to be greater in those countries than in Russia and Ukraine, whose prospects of dual transition would be most affected by the relations between the two countries, the ethnic problems inside their borders, and their governments' ability to stabilize their economies. For Russia, the greatest challenge was to contain the rapidly rising ultranationalist forces represented by Vladimir Zhirinovsky's Liberal Democratic Party, defend the basic democratic institutions despite Yeltsin's apparent shift toward soft authoritarianism, forge a pragmatic moderate reform coalition, and prevent further disintegration and resurgence of Russian imperialism.

Croatia, Georgia, Armenia, Bulgaria, Romania, Moldova, Belarus, Kyrgyzstan, Albania, and Mongolia. In these states, democratization was less advanced and its consolidation more problematic and uncertain for various reasons. Among these negative factors were: armed conflicts with neighboring new states over disputed territories (Croatia and Armenia); internal ethnic conflicts and strong conservative political forces (Georgia and Moldova); weak new democratic governments (Albania, Bulgaria, and Kyrgyzstan); and the control of the new governments by autocratic former communists (Belarus, Romania, and Mongolia). There was also variation in the progress toward marketization among these countries. Croatia, Georgia, and Armenia all had large private sectors and higher levels of development prior to transition—structural factors highly favorable for democratic consolidation and marketization under peaceful conditions. The same prospects seemed to be more problematic for Bulgaria, Romania, Belarus, and Moldova, all of which had smaller private sectors, more severe economic crises, and stronger antidemocratic forces. The most problematic cases in this group were Kyrgyzstan, Albania, and Mongolia, which had weak democratic forces, low levels of development, and grim prospects for building a viable market economy. Except for Croatia, Georgia, and Armenia, the countries in this group were more likely to experience stagnation and frequent reversals in democratization and marketization than the countries in the above groups. The temptation to pursue the authoritarian route was also higher among the ruling elites in these states.

Serbia, Kazakhstan, Uzbekistan, Tajikistan, Turkmenistan, and Azerbaijan. With the exception of Serbia, the countries in this group were the poorer republics in the former Soviet Union. Their economies were more dependent on the production of primary commodities (oil and monoagriculture), less market oriented, and less industrialized than the other former republics. Despite the holding of elections in these countries, substantive democratization had not taken place. They might have changed their forms of government, but not their regimes. The opposition remained weak and nonexistent in the former Soviet Central Asian republics, and was repressed in Serbia. Without exception, governments in these countries were under the control of autocratic communist elites of the old regime. Compared with other groups, these countries were the most likely to follow the authoritarian route taken by China and Vietnam.

What factors accounted for the above variations in transition from communist rule? Elite choice might be an important factor, but choice alone cannot explain the diversities in regime transition from orthodox communist rule. In making their choice, elites were also constrained by historical-structural factors of their societies—as much as they were affected by their personal values, the severity of the initial crisis, and political calculations of the costs and benefits of the various strategies of transition. It is doubtful that the present status of social science, the dearth of precise empirical data about these elites and their decision-making processes, could ever allow scholars to make an exact determination of how extensively elite choice influenced patterns of transition. This leaves the task of analyzing two general characteristics of these societies and states: their level of attained modernization and their political and economic histories, which may provide more illuminating explanations of the variations in regime transition from communist rule. In other words, the patterns of transition were most likely affected by the initial historical, structural, and institutional conditions of these societies. The importance of *initial advantages,* therefore, is worth analyzing.

The level of attained economic development in the different countries mentioned could explain the many variations in their progress toward democratization. More modern societies achieved more rapid democratization. Ex-communist countries that had made the greatest progress in democratic consolidation were, almost without exception, the more modernized countries. Ex-communist states that experienced setbacks and reversals in the same process were, also without exception, the less modernized countries.

Legacies of the political and economic histories of these societies were both real and significant in influencing the dual transition from communism. Ex-communist states that enjoyed certain initial advantages made more rapid progress than those that did not. Briefly, these initial advantages consisted of the following factors.

Insufficient penetration of the planned economy and the socialist welfare state.   This historical-institutional factor significantly influenced the transition to a market economy in ex-communist states. In countries where the planned economy and the socialist welfare state failed to penetrate sufficiently or dominate certain sectors of the economy, the progress toward marketization was more rapid in these sectors. In Poland and Hungary, for example, agriculture remained essentially semiprivate. In China, the socialist welfare state did not reach the countryside. In southern Vietnam, where market-oriented reforms had made rapid progress, agriculture on the eve of *doi moi* was essentially private, with cooperatives employing less than 30 percent of south Vietnamese farmers.[74] Neither had the industrial sector gained dominance in southern Vietnam. In 1987, about 40 percent of industrial workers were employed in the private sector, compared with 18 percent in northern Vietnam.[75]

Legacies of previously limited reforms.   Initial structural-institutional conditions favoring a rapid transition toward a market economy varied from one ex-communist state to another. An important reason for this variation was the countries' prior experience with market-oriented partial reforms undertaken by the old regime. In ex-communist systems that had experienced such reforms, including Hungary and Poland, there were embryonic and informal market institutions, a small but energetic group of private entrepreneurs, a semifunctioning network of commercial relationships built on past transactions, and a higher degree of public tolerance for private property and relative income inequality. Compared with ex-communist states that had not undertaken similar reforms, these countries experienced real advantages that made a significant difference in lowering the costs and accelerating the transition to marketization. In Poland, the private sector accounted for 30 percent of the country's employment and 17 percent of the national income in 1987.[76] In Hungary, the nonstate sector employed 30 percent of active income earners and contributed nearly 35 percent of the national income before the collapse of communism.[77] The preexisting private sector in Poland, for example, was credited with having provided most of the growth during the country's shock therapy, which failed to revive the state-owned firms while allowing private businesses to flourish.[78]

Similarly, partial political openings under the old regime had loosened up the political system in these states. The most important example here was the Soviet Union under Khrushchev between the mid-1950s and early 1960s. Significantly, most of the reformers and intellectuals who were identified with *glasnost* came of age during Khrushchev's Thaw. The dissident movement that overthrew the hardliners in Czechoslovakia also emerged during and after the Prague Spring in 1968.

Past resistance. In countries with histories of mass resistance to the old regimes and their Soviet sponsors, including Hungary, Poland, Czechoslovakia, and East Germany, democratization proceeded faster and experienced fewer setbacks during consolidation. In fact, the old communist regimes in these four states were imposed twice by the Soviet Union. In East Germany, the reimposition of communism took place in 1953 with the Red Army's suppression of the workers' uprising. In Hungary, it occurred after the Hungarian revolt in 1956, and in Czechoslovakia, it followed the Soviet-led invasion in 1968. In Poland, the reimposition was carried out by the Soviet Union's surrogate regime headed by General Wojciech Jaruzelski in December 1981. Among other things, past resistance to the old regime had helped to bring opposition leaders to public prominence (Lech Walesa and Vaclav Havel) and create antiregime coalitions. In contrast, in countries where past resistance to the old regimes was weak, the opposition lacked credible leaders and mass support. Democratic transition and consolidation in such countries was more problematic, as evidenced in Romania, Bulgaria, and Albania.

Numerous factors influence regime transition from communism. The most important include the clear presence of a profound systemic crisis, critical decisions made by top political elites to launch transition along one of the three routes, and socioeconomic structural factors. These factors affect the top elites' calculation of the level of support and degree of participation from key social groups. The complex interaction among crisis, elite choice, and socioeconomic structural factors significantly increases the uncertainty of the dual transition. Transitions may not occur when top political elites resist change despite mounting systemic crisis, as was the case in Cuba and North Korea. Transitions may fizzle out even after top elites accept the need for change, initiate reforms, but receive little support from major social groups. Depending on the choice of top elites, transition toward a market economy may occur only in the absence of democratization; and democratization may proceed without much movement toward a market economy. After launching the initial reforms, top political elites may also lose their ability to control the transition process to the newly unleashed social, political, and economic forces, which quickly turn reform into revolution.

Explaining the Tocqueville Paradox

2

hat most distinguished the wave of reforms and revolutions between 1979 and 1991 from earlier political and economic changes in communist states was that regime-initiated reforms failed to revitalize the communist systems. Instead, they had led to the speedy demise of all Soviet-imposed communist regimes in Eastern Europe by the end of 1989, caused a near collapse of China's government in the spring of 1989, and culminated in the total collapse and disintegration of the Soviet Union in 1991.

Few may disagree that Gorbachev's limited political reforms unleashed a political-nationalist revolution in the Soviet Union, but many may question whether China's economic reforms had triggered a similar revolution. In fact, a capitalist revolution did break out in China in the 1980s, and it destroyed orthodox communist rule in that country. The quantitative dimensions of this economic revolution were reflected in the doubling of China's GNP, the internationalization of its economy, and rapid industrialization. But the most significant changes resulting from this revolution were institutional-structural and manifested themselves in the fundamental change of China's economy from state-dominated to increasingly market-oriented. This capitalist revolution, moreover, was carried out by societal forces through the market, and not by the state.

Except for its initially limited agricultural reform, the Chinese government neither explicitly endorsed nor actively pursued a comprehensive and consistent program of transforming China's planned economy into a full market economy. Its stated goal of reform was an economic system dominated by the planned economy, with market mechanisms playing a secondary role, or, to use the famous "Bird Cage" analogy of the arch-conservative Chen Yun, the market was to be the bird set free only inside the cage of the planned economy. Unlike the postcommunist governments in Eastern Europe and the former Soviet Union, the Chinese government did not launch any substantive programs to privatize state-owned economic entities. In fact, during the brief conservative counterattack between 1989 and 1990, the government even attempted—though unsuccessfully—to reverse the growth of the private sector.

As China entered the 1990s, this capitalist revolution from below became more visible, and it received, however belatedly, the notice of the world community. Leading Western publications such as the *Economist, Far Eastern Economic Review, Business Week, Fortune, Time,* the *New York Times,* and the *Financial Times* gave extensive coverage to China's "Economic Miracle." By 1991, for example, more than half of China's Gross Social Product (GSP) was generated by the private and quasi-private sectors.[1] In 1992, the nonstate sector accounted for 617 billion yuan (61 percent) of the total industrial value-added.[2] In terms of the gross value of industrial output, the state sector's share fell to a record low of 48 percent in 1992.[3] The most dynamic part of the private sector—quasi-private rural industry—generated more net profits than the state's industrial sector, excluding transportation and building industries.[4] Government figures revealed that in 1992 rural industries alone generated 40 percent of China's gross industrial output and 48 percent of the government's tax revenues from the industrial sector.[5] This means that the rural industries, which grew rapidly after decollectivization of agriculture in the early 1980s, are on the verge of overtaking, after just 15 years, a colossal industrial sector that had taken the Chinese state 45 years and massive amounts of capital to build.

The significance and impact of China's capitalist revolution was more than economic, for it was also a *societal revolution,* as was the Soviet Union's nationalist-democratic revolution. Despite sharing some key similarities with other political or social revolutions in history, a societal revolution is unique in several important ways. In terms of the similarities, the societal revolutions that dismantled the communist states in Eastern Europe and the former Soviet Union instantly changed the leadership and forms of government. The capitalist societal revolutions in China and Vietnam, and the radical economic changes following the revolutions in Eastern Europe and the former Soviet Union, have also fundamentally altered the social structures of these countries with the creation and rise of a property-owning class.

Unlike earlier political and social revolutions, however, the upheavals in China, the Soviet Union, and Eastern Europe share several characteristics peculiar to societal revolutions. The first of these—and the quintessential characteristic of a societal revolution—is society's rising against the state to free itself from the latter's domination. Whereas earlier social and political revolutions typically led to the strengthening, expansion, and centralization of the state and its power, the societal revolutions in the late twentieth century, without exception, have caused a significant erosion, limitation, and decentralization of the state and its power.

Second, unlike most social revolutionaries, who were driven by collective visions of employing the power of the state to reshape social structures and institutions, the societal revolutionaries set out to extricate the power and influence of the state from society and to entrust society with the task of remaking itself. Third, the organizers and participants in these societal revolutions were not the representatives of a particular social class defined in economic terms. They included members of diverse social groups, such as ethnic minorities, the intelligentsia, industrial workers, religious believers, private entrepreneurs, and peasants. These were the members of a society long dominated by the state, and they often shared little more in common than their antagonism toward the state.

How did reforms in China and the Soviet Union, homes to the two most significant social revolutions in the early part of the twentieth century, which resulted in the creation of the world's two most formidable communist regimes, become great societal revolutions toward the end of the twentieth century?

History has offered numerous cases of revolutions triggered by reforms. The French political sociologist Alexis de Tocqueville was among the first to identify this paradox. "For it is not always when things are going from bad to worse that revolutions break out," wrote Tocqueville in a celebrated passage, "generally speaking, the most perilous moment for a bad government is one when it seeks to mend its ways."[6] The primary danger for reformers of despotic regimes, Tocqueville noted, was psychological in nature and originated from two sources: the sudden disappearance of fear in the masses and the loss of legitimacy in the old regime. Improvement in the standard of living, reduction of repression, and expansion of liberty, instead of bolstering the fortunes of the old regimes, may actually raise expectations and radicalize demands from a long-suffering people.

> The social order overthrown by a revolution is almost always better than the one immediately preceding it . . . Only consummate statecraft can enable a King to save his throne when after a long spell of oppressive rule he sets to improving the lot of his subjects. Patiently endured so long as it seemed beyond redress, a grievance comes to appear intolerable once the possibility of removing it crosses men's minds. For the mere fact that certain abuses have been remedied draws attention to the others and they now appear more galling; people may suffer less, but their sensibility is exacerbated.[7]

The Tocqueville Paradox, however, was a political risk rulers had to take, according to Edmund Burke, who viewed reform as an essential means of self-preservation for the state. "A state without the means of some change is without the means of its conservation," Burke observed in another often-quoted sentence.[8] Burke suggested, for example, that reform could avert potential revolutions mainly through institutional renovation, by regenerating "the deficient part of the old constitution through the parts which were not impaired." Of the parts of the old constitution that could serve the regenerative function, Burke implied, the most vital was the fundamental constitutional principle of the old regime.[9]

In his classic study of reform and revolution, Samuel P. Huntington advanced a solution to the Tocqueville Paradox. He observed that reform could serve either as a catalyst to or a substitute for revolution—depending primarily on the types of social groups rulers chose to ally themselves with and who their reform policies would benefit. Reform policies catering to the urban intelligentsia and alliances built with them typically became catalysts of revolution, whereas initiatives aimed at improving the lives of the peasantry and forming coalitions with them tended to avert revolution.[10] Albert Hirschman similarly viewed coalition-building (which he called "reform-mongering") as the most important factor in achieving progress without inciting revolution.[11]

The sudden disappearance of fear on the part of a long-oppressed people, the rapid loss of legitimacy of a repressive old regime, the inability of reformers to reinvigorate the decaying institutions of the state *within* the existing constitutional framework, and poor statecraft in selecting allies and beneficiaries of reform are all important factors that may turn reforms into revolutions. Indeed, all these factors were present, in varying degrees and at different times, during Gorbachev's *perestroika* from 1985 to 1991 and Deng Xiaoping's reform from 1979 to the early 1990s.

Although in exploring the connections between reform and revolution Tocqueville, Burke, Huntington, and Hirschman emphasized the different components of the political system and process (respectively, legitimacy, institutions, political leadership, and coalition-making skills), their analyses shared two important assumptions: (1) reforms could be managed by what Tocqueville called "consummate statecraft" and what Huntington termed a combination of "Fabian strategy and *blitzkrieg* tactics" employed by the reformers; and (2) the state, through the individual leaders and the resources controlled by its institutions, provided the primary source and momentum of change. Revolutions, in other words, do not necessarily erupt from a reform process if skillful reformers are able to protect the basis of legitimacy of the system, maintain the integrity of the key institutions of the state, and utilize the right policies in building coalitions.

The experiences of reform and revolution in the communist world between 1979 and 1991 in general, and the Chinese and Soviet experiences in particular, raise questions about these assumptions and call for alternative explanations. In the case of the Soviet Union, Gorbachev appeared to have followed Burke's advice. He attempted to shift the basis of legitimacy and political power away from the Party to the state and from Marxist-Leninist ideology to some form of popular participation. Meanwhile, he tried to defend the constitutional principles of the Soviet Union—the leading role of the Communist Party and the Soviet multiethnic empire centered on Russia—until the early part of 1990, when his ability to control the course of reform was exhausted.

In China, Deng Xiaoping was also aware of the importance of preserving the basis of legitimacy of the communist regime by, on the one hand, championing market-oriented reforms and, on the other, insisting on the monopoly of political power by the Communist Party. Deng's mixed legitimation principles, which subsumed limited promarket reforms under an authoritarian political-institutional framework, had little success in curbing the intelligentsia-led democracy movement. Toward the beginning of 1992, the legitimacy of the regime was more performance-based than ideology-based, and Deng viewed the continuation of one-party rule in China as increasingly dependent on the economic results it could generate. In his famous tour of southern China in early 1992, Deng declared:

> I can say that without the economic results of reform and opening, we would not have survived through June 4 [1989]; then there would have been chaos and civil war. Why did our country remain very stable after June 4? This was because the reform and opening promoted economic development and improved our people's lives . . . The key to reform and opening at the moment lies in the development of the economy. Right now, the economies of our neighboring countries and regions are growing faster than ours. If we do not develop, or develop more slowly, there will be trouble once our people start making comparisons.[12]

Both the Chinese and the Soviet cases demonstrated that the preservation of the constitutional principles or the basis of legitimacy was more difficult in practice than in theory. Policies designed to reduce citizens' political alienation toward the regime through increasing popular participation invariably helped raise more disturbing questions about the legitimation principles of one-party rule. Improvement in the standard of living often made its beneficiaries yearn for expansion of their political freedom. Meanwhile, the political fluidity of reform and the complexities of coalition-building made it equally unrealistic to expect reformers consistently to make the right decisions in adopting institutional reforms and picking allies.

In Gorbachev's case, even if one concedes that he might have wisely implemented certain institutional reforms, he picked the wrong partners by allying with the radical intelligentsia, who eventually deserted him and attacked him from the left. In China, even adopting policies that benefited the more reliable social groups failed to generate timely political support for the regime. Although Deng's agricultural reforms improved the welfare of the peasantry, he did not translate the economic results of his reform into political support in countering the radical intelligentsia. When confronted with the political crisis of the spring of 1989, Deng was compelled to turn to the hardliners and the military to put down a radicalized opposition.

In light of the Chinese and Soviet experiences of the 1980s and early 1990s, an alternative explanation focusing on the shifting balance of power between the state and society and the institutional vitality of the state during reform may shed new light on the Tocqueville Paradox. This explanation posits that in a reform process, the relationship between the government's ability to control the pace, direction, and agenda of reform and the extent of change is affected by a shift in the balance of power—mainly in the form of a transfer of political and economic resources—between the state and society.

In a previously closed political system in which the state monopolized economic and political resources, as all established prereform communist systems did, the balance of power was overwhelmingly in favor of the state. But once reform was initiated, the balance of power started to shift in favor of society, as the government, seeking renewed popular support or abandoning an increasingly costly institutional arrangement that maximized political control at the expense of other goals, namely, economic efficiency and public loyalty, began to permit measures resulting in the transfer of resources to the various components of society. There are two reasons such sustained reform efforts are likely to cause the balance of power to shift in favor of society.

First, there is an *absolute* decline of state-controlled resources (mainly economic assets, mass support, and political mobilizing capacities) either through the nongrowth or net loss resulting from their transfer to society. In the case of nongrowth of state-controlled resources, reform programs fail to generate new resources for the party-dominated state. For example, the state-owned sector continues to stagnate; the Party and its auxiliary organizations fail to bolster its mobilizing capacities or attract a new mass following. Meanwhile, the same reform programs produce significant resource gains for society by spurring the growth of the private sector, unofficial political organizations, and civic groups. In the case of negative growth, or net loss, state-controlled resources are depleted through various transfer programs, either state-initiated or society-initiated. Typical forms of state-to-society resource transfer include privatization's channeling productive assets from state control to private control; diversion of elites from the organs of the party-state to the emerging private sector and opposition groups; and the state's loss of control over key socioeconomic activities as a result of the rising influence of market forces controlled by societal actors.

Second, there is a *relative* decline of state-controlled resources. In this case, reform measures might generate growth for both the state and the society, but the resource gains for the state lag behind those for society.

The shift of balance of power between the state and society resulting from this transfer-cum-decline process in a dual transition undermines the regime's ability to control reform. To the extent that individual societal groups such as nationalists, religious organizations, intellectuals, industrial laborers, and the peasantry have their own agendas and interests that are different from, and often in conflict with, those of the reformer and the state, the gains from the resource transfers provide these groups with enhanced capacities to radicalize reform. The power shift between the state and society subsequently turns initially reformist programs into radical revolutionary ones—in a phenomenon that might be called "societal takeover," when the government effectively loses control of the pace, direction, and agenda-setting of reform to autonomous or organized social groups.

Although the shift of balance of power thesis provides a more obvious explanation of the difficulty of managing reform, it addresses only half the puzzle raised by the Tocqueville Paradox. The other half centers on another issue: Why is the state seldom able to take effective countermeasures to restore the balance of power and contain the expansion of certain societal groups and forces that pose a serious threat to its authority and control?

The answer lies in the process of progressive institutional decay of the old regime prevalent in nearly all transitions from communism. Ironically, reform in the communist systems tends to generate and accelerate the decay of the key institutions it seeks to preserve and revitalize. The causes for accelerated institutional decay are numerous and complex (more concrete causes for this process will be addressed later). Exogenous factors responsible for this process principally consist of the introduction of new autonomous forces, such as rival economic and political entities, which directly compete against these organizations and exploit their weaknesses, and the influx of new information and values that challenge the underlying authority and routine practices of these organizations. Internal factors chiefly include the low level of organizational complexity and adaptability of the agencies of the old party-state that traditionally rely on bureaucratic coordination and coercion as the only *modus operandi*. As the reform process increasingly emphasizes self-interested, voluntaristic *modi operandi* and reduces the use of coercion in coordinating public action, the performance and integrity of these organizations begin to decline precipitously. Other internal factors responsible for the institutional decay of the state prior to reform continue to erode the state even more potently after reform is launched. They often include the persistent corruption of organizational norms, declining ideology as a cohesive force, and rising cynicism among the personnel of these organizations.

Accelerated institutional decay contributes to societal takeover for the following reasons: (1) it reduces the regime's capacity to absorb and control newly generated resources (wealth and political participation being the two obvious resources produced by marketization and democratization); (2) it undermines the cohesion of the ruling elites and coordination among the different agencies of the state; and (3) it deprives the regime of its capacity to monitor and contain activated societal groups.

The institutional decay thesis thus explains the state's progressively declining ability to control, co-opt, neutralize, and counter societal actors who have made enormous gains through the resource transfer process of the reform. In short, the parallel processes of resource transfer from the state to society and accelerated institutional decay within the state produce the Tocqueville Paradox: reform generates forces that simultaneously strengthen the societal groups and social movements directly challenging the old regime and erode the institutions and legitimating principles it depends on for self-preservation.

The Dynamics of Control and Change

Historically, communist regimes initiated reforms when confronted with political and economic crises. Why, then, was it not until the 1980s that these reforms became revolutions or assumed increasingly revolutionary characteristics?

Table 2.1 illustrates the relationship between control and change during reform and depicts various reform outcomes. The table captures the Reformer's Dilemma: how to generate change without losing control. Reform, however, is not always necessary or inevitable.[13] Some polities lack the leadership and institutional capabilities for initiating reforms. Without internal stimuli or external pressures, countries may stagnate and further deteriorate. Or, in the case of "Burkian reform" (peaceful and gradual transformation of the key institutions of a polity), a rare historical occurrence that

Table 2.1   A typology of reform outcomes

		Amount of change	
		Low	High
Degree of control	High	(I) Limited reform	(II) Revolution from above
	Low	(III) Instant break-down	(IV) Societal take-over

has been called the "revolution from above," the regime manages to maintain control in spite of massive political and economic changes generated by reforms. Managing a Burkian reform is so difficult that historians and political scientists seldom agree on which historical cases qualify as "revolutions from above," with the exception of the Meiji Restoration in Japan, Bismarck's reforms in Germany, and Kemal Ataturk's modernizing reforms in Turkey.[14]

In all three cases, the consummate statecraft of individual leaders notwithstanding, the ruling elites reached a consensus on the need for change, built a strong conservative-moderate coalition (typically supported by key elements of the state, such as the bureaucrats and the military), methodically removed the antireform forces entrenched in the old regime, and succeeded in preserving and rejuvenating parts of the old political institutions of the state through the political and social changes generated by the reform. When these conditions are met, revolution from above is usually the outcome.

Conversely, reform movements are unsuccessful when the ruling elites and key segments of society, deeply divided over the desirability, pace, and goals of reform, are unable to form a sustainable coalition to guide the resulting changes. The regime quickly reverses course when there are signs of erosion of government control, activation of opposition forces, and symptoms of institutional decay of the state. Such was the case with Nikita Khrushchev's reforms in the Soviet Union in the late 1950s and early 1960s. His attempts to initiate change resulted in his ouster from power and replacement by an antireform coalition headed by Leonid Brezhnev.

In other cases, external counterreform intervention stemmed reforms before they came to revolutionary fruition, as with the Soviet invasion of Czechoslovakia in 1968, which ended the Prague Spring. Consequently, fear of triggering similar Soviet intervention deterred some progressive rulers from implementing bolder initiatives, as was the case with Janos Kadar and his partial economic reforms in Hungary in the late 1960s and early 1970s (he launched the New Economic Mechanism in 1968). The tragic historical experiences of the Soviet reimposition of communist regimes in East Germany in 1953, in Hungary in 1956, and in Czechoslovakia in 1968 also compelled the antiregime forces in these countries to exercise self-restraint in their opposition activities.

These three interrelated factors—the conservative mentality of the Soviet ruling elites, the threat of Soviet antireform interventions in Eastern Europe, and the self-imposed restraint on the part of the opposition forces—explain why only limited changes occurred in these systems during the two waves of reform (in the 1950s and the mid-1960s to mid-1970s) in the communist world prior to the 1980s.[15]

For communist regimes devoid of legitimacy as a result of not having led a successful social revolution against a corrupt autocracy, such as the Soviet-sponsored communist systems in Eastern Europe, instant regime breakdown is the most likely outcome once changes are introduced and external constraints (the threat of Soviet military interventions) are removed. In these instances, even a small amount of change may trigger a massive and instantaneous loss of control, causing a quick collapse of the old regime. This occurred in Eastern Europe in 1989 when the Soviet leadership decided to discontinue its support for the communist regimes there.

Factors Contributing to Societal Takeover

Reform may also become revolution when the government's control declines in proportion to the amount of change introduced into the political system. As stated, a sudden shift in the balance of power between the state and society, in combination with the accelerated institutional decay of the old regime, lies behind the Tocqueville Paradox. At a more concrete level, four factors precipitate and accelerate the dual process of state-to-society resource transfer and institutional decay within the state: the size and arena of the initial opening created by the reformist elites; the activation of major social groups; the formation of takeover coalitions; and favorable external factors.

The Initial Opening

Reform, by definition, is initiated by the ruling elites and, unlike revolution, involves gradual, peaceful, and generally progressive changes in the political and economic systems of a given country.[16] One of the necessary conditions of a peaceful transition from communism is the initial political or economic opening created by the reform-minded ruling elites. Although its size and arena vary from one communist state to another, the initial opening typically includes a measurable degree of decontrol of socioeconomic activities by the state. This process of decontrol is the result of deliberate action by the regime, either because its capacity to control these activities and penalize offenders has declined or because its top leadership consciously selects the opening in these areas as part of its liberalization program. Examples of such decontrol include an increase in social mobility, access to information, and general civic and economic freedom.

The state withdraws from certain socioeconomic activities for similar reasons: it no longer has adequate resources to maintain its preeminence at the prereform level or its top leadership, realizing the limits of the state, decides to let society assume the responsibility of conducting such activities on its own. To the extent that the state's previous provision of services and benefits guaranteed it various means of control over society, the reduction of these services inevitably results in the state's loss of such control. The most obvious examples include (1) the transfer of certain services and activities to the private sector as part of the privatization program; (2) a decrease in the provision of services and benefits provided by the socialist welfare state; (3) the reduction of the state's involvement in the civic and professional activities of private individuals as part of political demobilization; and (4) economic deregulation and liberalization.

In theory, the larger the size of the initial opening, or the greater the degree of initial liberalization, the more favorable the conditions created by the reformers for the state-society resource transfer process and the activation of social forces. In reality, however, initial openings of most reforms tend to be small as a result of strong conservative resistance and the compromises made by a reformer to launch his programs. The size of the initial opening thus matters less than the *arena* of the opening; that is, where the initial liberalization program is launched, for a relatively small or weak opening in a significant or strategic area may unleash, after a short period, enormous amounts of energy stored in that particular area. Preferably, the initial opening is created in a strategic area whose liberalization may result in the mobilization of important social groups, which can then be recruited as dependable coalition partners for the reformer and are capable of generating self-sustaining reform momentum.

Generally, the initial opening created by the reforming elites is a necessary—though not a sufficient—condition for societal takeover. The contribution of the top reformers in this phase usually consists of reaching a minimum level of consensus on the need for change, making the necessary personnel changes within the government to ensure the implementation of limited reform measures, and providing some protection and reassurances for the social groups being mobilized for the reform. Another contribution of the initial opening is its creation of a conducive environment in which to accelerate the activation of social forces. This environment is often the product of the consequences, some intended but most unforeseen, of the liberalization project that led to the decontrol of socioeconomic activities by the state, dispersion of power within the state, an overall decline in repression, and expansion of the influence of nonstate actors, that is, foreign, societal, and market forces.

It has often been observed that a higher degree of decentralization of economic decision-making, widespread official corruption as part of the institutional decay of the party-state, limited price reforms, and expansion of foreign economic contacts contribute to the growth of the private sector in communist states (such as Hungary and Poland in the 1970s and China and Vietnam in the 1980s). Even though the original intention of the reformers in nearly all cases was to improve the performance of the state sector with an injection of material incentives, their policies created a favorable environment for the private sector—which directly enhanced the autonomy and strength of major social groups and functioned as a vehicle for societal takeover—to grow rapidly.

Politically, when the regime pursues partial democratization leading to a decline in repression, a corresponding decline in the population's fear of the regime, and a loosening of certain aspects of the political process, openings in these areas provide the democratic opposition with opportunities for a direct seizure of critical resources from the state. Indirectly, such partial reforms often lead to the formation of society-based mass democracy movements and, eventually, the institutionalization of democratic politics, even though the regime does not intend such results. The best example here was the proliferation of political parties, the takeover of a significant part of the mass media by the liberal forces, and the mushrooming of political and religious groups in the Soviet Union in the late 1980s and early 1990. These mobilized groups and movements went on to capture elective offices, as well as republican and local governments in the Baltic republics, Moscow, and Leningrad.

The contribution of the initial opening to a societal breakthrough in regime transition is essential but not decisive. Whether greater momentum can be added to the weak, regime-initiated changes depends on the second factor: the activation of major social groups.

Activation of Major Social Groups

In transitions from authoritarian and communist rule, the initial opening created by the regime produces "a sharp and rapid increase in general politicization and popular activation."[17] But scholars have yet to explain the variations in the participants, speed, level, and form of sudden and dramatic popular activation. Frequently, the political and economic mobilization of major social groups fails to occur, or it is too weak to make an impact on the transition. The postopening mobilization of such groups offers a more powerful explanation for societal takeover. Whether they are able to seize the opening and acquire the resources and capabilities necessary to reset the political agenda is basically determined by three characteristics of these groups: their autonomy, strength, and value orientations.

First, they must possess a relatively high degree of autonomy—which means that, even prior to the initiation of reform, certain social groups were relatively independent from and unconstrained by the political and economic institutions of the party-state. The autonomy of a given social group here is defined as its ability to resist the total assimilation or co-optation into the dominant value system and sociopolitical institutions of the communist party-state. This ability manifests itself in the group's capacity for independent collective action, both coordinated and uncoordinated.

As a rule, those groups that remain on the periphery of the communist political system and welfare state, such as minority ethnic groups, peasants, and the intelligentsia, tend to possess a higher degree of autonomy relative to other groups, including industrial workers, state employees, and technocrats. The relative autonomy of these groups is usually the consequence of their deliberate exclusion by the prereform regime. For instance, the Chinese communist regime had pursued a policy of excluding intellectuals from positions of power and membership in the Party prior to the early 1980s. Before reform, only 4 percent of party members were college graduates and 6 percent of the 810,000 officials in the government and party organizations had college educations.[18] The regime's inability to fund an inclusive welfare state forced it to exclude the Chinese peasantry from its socialist welfare programs, which consisted of food subsidies, free health care, guaranteed employment, and income security. In contrast with industrial workers, Chinese peasants retained a high degree of independence from the state.[19]

Relative group autonomy may also result from the failed efforts of the old regime to co-opt such groups. Observers of the precollapse Eastern European countries noted that the ex-communist regimes' co-optation of the intelligentsia remained superficial.[20] Post-1989 studies of the causes of the collapse of communism in Eastern Europe reveal much evidence of resistance within these groups to state domination.[21] In the Soviet Union, recent studies also show that the intelligentsia, compared with other social groups, were more likely to engage in independent antiregime activities prior to *perestroika*.[22] Except for the Solidarity in Poland in the 1980s, few groups openly challenged the authority of prereform regimes. But scholars who have examined the relationship between the communist party-state and the intelligentsia have found that the latter, although not engaged in organized opposition, were able to act with relative autonomy in their traditional strongholds, such as universities, news organizations, and professional associations. They even periodically used these forums to attack the old regimes.[23]

In China, although the majority of the intelligentsia did not openly challenge the prereform Maoist regime, a considerable number of liberal intellectuals, who were admitted into the various organs of the regime but whose liberal views remained unchanged, constantly tested the limits of the regime's tolerance by publishing veiled attacks against it and urging political liberalization. They might be called the "outsiders" attacking from within.[24] Generally, the autonomy of major social groups tends to be higher in authoritarian states than in communist states, largely owing to the less penetrative reach of the state in the former than in the latter.

Second, major social groups must have a minimum amount of strength in certain areas—their membership size, organizational or entrepreneurial capacity, and access to political and economic resources—to have an impact.

As a result of the withdrawal of the state during reform, the strength of such groups usually gains, although such gains are distributed unevenly among different groups. But what makes certain social groups more likely candidates for "revolutionaries from below" than others is probably related to their prereform individual group characteristics. For example, the strength of the Chinese peasantry as a social group has much to do with its huge size and strategic position in the maintenance of political stability for the regime. Another strength of this group comes from its ingrained entrepreneurship, which the commune system had failed to eradicate. The ethnic groups in the Baltics became a powerful political force during *perestroika* because of their group cohesion and shared goal of national independence. The Eastern European and Soviet intelligentsia demonstrated their political power during regime transition mainly through their organizational capacity, political entrepreneurship, and influence in the mass media.[25]

The last factor affecting the activation of key social groups may be called "group value orientations." This term is distinct from the more inclusive phrase "cultural values" in that cultural values typically refer to the dominant beliefs of a given society, whereas "group value orientations" are defined as a set of political and economic values certain social groups are more likely to possess than others. Group value orientations influence the political and economic behavior of the members of these groups when they are presented with opportunities created by regime-initiated openings, principally because these values affect their perception and calculation of the costs and benefits of activation.

For instance, one can argue that ethnic pride and nationalist values were the most powerful motivating forces behind the independence movements in the Baltics, the Ukraine, and other former Soviet republics; similarly, strong belief in political participation and democratization also propelled the intelligentsia-dominated democracy movements in China and the Soviet Union. Peasants' entrepreneurial attitudes provided an important explanation for the grassroots reform movement in the Chinese countryside. In contrast, other group value orientations can help explain the failure of certain groups to take advantage of regime-created openings.

The increasing availability of opinion polling data from communist states makes it possible to examine the relationship between group behavior and group value orientations. In general, the level of motivation for political participation is associated with the level of education, as has been repeatedly reconfirmed by opinion survey data collected in both China and the Soviet Union.[26] The degree of motivation for taking economic risks, however, may be correlated with the given groups' stake in the economic *status quo*. Because of their relatively privileged position in the socialist welfare state, industrial workers were rarely at the forefront of market-oriented reform despite their enormous group strength and the potential benefits of such reform. In fact, they often appeared to oppose reforms that would harm their security, benefits, and status.[27] The postcommunist transition toward a market economy in nearly all Eastern European states demonstrated the opposition of the industrial workers and state employees to market-oriented reform measures that threatened to deprive them of some of the most sacrosanct benefits they had enjoyed under the old regimes—above all, job security.

This argument does not suggest, however, that the industrial labor force in ex-communist states is composed of *homo sovieticus* inherently incapable of undertaking entrepreneurial activities. Rather, workers' unfavorable collective attitudes toward a market economy must be traced to the effects of socialist welfare institutions on their value-formation. Such welfare institutions shape the values of individuals included by developing certain basic expectations about job security, social justice, and equality. The absence of competing or alternative institutions such as markets (1) raises doubts and fears about the effectiveness of these alternative institutions and the values they embody (the profit-motive and risk-tolerance) and (2) reinforces the long-standing values embodied by the monopolistic existing institutions of state-socialism.

Promarket group attitudes should thus be expected to be strong where (1) there are competing, however weak, market institutions (as in certain parts of rural China and Eastern Europe where some market institutions managed to survive collectivization); (2) the monopolistic institutions of the planned economy are relatively weak or have been eroded by limited marketizing experiments (as in Hungary and Poland); (3) the old regime fails to extend the socialist welfare state to all social groups (as in the Chinese and Vietnamese countryside); (4) new market institutions take root and grow.

Although the less educated and underprivileged peasantry has proved to be the leading force in the development of a market economy, the same group is rarely an active participant in the democratization process. This fact can also be explained by the value orientations of this group as a whole. As polling data in China revealed, the Chinese peasantry tended to be less supportive of democracy and more submissive to authority than other groups. A survey of Chinese citizens in 1987 showed that 26 percent of peasants thought that "China does not need democracy right now," compared with 21 percent of workers and 11 percent of intellectuals. When asked what they would do when there were differing views, 33 percent of the peasants interviewed said they would "listen to the leader," compared with 27 percent of workers and 13 percent of intellectuals.[28]

In other ex-communist countries, peasants were, at least initially, reluctant to embrace new democratic forces. In the first free elections held in Albania, in March 1990, the communists won most of the rural votes. Bulgaria's democratic coalition, the Union of Democratic Forces, was defeated in the June 1990 elections largely because of its weak rural support.[29] In the local elections held in Romania in February 1992, the National Salvation Front dominated by ex-communists received the majority of its support from rural areas.[30]

The peasantry's initial lack of support for democratic forces should not be construed as an unwavering endorsement of dictatorship. Even authoritarian regimes cannot afford to take the political support of this group for granted—it must be cultivated, rewarded, and institutionalized, for peasants, angered by taxes, levies, and declining standards of living, can also imperil the survival of an authoritarian regime through the withdrawal of their political support, riots, and other forms of protest. A case in point was the overwhelming electoral victory by the opposition in Albania in March 1992, when angry peasants joined forces with the Democratic Party and voted the former communists (the Socialist Party) out of office.

The explicit proposition here is that the likelihood and form of societal takeover may be significantly influenced by a country's *social mobilization profile,* which includes, primarily, level of education, urbanization, and structure of the labor force. When a given country's social mobilization profile corresponds closely to that of societies on the eve of the inauguration of democratic regimes (high rates of urbanization and literacy), a democratic breakthrough is more likely. When a country's social mobilization profile shows no significant deviation from that of societies during the early stages of the development, a democratic breakthrough may be less likely, but the chances for a capitalist breakthrough are enhanced by the presence of a large peasantry excluded from the socialist welfare state. Table 2.2 provides the social mobilization profile of the major ex-communist states. The patterns of regime transition in these countries support this argument, with ex-communist states at the lower level of development, namely, China and Vietnam, moving more rapidly toward marketization but making little progress in democratization. More developed ex-communist states have made greater progress toward democratization but lag behind China and Vietnam in marketization.

The Formation of Takeover Coalitions

Whether autonomous social groups can seize resources from the state, in many instances, depends heavily on the ability of these groups to form takeover coalitions. The cooperation, support, and participation of other groups and actors are required to gain the resources needed for a societal breakthrough. Given the general weakness of civil society in pretransition communist states, individual societal groups often join forces, for however enfeebled and corrupted, the old regime normally possesses enough resources to defeat takeover efforts attempted by individual societal groups acting inde-

Table 2.2 Social mobilization profiles of established communist countries prior to transition (in percentages)

	Urbanization	Labor force in nonagricultural sector	Population with a secondary education[a]	Population with a higher education
More developed communist states				
Soviet Union	65.7 (1986)	81.0 (1987)	63.3 (1989)	13.9 (1989)
Czechoslovakia	75.6 (1985)	88.0 (1988)	45.9 (1980)	6.0 (1980)
East Germany	76.8 (1984)	96.0 (1988)	52.6 (1981)	17.3 (1981)
Hungary	59.6 (1988)	81.0 (1988)	80.6 (1980)	7.0 (1980)
Poland	61.2 (1988)	73.0 (1988)	33.9 (1978)	5.7 (1978)
Yugoslavia	50.2 (1987)	95.0 (1988)	23.4 (1981)	6.8 (1981)
Moderately developed communist states				
Bulgaria	67.0 (1988)	79.0 (1987)	—	—
Romania	51.3 (1987)	71.0 (1985)	39.8 (1977)	4.6 (1977)
Cuba[b]	71.0 (1985)	76.0 (1976)	—	—
Less developed communist states				
Albania	35.0 (1987)[c]	48.0 (1988)[d]	—	—
China	18.9 (1979)	24.6 (1979)	21.8 (1982)	1.0 (1982)
Vietnam[e]	21.0 (1987)	32.0 (1980)	—	1.3 (1989)

Sources: Statistical Yearbook of China, 1991, pp. 79, 95, 822–823, and 852; *Statistical Yearbook of China, 1988,* pp. 997 and 1023; *Statistical Yearbook of China, 1989,* p. 946.

a. Including both middle-school and high-school education.

b. The World Bank, *World Development Report, 1987,* pp. 265 and 267.

c. The World Bank, *World Development Report, 1989,* p. 233.

d. Per Sandstrom and Orjan Sjoberg, "Albanian Economic Performance: Stagnation in the 1980s," *Soviet Studies,* vol. 43, no. 5 (1991), p. 936.

e. The World Bank, *World Development Report, 1987,* p. 264; *World Development Report, 1989,* p. 224; David Marr, "Education, Research, and Information Circulation in Contemporary Vietnam," in *Reinventing Vietnamese Socialism: Doi Moi in Comparative Perspective,* ed. William Turley and Mark Selden (Boulder, Colo.: Westview Press, 1993), pp. 341–342.

pendently. A case in point was the intelligentsia-dominated democracy movement in China during the 1980s, which suffered repeated setbacks chiefly as a result of the intellectuals' inability to form a broad-based coalition in their push for democratization.

Crafting coalitions is one of the most critical skills of the reformer and the deciding factor in the success or failure of his programs. In the case of societal takeover or instant breakdown of communist regimes in the late 1980s, however, the extraordinary ability of key societal groups to form takeover coalitions when individual reformist leaders were incapable of maintaining their own alliances shows that coalition-building is also a powerful instrument that societal groups can use against the state.

Depending on the compatibility of the values, interests, and goals of the partners, societal coalitions may vary in terms of their durability, strength, and organizational forms. Societal coalitions whose central mission is to seize resources from the state as opposition coalitions, rather than to allocate resources or payoffs as governing coalitions, are often large in size and have considerable strength. These two characteristics, however, tend to reduce their durability and organizational cohesion over time, as a result of the costs and complexities involved in maintaining an oversized coalition.

Because of the fluidity of coalition politics and the high costs of political opposition under prereform communist rule, most societal coalitions were formed during or immediately before transition. In most Eastern European countries, hastily formed coalitions sprang up on the eve of transition to seize power from collapsing regimes. In the Soviet Union, most societal coalitions were built during the course of *perestroika* in pursuit of increasingly radical goals of change. In China, while the radical intelligentsia were unable to rally other social groups, the newly emerging rural entrepreneurs were successful in forging an informal alliance with members of the local elites, peasants, and foreign investors in the rapid development of a vigorous private sector.[31]

Societal actors may form a predominantly society-based takeover coalition incorporating many groups—the intelligentsia, religious groups, ethnic minorities, and industrial labor—such as the coalitions forged between the anti-Russian nationalists and the antiregime democratic opposition in Eastern Europe and the Baltic republics. Experiences of regime transition in both authoritarian and communist systems demonstrate that purely society-based takeover coalitions were quite rare. Some participation by the progressive elements within the old regime was the rule rather than the exception.[32] The latter's inclusion in the takeover coalition reduces the costs and accelerates the speed of transition.

Transition in the Soviet Union received added momentum when the radical intelligentsia established an alliance with the radical reformers who had defected from the regime, Democratic Russia being the preeminent example.

In other instances, societal actors found allies in the *entrepreneurial* establishment of the government—mainly the managerial elites in local governments and state-owned enterprises. The diversion of these entrepreneurial elements from the state sector to the private sector constituted another form of state-to-society resource transfer and directly contributed to the strengthening of society and the erosion of the state. For instance, by 1991, China's quasi-private rural industrial firms had recruited more than 1.3 million engineers and technicians from the state sector with higher pay and other benefits, representing about 12 percent of the technical elites in China.[33]

Although takeover coalitions often accelerate resource transfer from the state to society during reform, in the post-takeover phase these coalitions tend to be fragile and short-lived. As the posttransition experiences in Eastern Europe and the former Soviet Union have shown, societal coalitions were more unified in opposition than in power, and they frequently broke down over long-term policy and ideological differences obscured and outweighed by the coalition's shared short-term interest in driving the old regime from power during the takeover phase.

Favorable External Factors

The involvement of external influences in transition from communism is necessitated by the relative weakness of society in communist states. The principal advantages of using external resources to bolster society-based democratizing and marketizing forces include: (1) the diversity of external actors over whom the old regime has little control; (2) their capacity to mobilize externally available resources; (3) the speed with which these resources can be introduced into the transition process; and (4) the multiplicity of means and channels through which external influences may be applied.

The introduction of foreign influence, both political and economic, can increase and diversify the resources available to society, thus accelerating the power shift between the state and society. Societal actors normally require a considerable length of time to mobilize their strength and resources in launching takeover attempts; this period of time can be significantly shortened, and the takeover process speeded up, if existing resources outside a sovereign nation-state can be made available to these societal groups. In other words, the readily available resources of the *international society* can assist the forces of the domestic society.

Students of comparative politics have long recognized the importance of favorable external factors in democratization.[34] However, the primary source of regime change in communist systems was domestic rather than foreign; the ascendance of reformers within the ruling elites and the political mobilization of societal forces constituted the main sources of change. The important distinction between the roles played by domestic and external actors in regime transition is that between *initiation* and *promotion*. Although external actors played virtually no direct role in initiating transition in communist systems at the end of the 1980s, they made critical contributions to the acceleration of the transition and the consolidation of new democratic regimes. In the dual transition, a further distinction needs to be made between external political contributions and external economic contributions.

In the democratization phase, external political actors—democratic governments in the West, their alliances, international organizations, and human rights groups—normally play a minor role because their ability to influence directly the events in a given country is limited. National sovereignty routinely provides the regime in power with a convenient—albeit increasingly porous—shield to defend itself against external criticisms and interventions. Larry Diamond noted that democracy may be "promoted," but not "exported."[35] Short of direct military intervention to install or restore democratic governments, there have been few instances of successful democratization carried out solely under the auspices of external political actors.

At most, external political actors may offer incentives for democratization and impose penalties for the continuation of authoritarian rule or the reversal of democratization. They act as international pressure groups that may moderate the political behavior of hardline regimes and raise the costs of repression through international sanctions.

A case in point here was the West's response to the crackdown on the opposition by the Chinese government after the Tiananmen Square incident in June 1989. Although the West could do little to revive the opposition movement within China or force the hardliners to liberalize the political process, it was able to raise the costs of repression. Western sanctions forced a degree of moderation on the Chinese government, as evidenced by the execution of fewer political prisoners than expected, the less severe punishment against opponents of the regime, and the early release of hundreds of political prisoners (with each release timed with the annual renewal of China's Most Favored Nation trade status with the United States).

In transition from communism in Eastern Europe, the political role of the West was nearly negligible. But the role of the Soviet Union was of exceptional importance—not for what it did, but for what it failed to do. Under Gorbachev's rule, the Soviet contribution to the collapse of communist regimes in Eastern Europe was its refusal to continue to support these regimes with force. The removal of this external constraint in 1989 was the single most powerful explanation as to why these regimes all collapsed in quick succession.

In the marketization process of the dual transition, both in the authoritarian model and in the democratic breakthrough model, the role of external economic factors assumes critical—though not necessarily decisive—importance for the following reasons. First, given the severity of the economic crises that accompanied nearly all regime change in communist states, external economic actors, such as Western governments, multilateral financial organizations, and private investors, could provide the much-needed funds to stabilize the macroeconomic situation. Without the West's multibillion dollar aid packages to the former Soviet republics and Eastern European countries, they could never have embarked on bold but high-risk programs of rapid marketization.

For most Eastern European countries, the inflow of large amounts of Western aid may have helped cushion the negative impact of shock therapy. As of November 1991, OECD countries, the IMF, and the World Bank had pledged $45 billion, including $8 billion in grants, to Eastern Europe, with close to $9 billion actually disbursed.[36] In March 1991, the member nations of the Paris Club waived half of Poland's $33 billion external debt.[37] In addition, the Eastern European countries, especially Poland, Hungary, and Czechoslovakia, received an increasing flow of foreign direct investment. Between 1990 and 1992, direct investment from private Western sources in Eastern Europe amounted to $11 billion.[38]

Second, perhaps more important than the provision of capital, a crucial external economic factor is the establishment of linkages between the world economy and the previously autarkic planned economies of communist states. These linkages speed up marketization by exposing the formerly protected domestic markets in these countries to the intensive competition of the world market, introducing new technologies, accelerating changes in the economic structure, and opening up access to the international markets to the emerging private producers in these economies. Unlike the short-term injection of massive aid aimed at stabilizing a crisis situation, such structural linkages to the world economy are, in the long-run, better able to generate self-sustaining growth in an outward-looking economy over which the state tends to exert dwindling control.

The case of China is, again, illustrative of the critical role of external economic forces in the marketization processes of the 1980s.[39] Between 1979 and 1991, China absorbed nearly $80 billion in foreign capital ($52.7 billion in loans and about $27 billion in investment) and imported $24.6 billion in foreign technologies and advanced equipment.[40] As a measure of the internationalization of the Chinese economy, the total volume of foreign trade was only $38.1 billion in 1980, but reached $165.6 billion in 1992, a fourfold increase over 12 years, moving China's ranking from the world's thirty-fourth trading nation to the eleventh.[41] In 1978, exports accounted for only 4.65 percent of Chinese GNP; by 1992, their share had jumped to 19.5 percent—well above the 12 percent average for very large countries (for the United States, this ratio was 7.5 percent in 1991).[42]

Strong evidence links the phenomenal growth of the private and quasi-private sectors in China to the role of external economic factors. The private and quasi-private sectors were most developed in China's coastal areas (especially in the South), where about 80 percent of foreign investment was concentrated.[43] The increasing access to the world market also benefited the private sector. The quasi-private rural industries alone accounted for 30 percent of the net growth in China's export earnings between 1986 and 1990, and 25 percent of China's total exports in 1991.[44]

The Vietnamese leadership similarly recognized the crucial role of foreign economic influence in transforming a backward planned economy and aggressively courted foreign investment. Despite the U.S.-imposed economic embargo, Vietnam's efforts between 1988 and 1992 achieved impressive results, attracting more than $4.6 billion in pledged foreign investments, with about $1 billion actually disbursed.[45] As in China, foreign-invested firms in Vietnam began to promote exports and tourism aggressively. These foreign investments were concentrated in the traditionally capitalist South, where the planned economy never gained dominance, as it did in the North; about 80 percent of total foreign investment was made in the South, and 50 percent in Ho Chi Minh City (Saigon) alone, where the private sector had experienced the fastest growth.[46] Aside from private foreign direct investment, Vietnam in the early 1990s began to receive sizable amounts of aid from Western governments. Japan resumed its official aid program to Vietnam in 1993, as did France in the same year. The flow of capital from private and official sources was expected to further accelerate Vietnam's progress toward a market economy.

External economic factors have been used to advance indirectly the cause of democratizing countries led by rulers who, although determined to maintain their monopoly of political power, were forced by economic necessities to open their countries to foreign investment and commerce, as China did in 1979, Vietnam in 1987, and Cuba and North Korea attempted to do in the early 1990s. In addition to the obvious economic benefits mentioned above, linkages with the world economy tend to increase the volume and speed of the flow of information and ideas through trade, tourism, and educational and cultural exchanges, all of which often quietly undermine the ability of these postcommunist authoritarian regimes to control their societies.

The desirability of favorable external influence should not, however, be confused with its availability, as illustrated by the case of the former Soviet Union, in which promised Western official aid and anticipated private investment were disappointing. Only a small portion of the pledged Western aid packages (the $24 billion promised in early 1992 and the repackaged $28 billion program in May 1993) was actually delivered in 1992–1993 because of the slow progress toward stabilization, lack of real U.S. leadership, and division among the principal donors. Continuing political turmoil and worsening economic conditions across the former Soviet Union also discouraged private foreign investments. External aid also comes with a price—reduction in national autonomy in economic policy-making and increased vulnerability to international competition, which is, in reality, not always fair or free. For instance, several new democratic Eastern European countries in the early 1990s found themselves subject to trade restrictions imposed by the European Community (on chemicals, agricultural produce, steel, and textiles) while they imported more goods from EC countries. This resulted in a trade deficit of $3.9 billion between 1991 and 1992 with the EC; but previously, Bulgaria, Czechoslovakia, Hungary, Romania, and Poland had had a trade surplus with the EC every year, totaling $2.7 billion in 1988–1990.[47]

Reform and Institutional Decay

The relationship between the institutional decay of the communist party-state and the empowerment of society is an interdependent one in the reverse sense: The more robust the institutions of the communist party-state, the more difficult it is for the forces of society to make a breakthrough during reform. In studying the forces contributing to the institutional decay of the state in communist systems during reform, one must distinguish between the level of *prior* institutional decay and the *accelerated* institutional decay caused by the reform process.

Reform in communist states is invariably precipitated by a systemic crisis, a fact implying prior failures of the regime's policies and institutions. But the degree of institutional decay—loosely defined here as loss of public trust, organizational deterioration, internal corruption, and declining effectiveness—varies from country to country at the initiation of reform. In countries where the prior level of institutional decay was higher, such as post–Cultural Revolution China, where a decade of internal political chaos had ravaged the key institutions of the Party and the state, the initial institutional barriers to reform were low, giving the reformers an initial advantage over their counterparts in communist systems where prior institutional decay was less advanced.

Regardless of the level of prior institutional decay, moreover, a common feature found in all reform movements under communist rule during regime transition was accelerated institutional decay of the party-state. The key institutions of the communist party-state, compared with those of other types of authoritarian states, were especially vulnerable to accelerated decay because of their high level of interpenetration, interconnectedness, and interdependence. These unique features of the party-state constituted a major obstacle to the transformation and revitalization of these institutions into autonomous agencies of the state. As a result, the decaying of one institution of the party-state infected another, degraded its integrity, and reduced its chances for self-renewal.

Four additional factors were also responsible for the accelerated institutional decay of the party-state. First, these institutions suffered from a low level of adaptability to new missions, environments, and functions. Thomas Remington observed that "communist institutions . . . are ultimately incapable of accommodating the explosion of demands for participation that follows a liberalization of political rights."[48] Despite their renowned mobilizing capacities in a centralized and hierarchical system under orthodox communism, these institutions have great difficulties adapting to more decentralized, competitive, and pluralistic conditions during transition. In an illuminating study of the 1990 Moscow city council elections, Timothy Colton linked the ineptitude of the Moscow Party Organization of the CPSU with its humiliating electoral losses.[49] In the economic arena, as exemplified by China in the late 1980s, state-owned enterprises, despite their huge advantages in technology and capital, were bested by private and quasi-private producers in many markets. In the Soviet Union, economists also noted widespread managerial disarray and atrophying of the old administrative institutions of the planned economy during *perestroika*.[50]

Second, ideological and policy conflicts among the different groups within these institutions led to internal division and loss of cohesion. Opposition forces composed of liberal elements emerged from within the regime, rather than outside of it. This occurred, for example, in Vietnam in the late 1980s, when the Club of Former Resistance Fighters, based in Ho Chi Minh City, openly challenged Hanoi by calling for political liberalization.[51] In China and the Soviet Union, most of the radical reformers and liberal intellectuals were former functionaries of these institutions. The dispersion of power and resources within the party-state during reform, generating center-periphery disharmony, was another type of loss of institutional cohesion and coordination. A case in point was the growing fiscal tensions between provincial governments and the central government in China.[52]

Third, accelerated institutional decay was related to growing oppositional assault on the legitimacy, image, performance, and personnel of these institutions, and to the resulting politicization within them. Many peripheral institutions, such as the Komsomol in the Soviet Union and the Youth League in China, trade unions, and other formerly state-sponsored professional organizations, either dissolved because of a lack of material support and political guidance from the government or were taken over by radical elements and turned into organized antiregime forces. The central institutions of the party-state saw their prestige decline, and even fracture (such was the case with the formation of an in-party opposition group known as the "Democratic Platform within the CPSU" in the Soviet Union).

In the Soviet Union, accelerated institutional decay of the party-state was mainly caused by the forces of *glasnost* and *perestroika*. Radical opposition movements both in the center (the Interregional Group after March 1989) and on the periphery (popular fronts and nationalist groups in outlying republics) relentlessly attacked the old regime. A renewed media campaign of de-Stalinization after 1986 debunked the legitimating myths of communism. The potent delegitimizing impact of *glasnost* could best be gauged by an anguished outburst from Yegor Ligachev, the leading conservative in the CPSU Politburo:

> It created a gloomy atmosphere in the country. It affects the emotions of the people, their mood, their work-efficiency, when from morning to night everything negative from the past is being dumped on them. Patriotic topics have been squeezed out, shunted aside. People are longing for something positive, something shining, and yet our own cultural figures have published more lies and anti-Soviet things than our Western enemies ever did in the last seventy years combined.[53]

The same political forces were also responsible for the politicization and institutional decay of the Soviet military, debilitating it as the ultimate instrument of the state against society, as shown by the failed coup in August 1991.[54] Two key developments offered a glimpse into the extent of this decay:

(1) A large exodus from the Party of its demoralized members, with 4.2 million people—about a quarter of its total membership—leaving the CPSU between January 1990 and July 1991.[55] Most of the defectors from the old regime were the more experienced members constituting a key age group of the CPSU. Indeed, a study of CPSU members who left the Party between 1988 and 1990 in Dnepropetrovsky, where party membership declined by 11 percent between 1988 and October 1990, showed that half of those who had deserted the CPSU were from the 1960s generation—"the children of the 20th Party Congress."[56]

(2) A rapid decline of public trust in the key institutions of the party-state, captured by opinion polls in the Soviet Union between 1989 and 1990 and depicted in Table 2.3. Soviet political elites and the public perceived the CPSU as having lost most of its legitimacy and effectiveness. In a survey of 727 people's deputies, local officials, and political leaders in early 1991, 60 percent thought that the CPSU was incapable of leading the Soviet Union out of the crisis; only 28 percent thought it could.[57] In July 1991, a poll of 2,000 people in the Soviet Union found that only 8 percent thought the CPSU worked in the interests of the progressive forces in society, while 49 percent said the CPSU worked in the interests of the conservative forces. The same poll showed that only 14 percent wished to see the CPSU resume its leading role in society, while 36 percent advocated its immediate abolition and 31 percent supported turning it into one of the parliamentary parties.[58]

Finally, even in the absence of a mobilized democratic opposition, market forces unleashed by economic reforms contributed to the decay of the institutions of the party-state by attracting large numbers of their technocratic

Table 2.3   The level of complete public trust in key Soviet institutions, 1989–1990 (in percentages)

Institution	March 1989	December 1989	March 1990
Army	—	44	35
Council of Ministers	28	34	23
CPSU	38	27	16
Local soviets	18	16	14
KGB	—	38	32
Law-enforcement bodies	15	22	18
News media	39	36	37
Religious organizations	13	30	37
Supreme Soviet	43	45	34

Source: Moscow News, no. 21, May 20–26, 1990, p. 7.

elites into the private sector. The expansion of market forces rendered most grassroots organizations of the party-state redundant and ineffective. A study of 1,358 village Chinese Communist Party (CCP) branches in 1989 revealed a high degree of institutional decay; it reported that only 32.4 percent of the CCP branches "could fully play their role," 59.5 percent were "mediocre," and 7.9 percent were "basically defunct."[59] In Vietnam, the decay of the Communist Party was evident in the ruling party's declining ability to attract new members after the initiation of reform in 1986: in 1991 it managed to recruit only 36,000 new members, compared with 100,000 in 1987.[60]

The same market forces caused a breakdown of the state's institutional discipline by creating opportunities for quick self-enrichment that venal government and party officials found irresistible. During the transition to a market system, reforms introduced into planned economies facilitated the illicit conversion of political power into economic gains, exposed public goods to private misappropriation, and were closely associated with a dramatic rise in official corruption.[61] The danger of loss of public support and political legitimacy, though real for both the postcommunist authoritarian regimes and the democratic governments, was greater for the former than the latter, because postcommunist democratic governments might fall back on electoral procedures as a safety valve and means of self-cleansing, whereas postcommunist authoritarian regimes had no such institutional mechanisms for offsetting the delegitimizing effects of massive official corruption. Indeed, available evidence indicates a close connection between the rise of official corruption in China and the erosion of the legitimacy of the Party and the government. Although it is hard to gauge the degree of official corruption in

China systematically, official data on the number of criminal corruption cases brought against suspected officials and government workers showed that this problem was widespread.

Between 1982 and 1991, government prosecutors and disciplinary committees in the CCP investigated and prosecuted 1.78 million cases of corruption involving members of the Communist Party. More than 1.26 million CCP members were punished. A classified speech by Qiao Shi, a member of the Politburo Standing Committee in charge of security and law enforcement, pointed to a dramatic rise in corruption cases involving senior officials in the government and the military in the early 1990s. For example, of the party leaders punished for corruption in 1990, the number of officials above the rank of regiment commanders and county magistrates showed a 40 percent increase over 1989. Of the 11,000 "major" corruption cases exposed in 1991, 17 percent involved party and government officials at or above the level of county administration. Among the 41,000 criminals implicated in major corruption cases in 1991, more than 50 percent had held positions in party organizations, government agencies, and state-owned enterprises. Official corruption of this magnitude prompted Qiao to warn that corruption would cause the Party to "destroy itself."[62]

Such self-destruction, in fact, had gone a long way, as reflected by the rising negative image of the Party and the government in public opinion survey data. One poll of 12,000 urban workers in 16 Chinese cities conducted in August 1988 showed that 63 percent selected "the bad image of the Party as a result of official corruption" as the most pressing political issue.[63] Another survey completed in 1987 found that about 62 percent described the image of the CCP as "not good."[64] Widespread official corruption threatened the Party with the loss of rural support. In an internal poll of peasants conducted in late 1991, 49.5 percent identified "the corrupt practice within the Communist Party and government officials using their power for personal gains" as the "most pressing problem[s] in the countryside."[65]

There are two resources available to major social groups in initiating a takeover. One is the political mobilization of autonomous social groups into organized opposition. The Polish Solidarity, the Baltic independence movements, the informal groups in the Soviet Union, and the formal opposition parties in Hungary between 1988 and 1990 were obvious examples. In the late phases of *perestroika* in the Soviet Union and following the Soviet withdrawal of military support for Eastern European communist regimes, these groups broke the old systems' monopoly of political organization and directly seized power by converting their organizational strength into electoral gains, parliamentary seats, and executive offices. The other means available to civil society is market forces, which they can utilize after certain social groups have gained control of significant economic resources, such as capital, assets, and market share, that can be used to shift the balance of power in society's favor.

The first means of societal takeover—direct seizure of political power—is an exciting, visible, and quick way of replacing communist rule. By comparison, the second means—gradual ascendance of the market and its encroachment upon the power of the communist party-state—is a silent, subtle, and slow way of transforming communism. The effects of the former can be easily gauged by counting the votes cast for the opposition groups and the number of parliamentary seats and executive offices thereby captured; the impact of the latter is often elusive and difficult to measure.

Many scholars have emphasized the role of market forces as an indispensable precondition to freedom in general and democracy in particular.[66] Several Eastern European scholars, including Janos Kornai, Ivan Szelenyi, and Wlodzimierz Brus, see a general connection between the expansion of market forces and the expansion of civil and political freedom in communist states—primarily Hungary and Poland—that experienced partial economic reforms between the late 1960s and early 1970s.[67] As noted, the direct seizure of political power by the opposition has led to the establishment of genuine new democracies in only a small group of Eastern European countries, namely, Poland, Hungary, and the Czech Republic. Market-oriented economic reforms *alone* have not yet produced a successful transition from communism to democracy.

It is premature, however, to dismiss market-oriented economic reforms as a viable means of achieving a societal takeover during regime transition. In fact, complete and clear-cut seizure of political power took place only in those countries in which the communist regimes were installed and maintained by the Soviets prior to 1989. When tried in the replacement of home-grown communist regimes, this approach yielded ambiguous results, as shown by the postcollapse situations in the former Soviet Union and Yugoslavia.

In the postcoup Soviet Union, the seizure of political power by democratic forces proceeded unevenly, with former communist elites and leaders with dubious credentials still in control of many local and republican governments. Moreover, as demonstrated by the postcommunist experience of those countries where quick replacement rather than gradual reform was the primary form of regime transition, most problems resulted from the weakness or near total absence of market forces.

Finally, in communist states where the initial opening was created in the economy rather than in the political sphere, direct seizure of political power was not only impracticable but likely to elicit a violent response, Tiananmen-style, from a regime threatened with imminent overthrow. In this case, societal takeover could occur only through the use of market forces. Despite their apparent drawbacks (primarily their gradualism), market forces have their own advantages as vehicles of societal takeover.

First, the growth and extension of market forces take place gradually and quietly without posing an overt political menace to the hardliners inside the regime and causing an early closure of the opening. The prosperity—hence temporary tranquility—created by the flourishing of market forces lulls the vigilance of the hardliners and obscures the market's threat to the long-term survival of the communist regime. In fact, in China in the 1980s, the growth of the market became a "silent revolution," the implications of which did not become clear to the hardliners until it was too late to stem the growth. Although the contribution of market forces to the expansion of political liberty may not be as quick, dramatic, or intense as direct seizure of political power, it can substantially enlarge most civil liberties that were previously restricted under orthodox communist rule. This expansion of civil liberties, in turn, frequently contributes to the growth of certain political liberties. In short, the primary virtue of market forces during transition from communism is that they can usher in political liberalization through the back door.

Second, sustained operation of market forces can enhance the autonomy and capacity of existing social groups and individuals (such as the intelligentsia and the peasantry) while creating new ones (private entrepreneurs and small property holders). It may also help develop new social institutions, such as commercial associations, practices, and networks, that can compete with the state institutions in the acquisition and utilization of material resources, thus gaining the commensurate political leverage. If a direct political takeover is the short cut to rebuilding democratic political institutions, the growth and expansion of market forces are the only way to rebuild a civil society—and its pluralistic social institutions, which are the foundations of modern democracy.

Third, unlike organized political movements acting as the main vehicle of direct seizure but presenting an easily identifiable target for regime-sponsored repression, market forces are virtually repression-proof. Opposition parties can be disbanded by brute force and their leaders thrown into jail. But market forces affecting tens of millions of profit-seeking private entrepreneurs are impossible to dislodge short of a Stalinist mass terror campaign that would bring the entire country to economic ruin. Even during the brief return of the hardliners in China between 1989 and 1990, organized pro-democracy movements were either physically crushed or driven underground and abroad, while the expansion of market forces and the growth of the private sector continued relentlessly. Lastly, although market forces may not, on their own, drive communist regimes from power (and, to date, they have not), they have proved no less effective in weakening the communist party-state by transferring critical resources from the state to society, thus shifting the balance of power in favor of society, imposing economic constraints on the state, and providing another favorable precondition for transition to democracy.

The corollary to this two-pronged process of state-society resource transfer and accelerated institutional decay during transition is the radicalization of reform. That all communist states have proved to be uniquely incapable of employing their previously formidable institutional resources to manage regime transition can essentially be attributed to this dual-process and its contributory factors. Conversely, that all regime transitions in communist states have so far been marked by societal takeover in varying degrees and forms suggests that it is societal forces, rather than the power of the state, which determine the character, direction, and pace of regime transition.

Societal takeovers are, however, not without their ambiguities. Chief among these in the regime transitions of the 1980s and early 1990s were their unevenness, sectoral disparities, and regional variations. Depending on the arena of the initial opening, societal takeovers may occur in one sector, but not in another. For example, although Gorbachev's political reform elicited a political revolution from below, it failed to generate an economic revival, which had been his original goal. In contrast, Deng's economic reforms helped to unleash an economic revolution from below, but did not lead to a full-fledged political revolution. The transition process was often fragmented. In the same country, dramatic forward movement and even societal takeover occurred in certain sectors or sub-sectors—the economy, the media, education, the political process, local politics, and peripheral republics—but stagnation was the rule in others. Societal takeover also varied along regional lines. In China and Vietnam, market forces were far more developed in some areas (coastal areas in China and southern Vietnam) than in others. In most former Soviet republics, the direct capture of political power by genuine democratic forces appeared to be confined mostly to large cities, having failed to extend to remote areas.

Societal Takeover in China and the Soviet Union

How does this analytical framework apply to China and the Soviet Union? Several general observations must be expanded upon here if we are to gain insight into the different aspects of transition in the two countries. First, although regime-created openings determined the character of the ensuing societal takeover (radicalized marketization versus democratization), whether such a takeover could occur depended on the characteristics of the key social groups involved. As indicated by each country's social mobilization profile, social conditions in the Soviet Union were more favorable to a takeover in the political sphere, whereas those in China were more conducive to a takeover in the economy.

Second, takeover coalition formation influenced the occurrence and arena of societal takeover. For example, the informal coalition of the peasantry, foreign investors, private entrepreneurs, and enterprising local ruling elites in China drove the rapid development of the private sector in these areas. Conversely, the absence of a democratizing coalition composed of the intelligentsia and other key elements of society was responsible for the slow progress in democratization. The situation was reversed in the Soviet Union, where a takeover coalition consisting of nationalists, the intelligentsia, liberal elements among the ruling elites, and industrial workers (mostly miners) led the democratization process, while the absence of an economic takeover coalition in the marketization process was a factor in *perestroika*'s failure to create a market economy.

Third, external economic and political influences could explain the differences in the types of societal takeover that occurred in China and the Soviet Union. Deng's *kaifang* (open-door) policy, taking advantage of China's strategic geopolitical position in the waning years of the Cold War, integrated the Chinese economy into the international economy and gave societal actors access to foreign capital, technology, markets, and information, all of which accelerated marketization; the impact of foreign economic influences on the democratization process in China, however, was indirect and small.

For the Soviet Union, a factor contributing to slow marketization under *perestroika* was the absence of similar foreign economic influences. This was due to the lingering effects of the Cold War, which denied the Soviet Union access to foreign benefits, although, ironically, *perestroika* was the principal reason the Cold War ended, and an important motive for the Soviet ruling elites to initiate reform was to seek economic rewards from the West.[68] Although the ending of the Cold War played no direct role in speeding up democratization from below in the Soviet Union, the resulting improvement in East-West relations directly removed much of the political justification for maintaining a repressive regime inside the Soviet Union, and thus indirectly contributed to the democratization process. It was hardly conceivable that democratization in the Soviet Union could have occurred or been radicalized in a hostile international context.

These differences affected the direction and speed of transition in China and the Soviet Union. But the most fascinating feature of the two different transitional experiences was that, despite their structural differences and dissimilar routes of transition, the processes of societal takeover in China and the Soviet Union shared many striking *sequential dynamic similarities*, in that they proceeded through five identifiable phases between 1979 and 1991: (1) a limited initial opening; (2) a big surge in the activation of major social groups and their acquisition of critical resources; (3) the consolidation

and institutionalization of these newly gained resources; (4) the radicalization of reform, along with conservative attempts at a countertakeover; and
(5) formal assumption of power by the previously excluded social groups.

Phases of Societal Takeover in China and the Soviet Union

Limited initial opening. During the first phase—1979–1982 in China and
1985–1987 in the Soviet Union—both reformist regimes implemented a
two-pronged approach: limited decontrol of socioeconomic activities and
political decompression, especially reduction of repression. In the case of
economic decontrol, the Chinese leadership permitted peasants to exceed the
bounds of governmental restriction of agricultural reform and turn it into a
full-fledged decollectivization program; it also allowed urban private businesses to resume operation. In the meantime, the government actively
courted foreign investment by opening the special economic zones. Politically, the regime sought reconciliation with the long-persecuted intelligentsia
and the so-called exploiting classes (prerevolution rural landlords, rich peasants, and urban business owners) by rehabilitating millions of individuals
who had been branded as members of these groups. These early reconcilia-
tory gestures appeared to have provoked calls for more openness from a
small group of young liberals, represented mainly by the Democracy Wall
Movement in Beijing between 1978 and 1979, which the regime suppressed
quickly.

Gorbachev also took tentative steps toward economic decentralization
and limited political decontrol. He passed the Law on State Enterprises in
1987 to give managers in the state sector greater decision-making power.
The Law on Individual Labor and the Law on Cooperatives, permitting
small-scale private business activities, became effective during this period.
The Soviet jamming of the BBC and the VOA was suspended in early 1987.
More significantly, Gorbachev was especially aggressive in seeking reconciliation with the Soviet intelligentsia. He released dissidents from labor camps
or internal exile, the most dramatic case being the return of Andrei Sakharov
to Moscow from internal exile in December 1986. Long-suppressed literary
works and films were allowed to be published or released. The government's
censorship of the mass media was curtailed.

At this stage in both countries, there was a temporary convergence of interests between the top reformers and newly activated social groups, which
climbed aboard the bandwagon of reform despite harboring different long-
term interests. In both countries, the majority of the intellectuals were
among the earliest and most enthusiastic supporters of Deng's and
Gorbachev's reforms, as were various ethnic nationalists in the peripheral
republics of the Soviet Union.

During this phase, the top reformers' most important contributions consisted of appointments of liberals to key positions in selected state agencies overseeing the areas being liberalized. In the Soviet Union, the need for launching *glasnost* motivated Gorbachev to appoint Alexander Yakovlev as the CPSU's propaganda chief and Yeltsin as the head of the Moscow Party Organization. Soviet reformers also appointed liberals to the editorships of important publications such as *Moscow News, Ogonek, Moscow Pravda,* and *Novyi mir.* In China, Deng gave his trusted aide, Wan Li, the post overseeing agricultural reform; Zhao Ziyang, a moderate, was promoted to the premiership. Under the aegis of Hu Yaobang, the liberal general secretary of the CCP, many ex-Rightists (liberal intellectuals persecuted in the Anti-Rightist Campaign of 1957) were politically rehabilitated and returned to key media posts.

The Big Surge. The second phase may be called the Big Surge, which was marked, in both countries, by the rapid rise of autonomous social and political movements and the transfer of economic and political resources from the state to the newly activated social groups.[69] There were two notable features of the Chinese and Soviet experiences in this phase. First, hardliners in both countries, alarmed by the rapid decline of their influence, launched counterstrikes—the anti-spiritual-pollution campaign in China in late 1983 and the conservative backlash represented by Nina Andreeva's anti-*perestroika* manifesto in the Soviet Union in March 1988. These were defeated, in each case, by the efforts of a moderate-liberal alliance.

Second, the Big Surge of state-to-society resource transfer in China occurred primarily through the mechanism of the market and was reflected in the rapid gains of the private and quasi-private sectors. In the Soviet Union, the Big Surge was driven principally by the swift political mobilization of certain segments of society and expressed in the proliferation of political organizations and electoral victories by radical elements supported by these organizations.

The Chinese Big Surge spanned the years 1983–1986, which saw unprecedented private-sector growth, a dramatic decline in the state sector's share in industrial output, a considerable influx of foreign investment, and impressive gains in the liberal intelligentsia's influence over public opinion despite the short-lived campaign against "spiritual pollution." Measured in terms of gross industrial output, the state sector's share plunged from 74.44 percent at the end of 1982 to 62.27 percent by 1986—a drop of 12.17 percent in four years; the share of the private, quasi-private, and other nonstate sectors rose from 25.56 percent to 37.73 percent.[70] During the same period, the size of the private industrial sector rose 90 times (measured in gross output), while the quasi-private rural industries grew 315 percent.[71] The true magnitude of the state-to-society economic resource transfer was perhaps most dramatically reflected in the rapid formation of a critical mass of the private and quasi-private sectors by 1986, the end of the Big Surge phase, when decollectivized agriculture, quasi-private rural industries, private industrial and retail businesses, and foreign-invested firms jointly produced 42.64 percent of China's GSP.[72]

By the government's own admission, 1984 was a turning point in Chinese economic reform. Between 1978 and 1983, the state sector accounted for 68.4 percent of the increment of the gross industrial output; after 1984, the state sector contributed less than half of the increment and began to see its share decline steadily.[73] The external dimension of the Big Surge in China was evident in the increase of foreign direct investment during the same period. Between 1983 and 1986, foreign investors signed investment contracts worth $14.45 billion and actually invested $6.53 billion (mostly in joint ventures in southern China).[74]

An informal takeover coalition began to form during this stage, with its chief partners united by shared economic interests: the need of grassroots-level rural officials displaced by decollectivization to find lucrative commercial exits from government employment; the opportunities for peasant surplus labor newly freed from the now-defunct communes to escape subsistence farming and increase income; the fiscal necessities of provincial and local authorities after the central government revamped the tax-collection system; and the opportunities offered to foreign investors by China's cheap labor and huge potential market.

No Big Surge in democratization materialized in China, although the conservatives' anti-spiritual-pollution campaign was defeated by a joint effort of the liberals and the moderates, with the former fearing a repeat of the Cultural Revolution–type witch-hunt and the latter alarmed by reports of panicky peasants halting investment in agriculture. The mass media during 1985–1986 saw a rapid decline of the influence of party-controlled press and an unprecedented overall openness. But most of the gains in political liberalization remained insecure because no political takeover coalition capable of defending the emerging political openness was formed. Only a small minority of the intelligentsia engaged in the debates about democratization; no substantive mass mobilization occurred. Their efforts were thus fragile, as evidenced in the political isolation of the student-led democracy movement between December 1986 and January 1987, its failure to attract mass public support, and its brevity.[75] The dismissal of Hu Yaobang as general secretary of the CCP further set back the liberalizing trend, depriving the intelligentsia of their strongest ally among the ruling elites of the regime.

Soviet development during the Big Surge phase, beginning in early 1988 and ending with the country's first semiopen elections in March 1989, followed a different course from Chinese development. The initial opening in the economy failed to spark a spontaneous capitalist revolution similar to that which had occurred in China. But partial *glasnost*, introduced during the initial opening, ignited a true political revolution from below and caused a massive transfer of political resources—the capacity of political organization and mobilization—to newly motivated societal actors. The Big Surge in the Soviet Union saw a rapid proliferation of autonomous societal groups. Thousands of religious organizations (1,610 in 1988) successfully sought registration by the state and retrieved nearly 1,000 religious buildings from the government.[76] An independent labor movement also began to emerge.[77]

The most striking feature of the Big Surge in the Soviet Union was the mushrooming of informal civic and political groups and the transformation of these groups into popular fronts—regional takeover coalitions that later became voter-mobilization organizations in the March 1989 elections for the Congress of People's Deputies. During the initial opening, most of the newly organized informal groups remained largely apolitical; in the Big Surge phase, many of them turned decidedly political.[78] Estimates of the number of informal groups in the Soviet Union during this period varied from 30,000 in early 1988 to 60,000 in early 1989.[79] By the end of 1989, *Moscow News* reported that these informal groups had a membership of at least 2 to 2.5 million people.[80]

The most potent form of political organizing during the Big Surge in the Soviet Union was the mass movement called "the popular front" that first emerged in the Baltics in early 1988 and quickly spread throughout the Soviet Union in the same year. By the end of 1989, one estimate put the number of popular fronts in the Soviet Union at 140.[81] The political power gained by these newly formed cells of civil society was reflected in their helping to defeat conservative candidates for the CPSU and elect many radical elements of the intelligentsia and liberal reformers within the CPSU, including Andrei Sakharov, Boris Yeltsin, Gavriil Popov, and Anatolii Sobachk, to the Congress of Deputies in the March 1989 elections.[82] The popular fronts in the Baltic republics won overwhelming electoral victories and quickly transformed themselves into mass proindependence organizations.[83]

Consolidation and institutionalization of resources. This phase is usually marked by further gains for the newly mobilized social groups, as well as the cementing of their strength within the new economic and political frameworks. In some cases, the regime gave formal legal recognition to the gains in resource transfer made by societal actors; in other cases, regional disparities in societal takeover began to emerge, with democratization or marketization proceeding much more rapidly and the societal forces representing them obtaining a small advantage in some important areas of both countries. In the urban centers of the Soviet Union, democratic forces launched a *formal* takeover of governmental power through electoral victories. In the coastal areas in China, market forces began to play a more important role than state planning in the economy. The process of consolidation and institutionalization increased the irreversibility of reform and the political and economic costs of the regime's attempts at such reversals.

In China, despite the political setback that liberal forces suffered following the regime's campaign against "bourgeois liberalism," launched in early 1987 in response to the 1986–1987 democracy movement, 1987–1988 saw the regrouping of reformist forces around a seriously weakened, moderate-centered coalition that managed, with Deng's tacit endorsement, to put an early end to the antibourgeois liberalization campaign.[84] The same period was marked, more importantly, by the consolidation of the burgeoning private industrial sector; for example, with the formal legalization of private firms in late 1988.

The most important gains made by society-driven marketization were, however, in more substantive forms, and they were reflected in (a) the continuing trend of the rising share of wealth generated by the private and quasi-private sectors, which produced 46.43 percent of GSP in 1988;[85] (b) the expansion of market-determined pricing mechanisms in resource allocations following partial price reforms in the early 1980s, and the formation of embryonic market institutions (tens of thousands of local and regional commodities exchanges, wholesale markets, and various commercial networks) spanning the entire country;[86] (c) the further integration of the Chinese economy into the world economy, with the ratio between exports and GNP reaching 13 percent by 1987 (above the 12 percent international average for very large countries);[87] (d) *regional* marketization breakthroughs manifested by the overtaking of the state's industrial sector by the nonstate sector in the three most industrialized and economically important provinces in China: Jiangsu, Shandong, and Guangdong. By 1988, the nonstate industrial sector outproduced the state sector in four of the six most industrialized provinces in China.

In the Soviet Union, the consolidation phase occurred between 1989 and mid-1990. Beginning with the electoral victories by liberal forces in the March 1989 elections for the Congress of People's Deputies and the formation of the first parliamentary opposition coalition, known as the Interregional Group, in July 1989, this phase proceeded with the broadening of the social base and the political power of the takeover coalition, adding new partners—members of the recently mobilized industrial labor force who could supplement the intelligentsia's power of moral persuasion with strikes.[88] It concluded with further liberal victories in republican and local elections between the end of 1989 and the beginning of 1990, resulting in the *localized takeover* of political power by these coalitions. In the Baltic republics, these victories immediately installed the popular fronts in the government and led to the declaration of independence or sovereignty by these new governments. In the center of the Soviet Union, the consolidation phase was crowned by Yeltsin's election to the chairmanship of the Russian Parliament in May 1990.

In other parts of the Soviet Union, and especially in important urban centers, liberal forces expanded their gains during the republican and local elections held in March 1990, with their candidates winning elections in eighty major cities in the Soviet Union, fifty of which were located in the Russian Federation.[89] The most important victories won by the largest coalition—Democratic Russia—were in Moscow and Leningrad, where Popov and Sobachk were elected mayors after the coalition gained control of the city councils. The coalition also won 20–25 percent of the seats in the Russian Parliament.

In addition, this phase in the Soviet Union saw the genuine beginning of the institutionalization of a multiparty system, with the formation of more than a dozen all-Union political parties and many republican parties following the repeal by the Congress of People's Deputies, in March 1990, of Article Six of the Soviet Constitution, which granted the CPSU the monopoly on political power.[90] A second notable aspect of the consolidation-institutionalization phase was the spate of liberal legislation that poured out of the new Supreme Soviet and legalized the *de facto* societal takeover in many areas. The most important of such legislation included the Law on Freedom of Conscience and Religion, the Law on the Press and other Media, and the Law on Public Associations.

Radicalization of reform and conservative countertakeover. As the distribution of power shifts during the above-mentioned three phases, those groups that gain resources fastest and secure gains in new institutional frameworks are most likely to try to radicalize reform, even if that means directly challenging their erstwhile benefactors—the moderate reformers at the top of the old system.

In the Soviet Union, the nationalist movements in the Baltics that had successfully—and formally—taken over republican governments declared their republics independent (or ready to secede) in early 1990. A new radical-liberal takeover coalition, having consolidated its power in the Russian government, major cities, and leading media organs, openly broke its preconsolidation alliance with Gorbachev and started to urge far more sweeping reforms, for example, the 500-day plan for dismantling the planned economy.

In China, liberal intellectuals who had felt betrayed by Deng after his crackdown on the 1986–1987 student demonstrations renewed their demands for democratic changes and more radical economic reforms. Although they had been much less successful than their Soviet counterparts during the consolidation phase, the Chinese opposition forces initiated a struggle that led to a direct confrontation with Deng and sparked the Tiananmen Movement of May 1989.

In the meantime, China's private and quasi-private sectors continued their relentless growth and began to overtake the state-controlled sector of the economy. Although they made no open demands on the regime, Chinese private-sector forces had worked a quiet economic revolution by steering reform away from market-socialism and toward a full market economy. Their informal takeover coalition had gained much strength, both in membership size and in economic resources. It had nearly 600 billion yuan in registered capital assets, about one-third of the assets of the state's industrial firms, and employed more than 117 million people in the rural industries and the formal private sector by the early 1990s.[91]

In the late 1980s, this informal coalition, coordinated more by rudimentary market institutions and economic self-interest than by a clearly articulated grand program, made the drive toward a full market economy unstoppable. One measure of the extent of China's marketization was that, by late 1990, private and quasi-private networks and businesses, in the absence of shock therapy, controlled about 60 percent of China's market for consumer goods and 66 percent of the market for producer and intermediate goods.[92]

It was also during this phase, which overlapped somewhat with the consolidation phase in both countries, that a fierce conservative countertakeover was mounted in both China and the Soviet Union. The precipitating events and specific forms of conservative countertakeovers in each country differed. In China, the most immediate cause of the countertakeover in the economic area was the rampant inflation following the government's ill-conceived policy of lifting price controls, which led to panic buying throughout the country; its bloody crackdown on the democratic forces was an immediate response to a nationwide mass protest movement sparked by a confluence of forces: (1) public outrage against widespread official corruption; (2) popular resentment of the government's poor handling of the early phase of the Tiananmen Movement, especially its indifference to the hunger-striking students and the use of the military to intimidate the protestors; and (3) public agreement with some of the political demands made by the students.

In the Soviet Union, the earlier precipitating event was Gorbachev's decision to accept and launch the radical economic reforms embodied in the 500-day plan, leading to a revolt by a conservative coalition consisting of the military-industrial complex and hardliners inside the CPSU in the fall of 1990. Similarly, the event that directly triggered the abortive coup in August 1991 was the scheduled signing of a new Union Treaty.

Despite the differences in the precipitating events, the underlying causes of and circumstances surrounding these conservative countertakeovers were generally similar. First, the most important underlying cause of conservative countertakeover attempts was the fundamental power shift that had occurred between the state and society since the opening. In China, the conservatives belatedly felt that the state had lost too much economic power too quickly, especially with private-sector forces poised to overtake the state sector in total output and threatening an accelerated decline of the power of the state in the economy. Indeed, official statistics showed that in 1989 the state sector contributed 56 percent of the gross industrial output, meaning that, after a decade of reform, China had nearly undone the legacies of state-socialist development of the previous twenty years. (In 1957, the state sector's contribution to the gross industrial output was about 54 percent.)

The underlying cause of the conservative countertakeover in the Soviet Union was the even more rapid loss—if not evaporation—of the old regime's political power, to both the independence movements on the periphery and the democratic forces in the center. The extent of the CPSU's loss of power was reflected in opinion polls revealing that the Party wielded little influence in 1991. One poll in July 1991 found that 52 percent of the respondents felt that the Party did not have great influence in their districts, while only 24 percent felt that it did.[93]

Second, the countertakeovers occurred when the supreme reformers, isolated from the Left and the Right, were severely weakened. Deng's loss of the liberal support both within and outside the Party after the 1987 crackdown added to his vulnerability from the Right. Gorbachev found himself under attack both from the Left and the Right. He was reduced to issuing ineffectual presidential decrees, which met defiance from rebellious groups and republics.[94] And his popularity plummeted, with one poll taken in early 1991 showing that 45 percent of the respondents favored abolishing the presidency he occupied, while only 19 percent opposed such a move.[95] Therefore, it was no surprise that both Deng and Gorbachev initially reacted to the radicalization of the reform agenda with confusion, anger, and a sense of betrayal. Both resorted to a makeshift alliance with the alarmed old guard of the ancient regime.

In the Soviet Union, this countertakeover attempt occurred in late 1990 and early 1991 with the crackdown in the Baltics, which was planned in August 1990 and carried out in January 1991.[96] The 500-day plan was abandoned by Gorbachev, who also replaced a moderate reformer, Nikolai Ryzhkov, with an extreme hardliner, Valentin Pavlov, as prime minister. The hardliners attempted unsuccessfully to reimpose censorship in the mass media.

In China, the countertakeover began in late 1988. On the political front, the conservatives conspired to oust the moderate CCP general secretary, Zhao Ziyang. In this sense, the June 1989 massacre at Tiananmen Square and the mass repression that followed were merely the climax of this conservative political countertakeover. On the economic front, the countertakeover attempt was embodied in some of the austerity measures implemented between late 1988 and early 1991, which used massive state credit infusion to support money-losing state enterprises, and cut financing and raw material supplies to the more efficient private sector. The brunt of the economic countertakeover fell on the most important component of the nonstate sector—the rural industrial sector, which had become a fierce competitor of the state domain. According to Tian Jiyun, a vice-premier in charge of agriculture, conservative forces in some areas attempted to recollectivize agriculture and "nationalize" quasi-private rural enterprises under the guise of "state-sponsored buyout."[97] One million rural firms were closed in the first nine months of 1989.[98] Another figure showed that between 1989 and 1991 about three million private firms were closed, and job losses attributed to the downsizing of the rural private industries amounted to 2.8 million in 1989 and 1990.[99]

Although the conservative countertakeovers attempted in both countries displayed these similarities, their outcomes were extremely different—and served to reaffirm a critical lesson concerning societal takeover during regime transition: If societal forces can attain a position of parity or even slight advantage in certain sectors, such as the economy, the mass media, or urban centers, and maintain a sizable takeover coalition after the consolidation-institutionalization phase, they can resist a conservative countertakeover in those sectors.

The unsuccessful conservative countertakeover in the Soviet Union (including the failed coup of August 1991) and the equally futile attempt by Chinese hardliners to reverse marketization since Tiananmen support this observation. In the Soviet Union, for instance, the liberal forces had gained so much political power that the conservative countertakeover attempts had actually provided them with a golden opportunity to accelerate the takeover. The cooperation between the various partners of the takeover coalition in general, and the contribution by the striking coal miners in the spring of 1991 in particular, not only caused the makeshift moderate-conservative alliance to collapse quickly, but helped to install Boris Yeltsin as Russian president in June 1991 after a landslide victory.[100] The resulting new center-periphery and liberal-moderate alliance manifested in the nine-plus-one pact between Gorbachev and the republics more truly reflected the new underlying reality of power in the Soviet Union.

In China, the post-Tiananmen regime was able to suppress political dissent, but remained powerless to reverse the massive growth of the private sector—even though hardliners viewed it as the breeding ground of political subversion. The fragility of the 1989 democracy movement in China stemmed mainly from its relatively weak resource gains and inability to form a broad coalition encompassing other crucial social groups such as the industrial labor force and new private entrepreneurs.[101] Whereas the Soviet opposition benefited enormously from bringing together three diverse forces—the anticommunist intelligentsia, non-Russian nationalists, and disaffected workers—the pre-Tiananmen Chinese democracy movement remained separated from other groups and interests, and so lacked the momentum of its Soviet counterpart.

The same, however, could not be said of China's capitalist revolution from below, which was driven by a broad array of diverse groups and interests. Consequently, the private sector survived the conservative countertakeover virtually unscathed. It became even more efficient and competitive, and it continued to outperform the state sector and serve as the primary engine of growth and marketization.

The formal takeover. The Soviet hardliners' self-destruction through the failed coup of August 1991 transformed an informal societal takeover into a formal one. Radical takeover coalition leaders in the Baltic republics and Russia were catapulted into power. The *de facto* disintegration of the Soviet Union, which accelerated in early 1991, had become *de jure*. The Baltic republics seceded from the Soviet Union. The Ukraine, strategically and economically the most important Soviet republic after Russia, declared its independence on August 24, 1991; it was immediately followed by Belorussia and Moldavia. The CPSU itself was suspended at the end of August 1991. Gorbachev's central government, politically and economically bankrupt, was ousted from power by a Yeltsin-led coalition of republican leaders who formed the Commonwealth of Independent States in December 1991. Gorbachev himself resigned in late December, and the Soviet Union, as a multinational empire, officially collapsed.

In the former Soviet Union, however, the formal takeover yielded ambiguous results. Although the democratic opposition had clearly gained power in Russia and the Baltic republics, the political forces that replaced former communist rule in other parts of the Union were mixed, reflecting the unevenness of the degree of societal takeover in these areas prior to the collapse. In Ukraine, the new ruling coalition consisted of nationalists and former communist elites championing Ukrainian nationalism (chief among them was its new president, Leonid Kravchuk). In the Central Asian republics, with the exception of Kyrgyzstan's president, Askar Akaev, former communist elites retained power. They also remained in power in Azerbaijan under its newly elected president, Ayaz Mutalibov. In Georgia, political power fell to a short-lived personal dictatorship under Zviad Gamsakhurdia. In Moldova and Armenia, the nationalist-dominated opposition gained control. The sudden collapse of the center created new political and economic crises. Politically, struggles for power immediately erupted in most ex-Soviet republics—among former communist elites and the opposition, political factions, and ethnic groups. Economically, the collapse of political authority in the center completely destroyed what was left of the central planning system and the interrepublican trade system.

As of 1993, only Russia and the Baltic states had carried out programmatic, radical, market-oriented economic reforms after the formal takeover phase. The launching of Yeltsin's shock therapy program in January 1992, under the direction of his prime minister Yegor Gaidar, marked a turning point in economic reform for Russia. But leaders in several other republics, chiefly Ukraine and Belarus, delayed the drive toward marketization. Political turmoil, armed conflicts, and ethnic strife impeded economic reforms in Armenia, Azerbaijan, Georgia, Moldova, and Tajikistan. Despite relative domestic tranquility, the other Central Asian republics dominated by former communist elites implemented no systematic program of marketization.

In China, though there was no formal democratic takeover of the political system, a *semiformal* capitalist takeover occurred in 1992 following Deng Xiaoping's historic tour of southern China, where a *regional* capitalist takeover was, in a *de facto* sense, nearly complete. Deng's tour formally ended the post-Tiananmen, moderate-hardliner antitakeover alliance and revived the moderate-liberal coalition; regional leaders from coastal provinces, wielding increasing amounts of economic clout, gained new power, as evidenced by the inclusion of the party secretaries from Guangdong and Shandong into the Politburo elected in the Fourteenth Party Congress in October 1992.

On the surface, it seemed that Deng's strategic political move in early 1992 should have received most of the credit for reenergizing China's capitalist revolution after Tiananmen. In reality, it merely reflected, again, the changed balance of economic power, both between the state and society, and between the center and the periphery: in 1991, before Deng's tour, the size of China's private and quasi-private sectors had already surpassed its state sector in terms of GSP.[102]

The semiformal takeover in China since 1992 was notable for the following reasons: (1) for the first time since reform began, the Chinese political leadership openly endorsed the market economy as a goal, although, in appeasing the conservative remnants, this endorsement was vaguely phrased as support for a "socialist market economy"; (2) the government also permitted the takeover of small and medium state-owned enterprises by private entrepreneurs and foreign investors, taking a tentative step toward mass privatization; (3) there was a huge exodus of technical and political elites from the state sector and bureaucracies into the private sector; (4) the semiformal takeover was marked by an unprecedented expansion of the private sector into previously closed sectors, such as real estate, commercial aviation, and the financial market (private banking, secondary stock exchanges); (5) many provincial and local governments passed liberal laws expanding the formal private sector; and (6) the semiformal takeover was accelerated by a massive infusion of new foreign investments. Taken together, the economic developments in China in 1992–1993 marked the near total victory of its society-led capitalist revolution.

China's Capitalist Revolution

3

rivatization, the transfer of productive assets such as land, factories, shops, and so forth from the state to private ownership, is one of the most important steps in regime transition from communist rule. Generally speaking, privatization of a command economy may originate from two sources: the emergence of fully autonomous private producers in possession of their own capital, which they are allowed to accumulate and put to productive use; or the sale or free distribution of previously state-owned productive assets to private individuals or economic entities.

In the first case, the productive assets are created, accumulated, transferred, and utilized almost exclusively by private individuals and through private means, much like the development of capitalism in its earlier stages. In this process, the role of the state is, at best, indirect and restricted to enforcement of contractual obligations and market regulations. In transitions from communism, however, this society-driven or "ground-up" process of privatization requires the government to lift its restrictions on private property, protect the newly created private property and the rights derived from its ownership, and broaden the boundaries of legitimate commercial activities for its owners.

The second process of privatization, which requires extensive and direct government intervention in transferring state-owned productive assets to the private sector, is a state-driven or "top-down" program of privatization, attempted in most Eastern European countries and many parts of the former Soviet Union after the fall of communist regimes there.[1] Because privatizing ownership and management control can be accomplished both simultaneously and sequentially, this process of privatization can be divided into two sub-types: (1) full privatization, which transfers both ownership and management control from the state to society (free distribution or auction of state-owned enterprises); and (2) partial privatization, which initially transfers management control from the state to private agents for a fee without conferring ownership to new managers (leasing state-owned assets to private individuals).

The privatization of management can be the first step toward the privatization of ownership as the lessees of the state-owned enterprises (SOEs) accumulate enough capital to purchase the assets, provided that government policies allow such transactions. As the original capital stock of the leased enterprises depreciates and the lessees invest in upgrading the productive facilities, the share of private equity gradually grows, constituting another subtle form of privatization of ownership. If we characterize the process of market creation in a communist state as basically consisting of two sub-processes, marketization of resource allocation through price reform and privatization of assets, then comprehensive economic reform must include both sub-processes.

Before the 1990s, economic reforms in communist states had focused exclusively on decentralization of decision-making, organizational restructuring, and price reform to improve economic performance. The results were disappointing. In fact, in both China and the Soviet Union, these efforts failed to revive the state-owned industrial sector; partial privatization, in contrast, was quite successful, as in the case of Chinese agricultural reforms. Perhaps reflecting this shift in attitudes, the new democracies in Eastern Europe and Russia assigned top priority to the rapid and massive privatization of the state sector in the transition to a market economy.[2]

The Development of the Private Sector

In China, the government initiated no systematic program of privatizing the state industrial sector. On the contrary, it maintained that its primary goal of economic reform was improving the efficiency of the state-owned enterprises without changing their ownership.[3] However, a huge private and quasi-private sector emerged in China during the 1980s and became the engine driving economic growth and marketization.

This development can be explained by the analytical framework set out in Chapter 2. Many of the factors that facilitate a societal takeover in the marketization process were at work in China during the 1980s: (1) the initial opening created by government-inaugurated agricultural reforms and other half measures that indirectly accelerated the development of the private sector; (2) the existence of a relatively autonomous, collectively powerful, and highly motivated social group (the peasantry) and its economic mobilization in response to the opening; (3) takeover coalition formation; (4) favorable external factors (access to foreign capital, technology, and markets); and (5) the accompanying accelerated institutional decay of the communist party-state.

Privatization is both a matter of kind (private interests versus the state) and a matter of degree (less control by the state and more control by non-state actors). The complication here arises mainly from the fact that nonstate actors are often neither, strictly speaking, private entrepreneurs nor state agencies. In Chinese parlance, such nonstate actors are called "collectives." In this study, the nonagricultural private sector refers to private firms, private cooperatives, quasi-private rural industries, and joint ventures with foreign firms and wholly owned foreign firms and subsidiaries. This definition is predicated mostly on the degree to which these individual components of the private sector are autonomous from the direct influence of the state's economic planning, and on the genuine holders of the property rights to these productive assets. As a rule, the state exerts almost no direct influence over them and excludes them from economic planning; the genuine holders of the property rights who exercise effective control over the distribution of income from these productive assets are also predominantly private (firms and individuals) or quasi-private (local communities).

The largest quasi-private sector to have emerged in China in the 1980s was the rural industrial sector. Whereas the Chinese government, for obvious ideological reasons, classifies this sector as "collective," I will categorize it as "quasi-private" for the following reasons:

Management autonomy and hard budget constraint. Unlike the SOEs, Chinese township and village enterprises (TVEs) operate in a market environment; they procure raw materials and other key inputs at market-set prices; they determine their own wages and price their products at the prevailing market rates; their budget constraint is hard; bankruptcies, instead of state-sponsored bailout, are the sure consequences of poor management and failure in the marketplace (for example, 400,000 TVEs went bankrupt in 1990);[4] and they are largely immune to direct intervention by the state through the institutions of the planned economy.

Mixed ownership. Although in theory many TVEs are owned by local communities, in reality they are owned by a multitude of groups, private individuals, and local communities. Whereas the earlier TVEs were mostly established with the nonagricultural assets previously owned by communes and production brigades, new investment by groups of individual peasants, depreciation of the old assets, and the development of a private shareholding system have jointly increased the proportion of the genuine private share of the productive assets in rural industries. Government figures showed that, in 1989, the number of rural private and cooperate firms classified as TVEs totaled 17.29 million and made up 91.6 percent of all TVEs; together they employed 46.4 million workers (about 49.6 percent of the labor force in TVEs) and accounted for 34.6 percent of the gross output of TVEs. Their total fixed assets at the end of 1989 reached 51.4 billion yuan (about 24.5 percent of all the fixed assets of TVEs).[5] Another government report claimed that the cooperative firms set up between local communities (the collective) and private peasants in 1991 employed about 60 percent of the workers in TVEs and contributed to 70 percent of their gross output.[6]

Sources of capital formation. Except for the capital stock inherited from the industrial enterprises previously owned and run by people's communes and production brigades (valued at 97.7 billion yuan at the end of 1978),[7] the new sources of capital formation for rural industries in the 1980s were almost exclusively private and collective (the value of capital stock of rural industries in China in 1991 amounted to 530 billion yuan).[8] Tian Jiyun, vice-premier in charge of agriculture, acknowledged that the government "did not spend any money on the development of rural industries."[9] Another official report claimed that the start-up capital for nearly all rural firms came from peasants themselves, in the form of individual savings and other private assets, including residential houses-turned-workshops, privately raised capital, and community savings.[10]

Private firms disguised as collectives. This practice is widespread in both urban and rural areas, with many entrepreneurs registering their private firms as "collective." Despite the lack of national data on the percentage of private firms disguised as collectives in the rural and urban industrial sector, regional data show that their presence is substantial.[11]

The growth of the private and quasi-private sectors in China can be broadly measured by the combined contribution of the five principal components of these two sectors—semiprivate agriculture, quasi-private rural industries, private industrial firms, joint ventures, and private retail businesses—to China's GSP (its equivalent of GNP). Table 3.1 shows the dramatic rise of the share of the two sectors in China's GSP between 1983 and 1992. With the exception of 1989, when a national economic recession, combined with a conservative counterattack against the private sector, resulted in an insignificant decrease in the share of the two sectors, their contribution to the GSP rose some 25 percent, accounting for 58 percent of China's GSP in 1992.

In addition, the two sectors (excluding peasants engaged in agricultural production) employed a labor force which, by the early 1990s, nearly equaled that in the state and quasi-state sectors. In 1990, combined employment in the state and quasi-state sectors totaled 138.9 million, while combined employment in the rural industries and the private industrial and retail firms rose to 130.4 million.[12] Tables 3.1–3.4 summarize the development of the private sector in China in the 1980s and show the rapidity, breadth, and depth of its growth. In a decade, the private sector had penetrated nearly all spheres of economic activity. A careful examination of the data in Tables 3.1–3.4 also reveals the following characteristics of the private sector in China.

First, it is more developed and concentrated in the countryside, with its

Table 3.1 The rising share of private and quasi-private sectors in China's GSP, 1983–1992[a] (in percentages)

Sector	1983[b]	1984	1985	1986	1987	1988	1989	1990	1991	1992
Semiprivate agriculture	23.96	23.67	21.17	20.43	19.69	19.05	18.30	19.53	18.31	16.50
Quasi-private TVEs	8.74	12.58	16.10	18.23	20.31	21.40	21.15	21.90	26.22	31.80
Private industrial firms	0.06	0.10	1.07	1.61	2.17	2.65	3.06	3.39	3.69	4.50
Joint ventures[c]	0.44	0.57	0.70	0.85	1.20	1.66	2.19	2.73	3.69	4.40
Private retail	0.55	0.77	1.48	1.52	1.22	1.67	1.71	1.60	1.36	1.50
Total	33.75	37.69	40.52	42.64	44.59	46.43	46.41	49.15	53.27	58.70

Sources: Statistical Yearbook of China, 1991, pp. 26, 47, 315, 375, 379, and 395; *Digest of China's Statistical Data, 1992* (Beijing: Zhongguo Tongji Publishing Co., 1992), pp. 8, 67, 70, and 93; *Digest of China's Statistical Data, 1993*, pp. 8, 70, and 93.

a. Estimates based on the following methodology: excluding the share of state-run farms and labor camps in China's gross rural output; excluding the agricultural gross output component in the gross output of the quasi-private township and village enterprises (TVEs); using the private sector's share in the total retail turnover to estimate its share in the retail trade's contribution to China's GSP.

b. The decollectivization of Chinese agriculture was completed in 1983, with 97 percent of the communes converted to the household responsibility system by the end of that year.

c. Including both foreign and domestic joint ventures, with the share of foreign-invested firms totaling about 70 percent in this sector.

two principal components—semiprivate (decollectivized) agriculture and rural industries—jointly contributing 48.3 percent of China's GSP in 1992. Of the fully private industrial firms, the government estimated that nearly 80 percent were located in the countryside at the end of the 1980s.[13] It is significant that the primary source of the growth of the private sector was the output generated by private and semiprivate industrial sectors, the most important component being the TVEs that contributed the bulk (a net gain of 23.06 percent in 1983–1992) of these sectors' rising share in China's GSP.

Despite the success of the decollectivization of agriculture in the early 1980s, the contribution of this sector to China's GSP actually declined by 7.46 percent between 1983 and 1992. The secondary sources of industrial growth came from fully private firms and joint ventures (70 percent of them being foreign), which together contributed 8.9 percent of China's GSP in 1992. The predominantly rural character of China's private and quasi-private sectors is central to this study, because in order to explain why a capitalist revolution from the ground up took place in China in the 1980s, one needs to explain why such a revolution occurred in the countryside but not in the cities.

Second, from the perspective of state-society relations, the shift of economic power, that is, economic resources generated by privately controlled productive capacities, from the state to society was most dramatically reflected in the relative decline of the state's industrial sector in the growth rates and in the share of China's gross industrial output through the 1980s. Table 3.2 shows that, between 1980 and 1991, the state's industrial sector, despite its relatively strong growth record, lagged far behind the nonstate sectors in general, and the quasi-private and private sectors in particular. This decline in growth caused a dramatic relative decline in the contribution of the state sector to China's gross industrial output. As Table 3.3 indicates, between 1978 and 1992, the state sector sustained a net decline of nearly 30 percent—from 77.63 percent to 48.42 percent. The true magnitude of the deteriorating performance of the state industrial sector, however, is not fully revealed by these figures. By the government's own admission, a substantial proportion of the output of SOEs consisted of unsold inventories, or "paper output"; despite the government's preferential policies and massive financial subsidies, about one-third of the large- and medium-sized SOEs suffered heavy losses, one-third were "mediocre performers," and only one-third were profitable in the early 1990s.[14]

Third, there were significant regional variations in the development of China's private and quasi-private sectors. For instance, 54 percent of China's private firms in 1990 were located in the five coastal provinces of Guangdong, Zhejiang, Liaoning, Hebei, and Shandong.[15] This regional variation is also evident in the fact that, by 1991, in six of China's eight coastal provinces and two centrally administered municipalities—Hebei,

Table 3.2   Annual growth rates of different sectors in gross value of industrial output, 1979–1991 (in percentages)

Year	State	Collective[a]	Quasi-private TVEs[b]	Private	Other[c]
1979	8.88	8.57	—	—	—
1980	5.61	19.24	20.28	—	—
1981	2.53	9.01	13.72	134.57	31.60
1982	7.05	9.54	11.50	78.95	27.73
1983	9.39	15.53	17.19	120.59	33.90
1984	8.92	34.85	64.49	97.47	56.81
1985	12.94	32.69	46.72	1,089.60	39.54
1986	6.18	17.97	32.08	67.57	34.16
1987	11.30	23.24	34.41	56.59	66.39
1988	12.61	28.16	39.62	47.34	61.53
1989	3.86	10.48	15.78	23.77	42.68
1990	2.96	9.02	15.36	21.11	39.33
1991[d]	8.40	18.00	12.90	24.0	56.0

Source: Statistical Yearbook of China, 1991, pp. 378 and 395.

a. Including both urban collectives and rural industries.

b. Including the industrial gross output of rural industries.

c. Including various types of joint ventures, co-ops, and wholly owned foreign firms.

d. From *Asian Wall Street Journal Weekly,* March 9, 1992, p. 13; *China Daily: Business Weekly,* March 8–14, 1992, p. 4.

Shandong, Jiangsu, Shanghai, Zhejiang, Fujian, Guangdong, and Guangxi—the nonstate industrial sector had outproduced the state sector, as shown in Table 3.4. Collectively, these six coastal provinces are among the most industrialized, prosperous, and important regions in China, having accounted for 30 percent of the country's population, 41.6 percent of its gross industrial output, and 35 percent of its GSP in 1990. The fall of the state sector's share in industrial output below the 50 percent level in these six provinces represented a milestone in the development of the private and quasi-private sectors in China.

Fourth, although foreign direct investment is often regarded as a crucial source of growth for the private sector, the Chinese experience shows that the contribution of foreign direct investment tended to be small initially and, despite its spectacular growth, took at least a decade to form a small critical mass (in this case, producing about 5 percent of China's gross industrial output and 4 percent of its GSP by 1992).[16] Thus, an important lesson to be learned here is that foreign direct investment is slow to influence the process of marketization; it is, therefore, unrealistic to stake the success of the transition to a market economy on foreign investment or count on external assistance to generate rapid initial growth. The primary source of marketiza-

Table 3.3 The share of the private and quasi-private sectors in the gross value of industrial output, 1978–1992[a] (in percentages)

Year	State	Quasi-state[b]	Quasi-private[c]	Private	Other[d]
1978	77.63	22.37	—	—	—
1980	75.97	23.54	—	0.02	0.47
1982	74.44	24.82	—	0.06	0.68
1984	69.09	29.71	—	0.19	1.01
1986	62.27	15.05	18.46	2.76	1.46
1988	56.80	14.25	21.89	4.34	2.71
1989	56.06	13.86	21.83	4.80	3.45
1990	54.60	13.38	22.24	5.39	4.38
1991	52.84	4.92	30.81	5.70	5.71
1992	48.42	38.23		6.75	6.60

Sources: Statistical Yearbook of China, 1991, pp. 391 and 396; *Digest of China's Statistical Data, 1992* (Beijing: Zhongguo Tongji Publishing Co., 1992), pp. 67 and 71; *Digest of China's Statistical Data, 1993,* p. 70.

a. Figures may not add up to 100 because of rounding.

b. Quasi-state firms here refer to urban collective enterprises.

c. Quasi-private firms here refer to township and village enterprises and urban and rural cooperatives; there were no separate data for the share of industrial output by these firms before 1986.

d. Including various joint ventures; foreign joint ventures and foreign firms accounted for 70 percent of output in this category in 1990. *China Daily: Business Weekly,* November 25, 1991, p. 1.

tion must come from domestic forces, although foreign direct investment and other favorable external factors, such as imports of technology and especially access to foreign markets, can accelerate marketization when domestic forces take advantage of them.

The contributions of the private and semiprivate sectors were significant factors in the rapid growth of the Chinese economy during the 1980s, when the country's GNP doubled. They provided employment for about 130 million Chinese and thus helped the government to solve a potentially destabilizing social problem without expending any of its resources. The government admitted that, had it tried to absorb into the state sector the 92 million peasants who were working in the quasi-private rural industries at the end of the 1980s, the state would have had to invest more than 3 trillion yuan; but it took rural industries less than 200 billion yuan, most of which came from private and quasi-private sources, to create these 92 million jobs.[17] The threefold growth of the quasi-private TVEs alone constituted an enormous component of China's total growth during the decade (37.7 percent of the net growth in industrial output and 31.5 percent of the net growth of GNP between 1986 and 1990).[18]

Table 3.4 Provinces with the nonstate sector larger than the state sector in gross industrial output, 1983–1991 (in percentages)

Province	Sector	1983	1985	1987	1988	1989	1990	1991
National	state	73.4	64.9	59.7	56.8	56.1	54.6	52.8
	nonstate	26.6	35.1	40.3	43.2	43.9	45.4	47.2
Fujian	state	73.6	56.3	52.5	49.5	49.5	45.1	40.6
	nonstate	26.4	43.7	47.5	50.5	50.5	54.9	59.4
Guangdong	state	66.8	53.3	49.3	45.1	43.4	40.2	38.2
	nonstate	33.2	46.7	50.7	54.9	56.6	59.8	61.8
Hebei	state	79.8	70.3	53.1	50.3	50.4	49.4	47.9
	nonstate	20.2	29.7	46.9	49.7	49.6	50.6	52.1
Jiangsu	state	59.2	40.4	36.6	34.7	35.0	34.3	33.1
	nonstate	40.8	59.6	63.4	65.3	65.0	65.7	66.9
Snandong	state	71.3	54.7	50.5	45.5	43.4	41.4	39.7
	nonstate	28.7	45.3	49.5	54.5	56.6	58.6	60.3
Zhejiang	state	56.7	35.4	33.2	31.2	31.9	31.2	29.4
	nonstate	43.3	64.6	66.8	68.8	68.1	68.8	70.6

Sources: Statistical Yearbook of China, various years; Digest of China's Statistical Data, 1992 (Beijing: Zhongguo Tongji Publishing Co., 1992), p. 71.

The private sector also enormously improved China's service sector and contributed to a significant rise in social welfare and the availability of consumer goods. Government data revealed that, in the early 1990s, the private sector had gained control of 30 percent of China's retail market.[19] The quasi-private rural industries produced 80 percent of the consumer goods (in terms of gross value) and 70 percent of the apparel sold in China; in addition, this sector became an important source of producer goods, accounting for 40 percent of mineral products, 33 percent of coal, and 80–90 percent of agricultural machinery.[20] In short, as a result of the rapid development of the private sector, China became a mixed economy in the early 1990s.

If, as the preceding data suggest, a vibrant and expanding private sector has established itself in China since 1979, what was the role of the state in this development? What was the role of various societal actors? And how useful is the analytical framework of societal takeover in explaining this capitalist revolution in China?

Explaining the Capitalist Revolution

Most notable in the development of the private sector in China was the absence of a deliberate, government-initiated program of privatization. Except for allowing peasant-initiated agricultural decollectivization movements as a response to enormous pressures from the peasantry at the outset of reform, the Chinese government made no attempt to privatize the huge, inefficient state-owned industrial sector. Not anticipating the explosive growth potential of the quasi-private rural industries following the emancipation of hundreds of millions of peasants from a low-productivity and low-income rural economic life under the commune system, many government policies actually discriminated against the private sector, and the conservative forces within the government periodically launched campaigns against it.

If the government made any contribution to the development of the private sector in China, it was its permissiveness toward the grassroots decollectivization of agriculture in 1979–1982, the partial legalization of small urban private businesses, the opening to the West, and limited price reforms. These measures, particularly the first one, provided the critical initial momentum that was to create China's private sector. These policies, however, constituted the government's only contribution to China's capitalist revolution.

The Initial Opening
The old regime's initial response to a systemic crisis usually provides the indispensable first step in the transition from communist rule. In many in-

stances, despite its tentativeness and limited scale, such a response creates several favorable conditions for societal forces to exploit. This was precisely the case with the initial rural opening in China between the late 1970s and the early 1980s. After winning a crucial victory against the holdovers from the Maoist regime at the 3rd plenum of the 11th Congress of the CCP in December 1978, Deng's regime launched its rural reform program.

However, as posited in the two key documents adopted by the plenum and issued in January 1979, this program was limited to increasing agricultural productivity by making production teams smaller and more accountable. Specifically, the documents called for the implementation of a "group responsibility" system that did not require a full-fledged decollectivization of agriculture. Although this merely tightened financial accountability,[21] the encouraging pronouncement was that peasant family plots, rural retail trade, and cash-earning activities were protected by law.[22] The new rural policy also raised the state purchasing prices for eighteen main agricultural goods by an average of 24.8 percent.[23] Nowhere in these documents was the decollectivization of agriculture mentioned as a government policy. Rather, decollectivization in this sphere was principally due to the spontaneous, and initially unauthorized, efforts of peasants, first in Anhui Province in January 1979, then across the nation as other peasants followed suit. From the very beginning, the process received overwhelming support from the Chinese peasantry. By October 1980, 43 percent of the production teams in Anhui province had been disbanded and converted to a "household responsibility system"; by October 1982, 95 percent of the teams in the province had been converted to the new system. In the opening phase, the momentum for change was typically provided by a convergence of mass pressure *from below* and tentative elite support *from above*. During this period, individual reformers were likely to make a greater impact than in the later phases of reform. This was the case with the development of the private sector in general and the decollectivization of agriculture in Anhui in particular.

Wan Li, a close aide to Deng who was appointed provincial party secretary during these critical years, personally supported the grassroots decollectivization movement. Although he first allowed only one commune to experiment with the new system, the news spread to other communes, where peasants quickly began to decollectivize on their own.[24] In this case, Chinese peasants simply seized the opportunity offered by a limited government reform program ("group responsibility system") and replaced it with their own radical "household responsibility system," leading to the dismantling of communes.

Although the government did not publicly sanction this mass movement, Deng and Wan (the latter was soon appointed to oversee agricultural reform) announced their qualified approval of the household responsibility system in April 1980. The experiment was, according to Deng, restricted to poorer areas in Gansu, Inner Mongolia, Yunnan, and Guizhou. The government formally authorized it in January 1982. By that time, however, peasants had already disbanded nearly half the communes in the country and converted them to the new system.[25] Formal government approval accelerated the mass decollectivization movement; by the end of 1983, 97.1 percent of the people's communes were dismantled and converted to the new system.[26]

With the fall of the communes, which had kept the surplus rural labor on the land through a mixture of political coercion and the constraints of a subsistence economy, the emergence and rapid growth of the private sector became inevitable. The decollectivization of agriculture was thus bound to have a far-reaching impact on the transformation of China's state-dominated economic system. Decollectivization not only gave the peasantry a powerful incentive to produce more, but it also increased their mobility and vastly expanded their opportunities.

The peasantry gained more freedom because, under the new system, their contractual obligation to the state was the delivery of a set amount of grain and other agricultural produce at state-fixed prices; once the quota was met, they were free to pursue any line of business they chose. The collapse of the communes both as a growth-suppressing economic institution and as a control-oriented sociopolitical institution that restricted rural labor mobility lay at the source of the rapid development of China's private sector. No government could expect to enforce regulations designed to restrict the growth of the private sector in the countryside once its key institutions there no longer functioned.

Besides protecting the peasant-initiated decollectivization movement, top elite endorsement also appeared to have shielded the private industrial firms from conservative attacks in the opening phase. When told about the emergence of these firms in China in 1982, Deng vaguely responded, "Let us take a look at it"—a statement that, in a country where formal legality often provided less protection than the personal utterances of high dignitaries, seemed to give the private sector a tacit endorsement. This unofficial—and highly capricious—style of policy-making was, and often still is, a unique feature of the Chinese political process. The personal views of the dominant leader carried enormous weight and were routinely construed as the implicit official position of the government. In reality, Deng's edict was translated into a policy of three "No's"—"no official promotion, no propaganda campaign [for the private sector], and no crackdown"—that constituted a "hands-off" policy toward the private sector.[27] In this case, it appeared to have worked to the advantage of the private sector.

Another top Chinese leader who promoted the private sector was Zhao Ziyang. In his report to the 13th Party Congress in November 1987, Zhao publicly declared, "As facts show, the development of a private economy up to a certain degree is favorable to the development of the economy, invigoration of the market, expansion of employment, and greater satisfaction of the economic needs of the people; it is a necessary and beneficial addition to the state-owned economy."[28] In October 1987, after reading an internal report about widespread fear and insecurity among owners of private firms, Zhao instructed that regulations on private firms be drawn up quickly, "so that owners of private enterprises may run their businesses with confidence." His directive was soon translated into the State Council's landmark document of June 25, 1988, legalizing private firms.[29]

If the rural opening was the result of the convergence of massive pressure for decollectivization from below and the top elite's perception of a growing crisis in the Chinese countryside, the urban opening in the creation of a private sector (oriented mainly toward retail activity and services) was similarly created by the pressure from below and the elites' timely response to a looming crisis. In this case, urban China in the late 1970s was confronted with millions of unemployed high-school graduates and educated youths who had returned to the cities from their involuntary settlement in the countryside during the Cultural Revolution.

In 1979, the urban unemployment rate rose to an unprecedented high of 5.9 percent, with more than 8 million people, 57 percent of them youths, jobless.[30] Their street demonstrations and sit-ins at government buildings coincided with the Democracy Wall movement in Beijing and similar democracy movements in other major urban centers between 1978 and 1979, putting enormous pressure on Chinese leaders to avert another potentially explosive situation. However, since the bloated state sector, which contained between 15 and 20 million "hidden unemployed workers" (more than 10 percent of its total labor force) was unable to absorb the unemployed, the urgent need to find jobs for so many people overrode the government's ideological reservations about the private sector and forced it to permit the unemployed to find jobs in that arena.[31] At a special central government meeting on employment in 1979, opening up the private sector—which employed only 140,000 people nationwide in 1978—was identified as a key component of the government's employment policy, although formal legal status was not given to the urban private sector until July 1981.[32]

Initially, the government tried to restrict the growth potential of the private sector by setting strict limits on hiring (no more than five "apprentices") and permitting only a small range of business activities. For example, its early definition of "urban nonagricultural private economy" was "small-scale handicraft manufacturing, retail trade, restaurant operations, services, nonmotorized transportation, and housing repair." The government later expanded the range of business activities to include the use of motorized transportation equipment and long-distance shipping services.[33]

By the early 1990s, however, most of the private firms, or *siying* (73 percent in 1991), were engaged in manufacturing, construction, and transportation, thus competing directly with the state sector.[34] Only a minority (27 percent) were in the service and retail sectors.[35] Moreover, the government clearly favored private cooperative *(hezuo)* organizations over private individual *(geti)* firms, allowing the former relatively more freedom in business activities (such as a higher ceiling on hiring and a license for small-scale manufacturing);[36] consequently, this policy encouraged many individual private entrepreneurs to form nominally cooperative private firms.[37]

Following the opening phase, the Chinese government was unusually inactive during the hyper-growth phase of the private sector from 1983 to 1986. After launching a campaign against "economic crimes" that was partially aimed at the emerging private sector in 1982, the government took no substantive action either to promote or to restrain the growth of the private sector. Certain government reform measures, however, inadvertently benefited the private sector by contributing to its rapid development. Some of these important measures included the economic opening to the West, fiscal decentralization (which gave local authorities the power to collect their own taxes and fund local projects, thus providing them with the incentives to support local private-sector activities), and the introduction of limited price reforms through dual-track pricing (which cracked the state's monopoly on the distribution of producer goods).

The dual-track price reform, for example, began in August 1981, when the State Council approved a document that permitted enterprises to sell their output—mainly industrial producer goods—above the state-set production quotas at market-set prices. In the beginning, this was to be a transitional policy designed to provide incentives to managers of SOEs to increase production without disrupting the government's economic plan. The partial price reform significantly reduced the government's ability to control the allocation of critical resources, particularly producer and intermediate goods. By 1988, for example, prices for about 50 percent of all products were set by the market. In the early 1990s, about 60 percent of all producer goods (raw materials and energy) were traded on the market using the dual-track pricing formula, and only 40 percent of them were allocated by the central planning system.[38]

Ironically, this policy achieved results both unanticipated and abhorred by the central government that authorized it. The dual-track pricing reform did not create a full-fledged market, but it did open an enormous fissure in the planned economic system through which the private sector could grow and prosper. The new incentive structure set by the dual-track pricing system immediately induced managers of SOEs to divert an increasing quantity of producer and intermediate goods away from the state sector and into the private sector, since they could get much higher prices for the same goods on the market. Some enterprises even illicitly marketed the portion of their products that was supposed to be sold to the state at lower planned prices.

Before the implementation of the dual-track price reform, private entrepreneurs had to obtain scarce inputs through illegal means. After the policy was put into practice, they were able to purchase inputs legally on the market, albeit at higher prices. As dual-track pricing became the dominant price-setting practice toward the end of the 1980s, even SOEs, which saw their subsidized inputs gradually reduced by market forces, had to go to the market to purchase such inputs.[39] As a result, the state sector was forced to compete with the private sector both for scarce inputs on the producer goods markets and for the share of the consumer goods market.

This dual-pricing system, however, was also blamed for China's double-digit inflation and rampant official corruption toward the end of the 1980s, as market forces drove up the prices of scarce goods and officials who controlled the allocation of key inputs (such as coal, steel, and other raw materials) at subsidized prices engaged in the widespread practice of diverting them into the private sector at immense personal profit. This new pricing system also spawned a large number of private brokers *(daoye)* who made huge profits from buying scarce goods from the state sector at subsidized prices and selling them on the market at higher prices.

In any case, the initial opening created by the government's limited reform measures freed a huge social group, the peasantry, from the institutional control of the communes, and it created a number of favorable contextual factors, the most important being decontrol of socioeconomic activities, partial price reforms that broke the state's monopoly on the distribution of producer goods, the opening of China's economy to the West, and a considerable degree of fiscal decentralization. Noteworthy about the initial opening in China, as compared with that in the Soviet Union under *perestroika,* was the relatively low level of politicization in the emergence of the private sector. Despite intraelite policy and ideological dispute, most of the changes took place without engulfing the entire nation in a bitter and divisive ideological debate such as that which occurred in the Soviet Union.

The Activation of a Major Social Group: The Peasantry

Why was it that, of all the major social groups in China, the peasantry played the predominant role in the creation of a vibrant private sector? In this section, we will see that Chinese peasants, rather than industrial workers, took the lead in the speedy development of the private sector mainly because of their relative group autonomy, strength, and entrepreneurial orientations.

*   *   *

The autonomy of the Chinese peasantry can be measured by examining (1) the degree to which Chinese peasants were included in the institutions of the socialist welfare state; (2) the extent to which the institutions of the party-state (primarily the organizational reach of the Communist Party) penetrated the rural areas prior to reform; and (3) the extent to which the same institutions decayed in the countryside as a result of the Cultural Revolution prior to reform and as a consequence of agricultural reform during the 1980s.

Unlike more developed communist states such as the Soviet Union and the Eastern European countries, which had the economic means to maintain a more inclusive socialist welfare state, China could include only a relatively small proportion of its population—almost exclusively its urban population and employees in the state sector—in the socialist welfare state. According to government figures, the Chinese socialist welfare state, comprising income security, lifetime employment, pensions, free health care, and other benefits, covered only about 22 percent of the total labor force, with the peasantry completely excluded. It was estimated that employees in the urban state sector received 237 yuan per person in 1987 in direct work-related benefits, excluding various food and housing subsidies.[40] A 1990 study showed that state-sector workers and employees derived 23 percent of their income from state-financed social service programs, and various government subsidies provided another 16.6 percent of their personal income.[41] The socialist welfare state thus increased the costs of exit enormously for workers long dependent on these programs.

The overall costs of these social welfare programs were evident in government financial statistics. In 1988, the state provided free medical care, pension benefits, and various subsidies totaling nearly 40.9 billion yuan for only 124.78 million workers in the state and quasi-state sectors, while 400 million rural laborers received no such protection.[42] Its total outlay for welfare programs in the countryside (almost exclusively poverty relief) amounted to only a fraction of its socialist welfare program for state employees.

For instance, in 1978 the government provided only 230 million yuan for the rural welfare program, excluding disaster relief; in the same year, it allocated 5.1 billion yuan to the labor insurance program, consisting of death benefits, funeral costs, pension plans, and free medical services, for the employees in the state and quasi-state sectors—which represented an approximate 1:25 ratio. During the 1980s, this ratio increased further; in 1984, for example, it rose to 1:62.[43] The exclusion of the peasantry from the services provided by the socialist welfare state in China may have helped reduce the group's dependence on the state, thus allowing them to preserve their relative autonomy and improve their lives on their own. As we shall also see from polling data collected in China during the 1980s, peasants tended to be more willing to take risks and less beholden to communist-socialist values than the industrial workers in the state sector. This critical difference in attitudes arose from the disparate degrees of allegiance these groups felt for the institutions of the socialist welfare state.

The autonomy of the Chinese peasantry was preserved largely because the reach of the party-state in rural China was limited. The Chinese Communist Party, though rural in origin, had gradually transformed itself into an urban-based political establishment since its revolutionary victory in 1949. For example, in 1957 peasants made up the majority of party members (66.8 percent); by 1981, peasants became a minority (45.5 percent); and by 1987, they accounted for 39.5 percent of party membership.[44] As a result, the CCP's institutional penetration of society was much deeper in the cities than in the countryside. One rough measure highlighting the difference between the reach of the party-state in these two areas was the distribution of the *nomenklatura*. In 1982, 95 percent of the CCP cadres were concentrated in urban areas, while only 5 percent worked in rural areas. The Party's penetration of the backbone of the planned economy—the SOEs—was especially deep, with nearly 70 percent of its cadres assigned to these enterprises.[45] Another measure of the institutional reach of the CCP was the proportion of CCP members in the urban and rural general population. This comparison showed, for example, that in 1982, CCP members made up 10.22 percent of the general urban population, whereas they accounted for only 2.24 percent of the overall rural population.[46]

The Chinese peasantry derived its strength chiefly from its huge size (it accounted for about 75 percent of the labor force in 1980, for instance) and, in the regime's view, its critical role in the maintenance of political stability. In confronting the emergence of the private sector at the end of the 1970s, the Chinese leadership, especially the hardliners, faced two equally unpleasant choices. On the one hand, it could contain the growth of this sector via strict government control and even repression, as it had done periodically since the late 1950s, in order to prevent an ideologically heretical form of economic activity and a potential threat to its hold on political power. But massive unemployment and the deterioration of the standard of living for hundreds of millions of peasants and tens of millions of unemployed urban residents would pose a more immediate threat to stability. On the other hand, if it allowed the private sector to grow and absorb a significant portion of rural surplus labor, social peace would be attained at the expense of the regime's control over society.

The pressure for creating employment for young urban dwellers paled in comparison with the need to find employment for the surplus rural labor freed up by decollectivization. If 8 million unemployed urban residents at the end of the 1970s threatened social stability, the estimated 200 million peasants who constituted surplus labor after the demise of the communes would, when left unemployed, have become an explosive source of political unrest. Indeed, creating employment for tens of millions of peasants became a primary concern of the regime. In terms of solving this huge problem, however, the only alternative was to allow the private sector to operate, grow fast, and absorb rural surplus labor. It is interesting to note that, after quasi-private rural industries had employed tens of millions of peasants, Deng himself identified the emergence of the sector as "one of the extremely important experiences in our success."[47]

The amount of rural surplus labor freed up by decollectivization was truly astonishing. From this huge pool of surplus labor came both the political pressure on the government to keep its hands off the private sector and the principal momentum for the development of the sector. Despite the phenomenal success of the quasi-private rural industries in absorbing about 90 million peasants during the 1980s, more than 100 million were still in need of employment, forming an enormous mobile labor force from which most of the private vendors, menial laborers, and entrepreneurs were drawn.

It was estimated that about 33 million members of this force, who were not classified by the government as employees in the private sector because they were not registered with government agencies as such, became the so-called migrant population engaged in various economic activities in the private sector across the country.[48] In addition, more than 14 million peasants became rural traders in the 1980s.[49] It should be no surprise, therefore, that the overwhelming majority of private businesses (about 80 percent) and individual private entrepreneurs (about 75 percent) were concentrated in the countryside at the end of the 1980s.[50] According to government figures, the rural labor force in China will experience a net increase of 79.2 million in the 1990s; in addition, about 11 million will join the labor force every year, but the government will be able to create jobs for only 7 million in the early 1990s. Thus, the combined rural-urban pressure for employment will continue to provide an irresistible momentum for the growth of the private sector in China.[51]

Why were Chinese peasants more motivated than other major social groups to take risks and plunge into the uncertain world of the private sector? Two explanations—one institutional and the other attitudinal—may shed some light on this question. First, most of the channels of upward mobility in the state-dominated sectors—industry, education, and the civil service—were closed to peasants, leaving the private sector as the only means for advancement (with the exception of military service) available to them. This highly unequal situation created an incentive structure which provided peasants with a high level of motivation to better their lives on their own. The same situation, in contrast, appeared to have dramatically increased risk-aversion, exit costs, and dampened entrepreneurial spirit among state employees.

Second, perhaps because of their exclusion from the socialist welfare state and most channels of upward mobility, the Chinese peasantry, as a group, tended to have a more positive attitude toward risk-taking and the private sector than industrial workers and state employees. They did not identify with officially promoted values as deeply as other social groups. Responding to the question "Are you proud of living in a socialist country?" in a 1986 poll, about 44 percent of the peasant-interviewees said yes, while 34 percent expressed indifference and 19 percent said no. By comparison, about 54 percent of the worker-interviewees said yes. The same poll also found peasants to be more pragmatic and less trustful of the government than other social groups.[52]

Available polling data also showed that those who enjoyed the benefits of the socialist welfare state in China tended to be more risk-averse and favored the continuation of the socialist safety net. In a 1986 national survey of employees in the state sector, for instance, 84.1 percent of the respondents expressed the view that "after all, the present system of socialist welfare is more reassuring," and 77.3 percent of urban residents said that they would rather choose a life-style that "provided security but offered fewer opportunities to increase income." Only 13 percent of the employees in the state sector said that they would enter the private sector if they lost their jobs.[53] Two other surveys of workers in the SOEs in 1987, conducted after the implementation of small-scale leasing and "contracting" (self-financing) experiments, found that these state employees overwhelmingly supported the job security provided by the socialist welfare state, with 71.7 percent of the respondents expressing their satisfaction with the "iron rice bowl" system (lifetime employment).[54] The Chinese experience of the rapid development of the private sector showed that the larger the state sector and the more complete the coverage of the socialist welfare state, the more difficult it would be for the private sector to emerge and grow.

This general observation is backed up by other attitudinal surveys indicating the adverse effect of socialist welfare institutions on individual entrepreneurship. A poll of 2,400 people in 1985 found a direct correlation between fear of the negative impact of reform (inflation, job insecurity, and elimination of government subsidies) and the respondents' receipt of benefits under the existing socialist welfare state. For instance, a huge majority of urban workers in the state-owned enterprises (77.7 percent) replied that they would rather choose a stable life with few opportunities for increasing income than enter the private sector. The peasants surveyed, however, showed a much higher level of risk tolerance and were ranked by the poll-takers as the most risk-taking social group in China.[55]

Formation of an Informal Takeover Coalition

The formation of a takeover coalition between diverse actors with respective motives is a critical factor in the acquisition of the resources to be controlled by various societal forces. In the development of the private sector in China in the 1980s, it can be argued that, driven by different motives, an informal takeover coalition consisting of the peasantry, private entrepreneurs, local political elites, and foreign investors played an instrumental role in accelerating the speed of the private sector's development and defending its gains. Given the participation of local political elites, this informal takeover coalition was not purely societal in nature.

The complex composition of the informal takeover coalition was the result of the interaction between the tensions generated by two sets of cleavages: (1) state-society cleavage and (2) center-periphery cleavage. In their efforts to gain autonomy from the state, societal actors frequently exploit the center-periphery tensions by establishing informal alliances with local elites in the latter's bureaucratic-institutional rivalry with the center of the state. In regime transition, cooperation from elements within the regime (even minor players on the periphery) often makes a crucial difference in terms of speeding up the transition and reducing its political costs. In such cases, the eventual resource gains for various societal actors may not be as clear-cut as when the takeover coalition is predominantly societal in nature (with no participation by any partners in the state apparatus). Frequently, such gains are distributed between societal actors and the local agents of the state. But because a decentralized state apparatus is easier for societal actors to penetrate and capture than a centralized one, even this outcome should be viewed as a positive step for the expansion of the influence of society.

What was striking about the partners' motives for cooperation in this informal coalition was that they resulted from shared economic interests, rather than similar ideological beliefs. Indeed, no evidence suggested that any of the partners in this informal alliance were driven by a sudden ideological conversion to neoliberal capitalism. They were pragmatists primarily interested in problem-solving. And their problem was not to build capitalism because it was ideologically appealing, but to create wealth quickly to meet their respective needs, and market forces happened to be the most efficient problem-solving means in this respect.

It is not difficult to divine the specific economic interests motivating these partners to engage in cooperative behavior that resulted in the emergence of a huge private sector in China. For the vast army of surplus rural labor freed from the defunct commune system, participation was simply a matter of escape from subsistence farming, to which they had been confined by the pre-reform system. Because the bloated state sector held little room to absorb them, employment in higher-income, nonagricultural private sectors was the only way to increase their income and social status.

Official data showed that, between 1981 and 1990, quasi-private rural industries paid their peasant employees 500 billion yuan in wages. By the early 1990s, about one-third of rural per capita income was derived from rural industries, which also contributed nearly all the net growth in rural GSP (87 percent in 1990, for example).[56]

Motivation for private entrepreneurs was simple but powerful: the creation, expansion, and defense of private wealth. Almost taken for granted in noncommunist states, such opportunities had been denied to the entrepreneurial groups in China since 1949. For foreign investors in general, and overseas Chinese investors in particular, the lure of China's huge supply of cheap labor and vast potential market was clearly the most powerful motive for supplying much-needed capital, technology, management, and marketing skills to the private sector.

The more complex case here involved the local elites who participated in this informal coalition.[57] They were also driven by an assortment of motives. Some—and in many areas, a significant portion—of the local elites had built up sizable personal financial stakes in the quasi-private rural industries because, as part of the process of the transformation of the *nomenklatura* into private entrepreneurs, they themselves had become owners or direct beneficiaries of these businesses. Anecdotal evidence suggested that a considerable number of private and quasi-private rural firms were owned and managed by relatives and close friends of local elites as part of the latter's patronage network; such firms required special care from the local elites involved.[58]

On a more political level, because the collapse of the commune system also brought an end to the use of overt political power in the maintenance of clientalist relationships in rural areas, local ruling elites were apparently under pressure to develop new economic resources to maintain such relationships (which could be converted into political power). In this context, rural industries provided an ideal means to meet this need, for TVEs supplied relatively well paying jobs (compared with farming), travel opportunities (as salesmen or on construction crews), and higher occupational prestige.

Local governments were thus driven by similar incentives to condone—if not actively support—the private sector. For local governments in general, the motive almost exclusively derived from their pressing fiscal needs in the wake of the reorganization of China's tax structure in the early 1980s.[59] The overhauling of the tax structure resulted in significant fiscal decentralization, which allowed local governments to collect and spend most of the tax revenues from locally owned enterprises and local tax bases, which included the private sector. Through the 1980s, additional measures of fiscal decentralization were implemented to reduce the central government's subsidies to local authorities through autonomy-enhancing devices such as "local financial self-accounting," or *baogan.* Under *baogan,* local governments had complete freedom in spending the portion of local revenues exceeding the level spelled out in the preset quota agreement between the local governments and the central government.[60] In the more open provinces such as

Guangdong, the provincial government encouraged further fiscal decentralization by allowing municipal and county governments to institute *baogan*.[61]

Generally speaking, Chinese local governments, especially at the county and township levels, were under severe fiscal stress and highly dependent on locally generated revenues. In 1990, for example, despite 6 billion yuan in central subsidies to county governments, nearly half the 2,182 county (municipality) governments in China incurred budget deficits.[62] Whatever ideological reservations local ruling elites might have harbored against the private sector, the dwindling subsidies from the center (which itself accumulated huge budget deficits in the 1980s) and the pressure for seeking alternative sources of funding forced them to turn to the private and quasi-private sectors to raise revenues.

The reform experiences of the 1980s demonstrated a strong connection between the development of the private sector and the increase in local fiscal dependence on the sector. In the coastal provinces, where the quasi-private rural industries were most developed, 70–80 percent of provincial and municipal revenues actually came from these rural firms.[63] According to Vice-Premier Tian Jiyun, in areas where rural industries were more developed, between 70 and 80 percent of the revenues for townships and villages came from rural firms; 40–50 percent of the revenues of the county governments came from these firms.[64]

This complicated web of economic interests thus helped to forge a powerful informal takeover coalition whose partners cooperated with one another tacitly. The cooperative behavior of local ruling elites deserves special analysis here. Because the extraction of fees and taxes from private entrepreneurs became an important source of revenue for local governments, the main contribution of these authorities to the coalition was twofold: protection and facilitation. For example, they shielded the private sector from discriminatory government regulations; typically, the full enforcement of such regulations would have meant the closing down of those many private firms that had violated such regulations.

A more revealing case here involved local governments' protection of private firms that falsely and illegally registered as "collective firms" in order to evade higher taxes and avoid political risks. In early 1990, as part of the post-Tiananmen countertakeover efforts, the conservative forces launched a nationwide campaign against such false collective firms. It was revealed that local governments, from neighborhood committees in cities to township governments, were not only well aware of obviously illegal practices, but actively supported them because these false collective firms created jobs, paid local taxes, and even, in some cases, helped to take over money-losing local enterprises and make them profitable. Without such false collective firms, as one local party official admitted to government investigators, "our local government could not have survived financially."[65]

In many cases, local governments received direct payments (in addition to taxes) from private entrepreneurs in return both for protecting the private sector by helping members maintain a "collective" front, and for providing many necessary administrative services that enabled them to operate in the still heavily bureaucratized Chinese economy. For a fee, rural governments would furnish private entrepreneurs with letters of introduction and allow them to use the corporate bank accounts of rural collectives (private individuals were not allowed to open corporate accounts) to facilitate commercial transactions.[66]

Favorable External Factors

The rapid development of the private sector in China between 1979 and 1991 benefited from several favorable external factors resulting from the dramatic shift in China's development strategy from import-substitution industrialization to export-oriented industrialization. The most important external factors included: access to foreign capital, technology, management expertise, and markets, following the government's "open-door" policy, which, in retrospect, opened the door of China not only to foreign capitalists, but to the emerging capitalists within the country. Foreign economic influence was especially important in China's coastal provinces (where external economic linkages were strongest) in general, and in Guangdong and Fujian (where most of the foreign investment from Hong Kong and Taiwan was concentrated) in particular. Altogether, about 80 percent, or $15.2 billion, of foreign direct investment in China between 1979 and 1990 was concentrated in the coastal areas.[67]

Nationwide, foreign businesses had invested in 7,000 quasi-private rural firms, or about 25 percent of the total number of joint ventures and wholly owned foreign firms in China, by 1991.[68] During the 1980s, 540,000 pieces of equipment, technology, and machinery were imported to enable quasi-private rural firms to produce goods for export.[69]

The opening of the consumer markets in the West was perhaps an even more important factor in bolstering the private sector in China that specialized in producing low-cost consumer goods. In 1991, 85,000 township and village enterprises were engaged in exports production, compared with 48 such firms in 1981.[70] In 1981, total exports from rural industries amounted to only 8.5 million yuan; in 1992, they reached 120 billion yuan.[71] Thus, the quasi-private rural industries had become a major player in China's export-oriented economy. Between 1985 and 1990, exports earnings from rural industries accounted for 30 percent of the net growth in China's exports.[72] Government figures also showed that exports from rural industries accounted for 25 percent of China's total foreign exchange earnings in the early 1990s.[73] Rural industries have now become China's main sources of exports in labor-intensive manufactures. For instance, roughly two-thirds of the apparel exported in 1990 (in terms of net value) was made by rural industries, and about 40 percent of China's total textile exports were produced by rural firms in the same year.[74]

Despite the foreign-invested firms' relatively small share in China's GSP (2.6 percent in 1991), the direct presence of foreign investment in China has constituted an important segment of the formal private sector since the early 1980s. All told, between 1979 and 1992, foreign direct investment in China reached $34.5 billion; these funds financed 84,000 joint ventures and wholly owned foreign firms.[75] In addition to contributing about 4.4 percent of China's gross industrial output value by 1991, foreign-invested firms, which are export-oriented, dramatically increased China's export capability. In 1991, foreign-invested firms earned $12 billion through exports and accounted for 16.7 percent of China's exports earnings.[76] Together, foreign-owned firms, joint ventures, and rural industries contributed about 43 percent of China's exports earnings in 1991. It is thus abundantly clear that the prime engines of China's export-oriented growth in the 1980s were the private and quasi-private sectors.[77] Without their contribution, the internationalization of the Chinese economy would not have occurred as rapidly or successfully as it did.

Some of these favorable external factors that accelerated the development of the private sector in China in the 1980s were, however, unique situational ones that cannot be duplicated in transitions to a market economy in other ex-communist states. Most important among them was the presence of more than 50 million overseas Chinese in Hong Kong, Macao, Taiwan, and Southeast Asia who had capital, management expertise, rich experience in foreign investment, and far-reaching business connections in the world trading system.[78] One estimate put the worth of liquid assets controlled by overseas Chinese at $1.5 trillion to $2 trillion.[79] Attracted by new business opportunities presented by Deng's open-door policy, motivated by deep emotional attachment to the land of their ancestors, and facilitated by their local connections, knowledge of the language and culture, these overseas Chinese private investors provided the most crucial *initial* sources of foreign direct investment when the actual investment climate in China might have discouraged non-Chinese overseas investors. It was their investment—usually in their ancestral towns and villages along the southern coastal provinces of Guangdong and Fujian—that constituted the critical mass which seemed to have both reassured capitalists from Western countries and spurred their investment. Between 1983 and 1990, about 60 percent of foreign investment came from Hong Kong and Macao alone.[80]

Moreover, certain changes in the East Asian international political economy at the end of the 1970s and early 1980s coincided with China's opening to the West in general and the development of the export-oriented private sector in particular. As the first-generation East Asian NICs—South Korea, Taiwan, Hong Kong, and Singapore—were shifting their export-oriented industries from low-margin, labor-intensive consumer products to higher-margin, more capital- and technology-intensive products, a valuable window of opportunity was created for newly opened rural China. The NICs targeted areas in rural China as offshore production sites for those goods that had become too costly to produce at home. At the same time, the relative openness of the American consumer market provided increasing access for these goods. By the end of the 1980s, the United States had become China's single largest market for merchandise exports, including reexports via transshipment through Hong Kong.

Accelerated Institutional Decay

China enjoyed a significant initial advantage over the Soviet Union owing to the devastation wrought by the Cultural Revolution on the economic and political institutions of the party-state. Because this higher level of institutional decay prior to the advent of reform lowered the barriers to change and spared China's reformers some of the frustrations Gorbachev encountered in the opening phase in the Soviet Union, it also enabled China's reformers to avoid the riskier reform path of using mass political mobilization to overcome bureaucratic-institutional barriers to economic reform.

Economic reform in China, moreover, unleashed market forces which further contributed to an acceleration of institutional decay, thus facilitating the rapid growth of the private sector while undermining the efforts by conservative forces to use the economic and political institutions of the state to control the growth of this sector. The decay of the party-state could be attributed to the institutional inflexibility of the state's economic administrative agencies and the CCP organizations, the corrosive influence of the market forces on the integrity of these institutions and their functionaries, and the new self-enrichment opportunities created by the private sector that induced a large exodus of elites from the state.

The Chinese economic administrative bureaucracy was established primarily to monitor and operate a centralized and inflexible state-controlled economy. Although this institutional framework was able to mobilize resources and develop certain high-priority projects, the same bureaucratic-institutional framework was incapable of dealing with a decentralized and flexible private sector. The institutional inability of government bureaucracies to confront the emergence of the private sector was evenly matched by the SOEs' lack of competitiveness with private and quasi-private industrial firms. The SOEs rapidly lost market share to these private upstarts.

The economic administrative bureaucracy in China underwent remark-

ably little organizational innovation during reform. The result was, predictably, bureaucratic chaos: more than a dozen government agencies claimed to
have a measure of authority to regulate the fast-growing private sector, but
few communicated and none assumed an exclusive and specialized role in
monitoring and regulating the sector. Consequently, the private sector grew
steadily in a bureaucratic no man's land. In many ways, this bureaucratic
chaos stymied private entrepreneurs, as each bureaucratic agency had the
power to deny a certain permit and each imposed some kind of fee on private entrepreneurs. One study showed that twelve different government
agencies were collecting twenty-three different types of taxes and levies from
the private sector.[81]

In other ways, however, this situation created favorable conditions for the
private sector. Poor communication between different government agencies
led to incomplete and inaccurate information about the true dimensions and
activities of the private sector. This resulted in an underestimation of the size
of the private sector and its potential threat to the state sector, precluding a
conservative crackdown on the former.

The rapid growth of the private sector quickly outstripped government
agencies' capacity to monitor and regulate it. One tax-collector exclusively
assigned to enforce tax laws on the private sector handled an average of 150
private businesses; in some areas, each tax-collector was assigned 300 private businesses to monitor. Such staff shortages in these government agencies seriously undermined the state's ability to enforce tax laws.[82]

Perhaps the most fascinating aspect of the politics of privatization in China
was the transformation of a large number of former rural party and government cadres into what might be called the "pioneers" of the private sector.
There was a positive correlation between the development of the private sector and the participation by the former, and sometimes current, members of
the ruling elites in that sector. Party members accounted for 15 percent of
the owners of rural private firms, while the percentage of party members in
the labor force was about 10 percent overall, and about 5 percent in the
countryside.[83] One study found that about 31 percent of rural private business owners were party members, and many were former village party leaders and government officials.[84] Another study concluded that the percentage
of party members among owners of private businesses in the countryside
was much higher than the percentage of party members among peasants at
large.[85] A survey of private business owners in Shaanxi Province revealed,
for instance, that 15.5 percent were former commune and brigade leaders;
another survey of private business owners in Tianjin showed that 22.2 percent were former leaders of communes and brigades or commune-affiliated
enterprises.[86]

In contrast, party cadres in the cities were for the most part absent from the ranks of owners of private businesses, largely because the bastion of power and privilege for the Party, the administrative agencies of the planned economy and party organizations in the cities, remained practically intact in the absence of a near complete dismantling of the Party's rural organizations following the collapse of the communes (although the upsurge of the capitalist revolution in China in the early 1990s did drive many members of the urban *nomenklatura* into private businesses). The transformation of former cadres into private entrepreneurs in the countryside was especially interesting because it suggested a way to overcome opposition to privatization from a group who apparently had everything to lose should privatization succeed.

In the Chinese case, however, it must be stressed that the government did not have a clear-cut policy to find suitable employment for rural party and government cadres displaced by decollectivization. Rather, these cadres simply helped themselves to the nonagricultural assets previously owned by the communes by leasing them initially on favorable terms and soon converting them into their private assets without a formal (legal) process of privatization.[87] After the dismantling of communes, the majority of the nonagricultural assets, such as factories and shops, were also leased to private individuals. One study showed that a large percentage of rural private firms were initially established with such assets.[88] Many former rural cadres used their power to pick and lease the most productive assets at extremely favorable rates.

For example, one study of 200 large quasi-private rural firms in 10 provinces in 1986 showed that village and former production team officials made up 55 percent of the founders of these rural businesses, while ordinary peasants accounted for 21 percent.[89] This process of spontaneous privatization converted most of the nonagricultural assets in the countryside from quasi-state ownership to private ownership. It was estimated that, at the end of 1978, nonagricultural assets of communes and state farms were valued at 97.7 billion yuan; but at the end of 1986, they dwindled to only 25 billion yuan, which meant a substantial portion of them had been effectively privatized (or stolen) in eight years.[90] By joining the postcommunist "gold rush" of privatization in the countryside, these cadres developed a strong personal stake in the process. This entrenched group was "bought off" by itself or economically "co-opted" by society. As a result, a group which would have otherwise most fiercely resisted privatization had become some of its most vigorous practitioners and defenders.

In the Chinese case, moreover, thanks to the connections they established while in government, these ex-*nomenklatura* were able to form business ties quickly, and they experienced fewer difficulties in getting supplies and credits. More important, their political influence, though somewhat diminished by decollectivization, also afforded them a high degree of protection for their private businesses. Of course, this process of transforming party cadres into private entrepreneurs was not an equalizing one. It converted a formerly politically powerful group into an economically privileged one. One study of income distribution in rural China found that new entrepreneurs who were ex-cadres benefited more than any other group in the market transition process.[91] The irony here is that, on the one hand, this was one of the few proven and effective options available for creating a viable private sector quickly, but its primary beneficiaries appeared to be those who were most responsible for the prereform economic collapse and least deserving of the pecuniary rewards generated by privatization. On the other hand, if public sentiment had denied the cadres the opportunity to make personal gains and contribute to the development of the private sector, they would have put up fierce resistance to reform, and privatization would have been impeded.

The process of institutional decay of the party-state, which began with the Cultural Revolution and accelerated following the decollectivization of agriculture, further eroded the state's hold on the peasantry. With the advent of a market economy in rural China, newly unleashed economic forces weakened the organizational discipline and integrity of the CCP through both corruption and attrition.

Venality in officials threatens the integrity of government and social justice, but curiously, in some unique circumstances, official corruption performs an unanticipated service for society, circumventing government red tape and removing barriers to the expansion of economic freedom. Although it is impossible to quantify the contribution of official corruption to the growth of the private sector in China, there was a strong connection between the rise of market forces and the increase in corruption. For instance, a large number of the official corruption cases brought to light involved bureaucrats who were put in charge of distributing scarce producer goods and who received bribes from private entrepreneurs to make such goods available to them. Such illegitimate "rent-seeking" behavior on the part of officials seldom failed to damage the image of the party-state.

The buying-off of government officials helped entrepreneurs to gain access to raw materials, credits, equipment, and information controlled by these officials, and it offset the competitive disadvantages of the private sector against SOEs, which acquired these key inputs free or below market value. Therefore, it is no surprise that rural industries and private entrepreneurs have been accused of causing widespread official corruption in China.[92] For these fledgling economic forces, corruption is merely an extension of the principle of market relations into their transactions with government officials; it has become an important means of ensuring survival and expansion.

In addition to corruption induced by the rise of market forces, the institutions of the party-state experienced a process of *attrition* in the new rural market society. Losing current elites to the private sector through corruption, the Party simultaneously faced a dwindling pool of qualified elite-recruits as new opportunities made joining the Party, which used to be a key route to upward mobility, much less attractive. For instance, although party membership expanded rather quickly in the cities during the 1980s, it remained stagnant in the countryside. About 6 million new CCP members joined between 1982 and 1987, but during the same period, peasant membership declined slightly from 18.2 million in 1982 to 18.17 million in 1987.[93] The Party also found it increasingly difficult to recruit new members from among the younger and better-educated peasants. One official study of the conditions of the CCP in the rural areas of 3 provinces revealed that, in the mid-1980s, more than 40 percent of the rural CCP members were over 46 years old. Overall, more than two-thirds of the CCP members in the countryside were either illiterate or had only a primary school education.[94]

This combination of an aging and poorly educated membership, the loss of power because of agricultural decollectivization, and the new social mobility of peasants caused most rural party cells to atrophy. A dramatic example of the basic incompatibility between the maintenance of a mobilization-oriented mass party and the use of such a party in directing an entrepreneurial marketized society, two official studies of the mid-1980s showed that, of the thousands of party branches surveyed, only one-third could be classified as "effective," while 20–25 percent were termed "poor" or "defunct," and about 50 percent were labeled "so-so."[95] Another survey of peasants in 1987 found that 45 percent of the respondents believed that the Party's leadership had been weakened, while 25 percent thought that it had not.[96] In any case, few peasants appeared to lament the massive deterioration of party organizations in the country. In a survey of peasants in 5 provinces, only 4 percent of the 1,200 respondents thought that "developing the organizations of the CCP" should be a priority.[97]

The Sociopolitical Implications of the Revolution

As the foregoing analysis has demonstrated, a capitalist revolution has broken out in China since economic reform began in 1979. This revolution is ongoing and will continue well into the early part of the twenty-first century. Although the enormous gains in economic resources made by society as a result of this revolution cannot conceivably be reversed by the state, one must judiciously recognize the limitations of this revolution and some of the important problems facing the burgeoning private sector in China.

The first and most critical problem confronting the thriving private sector is its structural imbalances and weaknesses. Despite their presence in nearly all spheres of economic activities, the private sector in general, and the rural enterprises in particular, are heavily concentrated in the labor-intensive and low-technology processing and light manufacturing sectors; their presence in the high-technology, capital-intensive industries is extremely weak. These high-value-added sectors are still heavily dominated and, in most instances, monopolized by the state. Given their small capitalization (80 percent of them had less than 1 million yuan in capital in 1991), these firms have weak research and development (R&D) capabilities.[98] Their engineering and technical talents are rather thin, for example, only 140 out of 10,000 workers in the rural industries in 1991 were engineers and technicians, compared with 1,045 out of 10,000 in the state sector.[99] In order to penetrate capital- and technology-intensive manufacturing, financial services, and other hitherto state-monopolized sectors, including civil aviation, railways, and telecommunications, the private sector needs not only more internally generated capital and managerial talents, but also a minimum level of government support and further opening in the economy. Signs in the early 1990s indicated that many local governments were increasingly willing to provide such support.

The second critical problem is the enormous regional disparities in the development of the private sector. It is most developed in China's south and east coastal regions and least developed in its interior. According to Tian Jiyun, the difference in the level of development of rural industries between coastal and inland areas in China is now the main reason for the disparity in the level of development between these areas.[100] Such regional differences may pose serious problems in maintaining political stability in the poorer areas and achieving economic reintegration in the future.

The third problem is continuing government discrimination against the private sector (high taxes and bureaucratic obstacles), weak legal protection for private property, and political unpredictability in the center, in spite of the numerous liberalizing regulations issued by the central and local governments in 1993. For example, the maximum corporate income tax is less than 55 percent for collective firms, but as much as 84 percent for private firms.[101] Such policy discriminations not only alienate the private entrepreneurs from the political system, but encourage widespread tax evasion and induce corruption.[102] Even though repeated conservative backlashes against the private sector have so far failed to restrain its growth, Chinese private entrepreneurs feel a high level of political insecurity. Private entrepreneurs disguise their firms as "collectives," as a government report revealed, because they lack confidence in the regime's policies.[103]

A fourth problem is that the market created by the private sector so far remains primitive and underinstitutionalized. Information gathering, legal protection of property rights, resource allocation, regulatory mechanisms, and enforcement of market discipline are haphazard at best, increasing the chances for market failure. It is evident that the private sector, in and of itself, lacks the ability to address the above problems in a fundamental way, because the societal takeover in the transition to a market economy in the 1980s was itself a partial one. For this process to be completed, a second breakthrough toward the market must occur; this breakthrough will require the close cooperation of the established private sector and the state. In any case, with a solid private sector producing more than half of China's wealth in the early 1990s, the second-phase breakthrough to a market economy can be expected to be less costly and disruptive than the shock therapy approach undertaken in most Eastern European countries and the former Soviet Union.

The revolutionary development of the private sector in China in the 1980s also has vast implications for China's overall modernization, future privatization of the most difficult part of the state sector (its large- and medium-sized SOEs), and prospects for democratization.

Mounting evidence from China now suggests that the development of the private sector has produced a self-sustaining rural modernization momentum originating from within society. The mushrooming of private and quasi-private rural firms, as one official study in Jiangsu (where rural industries were the most developed in China) showed, has enormously accelerated China's modernization and social transformation. For instance, in Jiangsu, income from rural firms has become the single largest source of rural capital investment, accounting for 72 percent in 1990.[104] Nationwide, rural industrialization driven by the private sector has led to rapid urbanization in the countryside, with more than 8,000 small towns springing up during the 1980s. Despite the absence of investment from the state, more than 15 billion yuan in income from rural industries was invested in building the infrastructure of these towns. Altogether, there were about 10,000 such small towns in China in the early 1990s, with a population of 61 million people, half of whom were former peasants.[105]

The successful development of the private sector and the creation of an expanding group of new private entrepreneurs not only helped change the Chinese public's attitude toward the private sector, but paved the way for the eventual takeover of SOEs by the private sector. It is revealing that, when the private sector was just emerging during the initial opening, there was much popular prejudice and resentment against the new entrepreneurs. But in the early 1990s, there were signs that, as the private sector made more economic gains, the public attitude toward it began to improve, and its status also rose. An opinion poll conducted by the Chinese Academy of Social Sciences in 1991 showed a dramatic change in the employment preferences of the public. When asked about employment, respondents picked private entrepreneurship as the most desirable form of work (followed by employment in foreign joint ventures); a job in the state sector was considered a third choice. Principally due to its poor economic performance, the state sector found it increasingly difficult to keep its more educated employees from being lured away by the private sector, especially foreign-funded firms, and to attract workers in areas where the private sector was most developed, such as Guangdong.[106] The Labor Department of the Guangdong provincial government reported that the SOEs there were losing nearly 30 percent (and in some cases as much as 50 percent) of their workers to the private sector in the early 1990s.[107] In Shanghai, more than 40,000 scientists and engineers quit their state-sector jobs to start 3,600 technology-intensive private firms by 1992.[108]

This trend is a welcome sign for the future, since the expanding private sector will be able to absorb a significant portion of the redundant workers from the dwindling state sector, reducing the transitional social costs of the eventual privatization of the SOEs. The emergence of a group of private entrepreneurs with market-oriented managerial experience and sufficient capital will also help privatize the SOEs. Indeed, this formal takeover was beginning to occur in the early 1990s, when thousands of small bankrupt state firms were sold or taken over by private and foreign investors.[109] In the future, this may well grow into a powerful national trend.

Undoubtedly, the most important sociopolitical implication of the development of the private sector in China is to be found in its impact on changing state-society relations in general and the prospects for democratization in particular (the second phase of the dual-regime transition). This development has already resulted in dramatic gains in economic resources for society and spectacular losses for the state, reflected not only in the rising share of the private sector in the composition of China's GNP, but in its distribution. For instance, in 1979, the central government's revenues amounted to 31.7 percent of the GNP; they declined to 26.2 percent in 1985 and plunged to 21.7 percent in 1990. The share of private income as a percentage of the GNP, however, rose significantly. In 1985, it was 59 percent; in 1990, it jumped to 62 percent.[110]

The rapid growth of the private sector has been accompanied by the emergence of a new social group potentially capable of penetrating the political system and accumulating political power in rural China. This may already be happening in some parts of the country. One study of 74,000 villages in Zhejiang province showed that, in the village councils that were elected in 1990–1991, more than 40 percent of the council chiefs and 70 percent of the council members were local entrepreneurs. This development apparently caused the government much concern, for the Central Committee's organization department reportedly issued a document in late 1991 banning the owners of private businesses from the Party and putting severe restrictions on party members who were owners of private firms (disqualifying them from becoming heads of party branches).[111] In the urban areas, however, the more individualistic private entrepreneurs with smaller business operations have so far been largely excluded from the political process. Eventually, it may be possible for China's fledgling democratic opposition to build a coalition encompassing these new entrepreneurial groups. Such an alliance will provide momentum for the transition from a market economy authoritarian system to a market economy polyarchy.

The rapid growth of the private sector has significantly increased the level of social mobility for Chinese citizens and broken down the government's system of social control. Once a communist state's ability to control its society through economic means dramatically declines, as in the case of the Chinese countryside, its capacity to enforce its rules and mobilize the masses is diminished.

The capitalist revolution in China has already produced many spillover effects, with the state losing control, in varying degrees, in such vital areas as the mass media and elite recruitment, while autonomous social forces are gaining influence in the same areas at the expense of the state. Moreover, the growth of the private sector could also lead to the establishment of various autonomous business organizations and networks, which may strengthen the degree of social institutionalization in a communist society in which such institutions used to be weak or nonexistent. Growing private economic resources could also financially support key social institutions such as the church and civic organizations.

Finally, it is interesting to note that, to date, the most marketized parts of China—Guangdong, Fujian, and other coastal locations—are also the areas that have seen a rapid increase in civic freedom and a dramatic decline in political repression. Even following the crackdown in Tiananmen in 1989, these areas were relatively unaffected by the conservative countertakeover efforts, and Guangdong became the favorite temporary refuge and the gateway to the West for most of China's leading dissidents fleeing government persecution.

The Private Sector under *Perestroika*

4

The Soviet economic reform experience in general, and the slow development of the private sector during *perestroika* in particular, were counterexamples of China's capitalist revolution. They illustrated how a combination of factors—an ill-conceived and poorly executed initial opening, the absence of relatively autonomous and strongly motivated social groups, unfavorable external factors, and the absence of a takeover coalition—contributed to the failure of a similar societal takeover in the former Soviet Union between 1985 and 1991. From a comparative perspective, the most puzzling question about the Soviet Union during its transition is: why, when *glasnost* quickly triggered a democratic-nationalist revolution from below, did *perestroika* fail to spark a similar *capitalist* revolution?

Obviously, the development of the private sector during *perestroika* took place in a political environment qualitatively different from that which prevailed in China. It was characterized by a high level of political openness, participation, and competition, yet despite the dramatic change in the emphasis of *perestroika* from economic reform to democratization in late 1986, many reforms undertaken by Mikhail Gorbachev between 1985 and 1991 were aimed at loosening up the state's overcentralized control over the economy and liberalizing the private sector. Specific measures were introduced, such as legalizing private enterprises and cooperatives to encourage autonomous economic forces to develop. And although managers of state-owned enterprises were granted considerable autonomy, the results were insubstantial. Despite limited gains in some service sectors, the private sector in the Soviet Union was an insignificant factor in the overall economic picture by the time the country disintegrated in late 1991.

The Development of the Private Sector, 1985–1991

As in other communist countries, the economic structure of the prereform Soviet Union was not monolithic. On the eve of Gorbachev's reform in

1985, the Soviet economy contained an oasis of the private sector that consisted of subsidiary farming (household plots) and a fairly large second economy. As a reform measure, subsidiary farming could be expanded to increase its output. Certain segments of the second, or "shadow," economy could be legalized. Such initiatives, without requiring a comprehensive program of privatizing the state sector, could provide quick fixes to the ailing Soviet economy.

For example, increasing the output of rural private households could ameliorate the country's perennial agricultural problems. In 1985, some 35 million rural families maintained an orchard and a vegetable garden alongside their houses and kept privately owned cattle and poultry. The produce from these private plots, which constituted only 3 percent of the agricultural land, amounted to 25 percent of the country's agricultural output.[1]

Legalizing part of the shadow economy to encourage private citizens to participate in this *de facto* private sector could presumably remove the bottlenecks in the distribution of consumer goods and services.[2] Leonid Abalkin, a deputy prime minister of the USSR, estimated that the size of the Soviet shadow economy was about 60 billion rubles.[3] The activities in the shadow economy that could be legalized included unauthorized trading activities, unlicensed public catering facilities, income from the leasing of state-owned housing and land, unlicensed construction businesses, and unregistered cooperative and private business activities. One Soviet estimate suggested that more than 20 million people were involved in these activities.[4]

Privatizing the state sector was not a top priority in Gorbachev's *perestroika*. His early reform efforts were directed toward improving the performance of the stagnant state sector by enforcing labor discipline and financial accountability.[5] The first indication of the government's desire to promote the private sector and legalize part of the shadow economy was the passage of the Law on Individual Labor Activity, in November 1986. This authorized moonlighting in certain consumer service sectors and specifically encouraged unemployed housewives, the disabled, pensioners, and students to engage in individual enterprise.[6] However, the 1986 law prohibited hired labor and liberalized only a limited range of entrepreneurial activities in the service sector. Moreover, it gave local officials enormous discretionary power in issuing permits for, monitoring, and closing down individual enterprises.[7] The tax rates on income from individual labor activity were high, with a 65 percent income tax on entrepreneurs making more than 500 rubles a month. (The average monthly wage in the state sector was about 250 rubles.)[8]

The salutary effect of the law was further reduced by a government campaign against "unearned income," launched in May 1986. "Unearned income" was vaguely defined as money obtained from "embezzlement, bribery, speculation, extortion, and so forth."[9] Local officials zealously turned this campaign into a crackdown on the shadow economy, creating a deterrent to private entrepreneurs. In particular, the loose definition of "speculation," which often covered many legitimate private-sector activities, gave conservative government officials a powerful legal weapon against private enterprise.[10] As a result, the growth of this sector was slow. By the middle of 1988, the sector had attracted only 627,600 individuals.[11] In any case, the law accomplished one goal: legalizing much of the underground economic activity concentrated in the service sector. According to Soviet economists, early co-ops were formed by the operators of the underground economy, whereas the co-ops formed in late 1987 (following the passage of the draft Law on Cooperation in the USSR) were truly new forms of economic organization.[12] This might explain the source of initial public resentment toward the private sector, since the early entrepreneurs appeared to be rather unsavory speculators and profiteers who dwelled in the underworld of the shadow economy. A poll of 3,000 Soviet citizens in 41 cities in April 1989, for example, found that 74 percent of the respondents believed that the growth of cooperatives could lead to a rise in crime.[13]

With the formal adoption of the Law on Cooperation in the USSR in May 1988—the second major initiative by Gorbachev in liberalizing the private sector—the focus of the development of the private sector shifted to the cooperative movement, which appeared to have absorbed most of the individual laborers. By June 1990, only 200,000 persons were engaged in individual labor activities in the Soviet Union.[14] The May 1988 passage of the Law on Cooperation permitted the formation and operation of economic entities outside of the state sector. Cooperatives had been a phenomenal success during the New Economic Policy (NEP) era in the 1920s, when they controlled more than 70 percent of retail trade in the Soviet Union.[15] However, the government's initial expectations of the economic potential of cooperatives were modest, and Premier Nikolai Ryzhkov predicted in June 1987 that the cooperatives would provide, in a few years, about 3 to 5 percent of the total volume of services and public catering.[16] The government permitted only pensioners, housewives, and students—not state employees—to participate in the cooperative movement.[17] This restriction would certainly have impeded the growth of the sector had it not been violated by most employees of the cooperatives.[18]

Although the Soviet government chose to define cooperatives as part of the "collective" (socialist) means of production, the majority of new cooperatives were formed with the leased assets of state-owned enterprises and were economically attached to these enterprises in various ways. This situation raised questions about how "private" the Soviet cooperatives were.

The passage, implementation, and modification of the law governing cooperatives provoked a heated public debate and involved intense bureaucratic infighting. Despite efforts by conservative officials at various levels to slow and restrain the cooperative movement, the cooperatives grew rapidly, as shown in Table 4.1, and, by early 1990, they produced 5.7 percent of the Soviet GNP and employed more than 5 million people.[19]

Compared with the dismal performance of the state sector, the cooperative sector grew rapidly, prompting Deputy Prime Minister Abalkin to claim that it constituted "one of the most dynamic sectors of the economy."[20] Its contribution was especially significant in the supply of consumer goods, one of the most deficient areas in the Soviet economy. In 1989, the cooperatives produced 7.1 billion rubles' worth of consumer goods and, in the first six months of 1990, turned out 4.8 billion rubles' worth of consumer goods.[21] Although the construction businesses accounted for the largest source of income (30 percent of the gross income for all cooperatives in 1989), co-ops producing consumer goods contributed about 17 percent, and research and information services co-ops produced about 8 percent of the total income for cooperatives in the same year.[22]

The development of cooperatives in the Soviet Union varied according to region. The data in Table 4.2 show that the private sector was more developed in non-Russian republics on the western and southwestern periphery of the Soviet empire, including Estonia, Armenia, Latvia, Lithuania, Georgia, Moldavia, and Belorussia, and less developed in the heart of the Soviet Union—the Russian Federation—and the Central Asian republics. By 1991, this trend was even more pronounced, with the Baltic republics leading the Soviet Union in the development of the private sector. For instance, more

Table 4.1 The growth of cooperatives in the Soviet Union, 1987–1990

Date	Number of cooperatives	Number of employees	Gross turnover (million rubles)
July 1, 1987	3,709	39,100	29.2
July 1, 1988	32,561	458,700	1,037.3[a]
July 1, 1989	133,000	2,939,000	12,864.0[b]
January 1, 1990	193,000	4,851,500	40,365.6
July 1, 1990	209,700	5,200,000	27,300.0[c]

Sources: Ekonomicheskaya gazeta, no. 3 (1988) and no. 43 (1988), quoted in Karin Plokker, "The Development of Individual and Cooperative Labor Activity in the Soviet Union," *Soviet Studies*, vol. 42, no. 3 (July 1990), p. 423; *Ekonomika i zhizn*, no. 49 (1990), *Foreign Broadcast Information Service: Daily Reports—the Soviet Union*, December 12, 1990, p. 53; the USSR State Committee for Statistics, *Moscow News*, no. 12, April 1–8, 1990, p. 10; *Pravda*, February 18, 1989, *Foreign Broadcast Information Service*, March 1, 1989, p. 82; John Tedstrom, "The Soviet Cooperative Movement: An Update," *Radio Liberty: Report on the USSR*, vol. 1, no. 40, October 3, 1989, pp. 4–5.

a. Between January 1 and June 30, 1988.
b. From January 1 to July 1, 1989.
c. Between January 1 and June 30, 1990.

Table 4.2   The size of the formal private sector in the Soviet Union, by republics

Republic	Number of cooperatives per 10,000 people (January 1990)[a]	Number of co-op employees per 10,000 people (January 1990)[b]	Number of individual workers per 10,000 people (April 1, 1988)[c]	Gross output of co-ops as percentage of net material product[d] (January 1990)
Armenia	25.7	418	30	13.19
Azerbaijan	4.8	88	10	3.43
Belorussia	5.2	121	15	3.23
Estonia	13.3	263	39	9.77
Georgia	11.3	251	22	9.39
Kazakhstan	5.9	134	8	5.64
Kirgizia	3.8	87	8	4.87
Latvia	15.2	499	42	14.93
Lithuania	12.2	220	85	7.09
Moldavia	7.9	188	16	13.38
Russia	6.9	181	12	6.19
Tajikistan	3.6	78	5	5.31
Turkmenia	3.7	84	7	4.15
Ukraine	5.8	150	13	4.81
Uzbekistan	4.5	123	9	8.22
USSR total	6.7	168	13	6.14

a. Darrell Slider, "Embattled Entrepreneurs: Soviet Cooperatives in an Unreformed Economy," *Soviet Studies*, vol. 43, no. 5 (December 1991), p. 803.

b. Estimates based on local 1989 population figures and the data collected in Slider, "Embattled Entrepreneurs," pp. 799–802.

c. *Narodnoe khozyaistvo, 1988,* quoted in Karin Plokker, "The Development of Individual and Cooperative Labor Activity in the Soviet Union," *Soviet Studies*, vol. 42, no. 3 (July 1990), p. 422.

d. Net material product (NMP) produced at current prices. Calculated from the data supplied by Slider, "Embattled Entrepreneurs," pp. 799–802, and the *Economist* Intelligence Unit, *USSR: Country Profile, 1991–1992* (September 1991), p. 9. It must be noted here that using the gross turnover of co-ops to calculate this sector's share in the Soviet NMP has a considerable upward bias because the NMP value of the gross turnover of co-ops should be much lower. Its share of the NMP should also be lower.

than 75 percent of the joint stock companies and 80 percent of the private farms in the Soviet Union in early 1991 were located in the Baltics.[23]

The public's attitude toward the private sector influenced its rapid growth in the Baltics and Armenia and its slow growth elsewhere, especially in Central Asia. A survey of 101,000 individuals found that, among the people of Latvia, Estonia, Armenia, and Azerbaijan, there were two to three times more unconditional supporters of cooperatives and individual labor activity than in Uzbekistan, Turkmenia, and Tajikistan.[24]

A similar interrepublican opinion survey of public attitudes toward privatization ranked the residents in Armenia, Lithuania, Estonia, and Latvia as the most supportive of privatization, whereas the residents of the Central Asian republics and the Russian Federation were the least supportive.[25] Interestingly, the results of this survey suggest a correlation between the public acceptance of privatization in a certain republic and the level of development of its private sector.

Another explanation for this regional variation can be found in the different positions of local government officials on the private sector. Those less beholden to the bureaucrats in the central government and less hostile to the private sector tended to create a more conducive environment for private businesses. Republican and local authorities in the Baltics were often mentioned as the most supportive of private enterprise. Latvia, Lithuania, and Belorussia allowed cooperatives to deduct investment outlays from taxes. Local authorities in Moldavia and Armenia also refrained from levying excessively high taxes on cooperatives, a common practice in many other republics.[26]

Evidence indicates that the private entrepreneurs experienced more frequent harassment at the hands of local government officials in certain Central Asian republics and the Russian Federation than elsewhere. For example, the republican authorities in Uzbekistan closed down 2,000 cooperatives in 1989; local government officials in Krasnodar Territory shut down about 1,000 cooperatives; officials in Stavropol Territory shut down more than 200 cooperatives; another 400 were closed in Alma-Ata; and more than 2,300 were closed down in Kazakhstan as a whole.[27]

In early 1991, political chaos, public hostility, penetration by organized crime, and harassment by local officials threatened the survival of cooperatives as a legitimate private sector in the Soviet Union. The government estimated, in 1991, that nearly 70 percent of the Soviet cooperatives either paid off racketeers or were involved in various racketeering activities themselves.[28] In February 1991, the national association of cooperatives, the Allied Cooperatives of the USSR, convened an emergency congress and issued an appeal to Gorbachev to save the cooperatives from arbitrary local authorities, government procurators, armed criminals, and confiscatory laws.[29]

With the Soviet economy in a free fall and political disintegration looming, the cooperative sector plummeted. When the Soviet Union collapsed at the end of 1991, the number of co-ops fell to around 150,000, and the number of their employees shrank from 4 million in 1990 to 3.2 million in September 1991.[30]

The third step taken by the Soviet leadership in the development of the private sector, with the issuance of the Decree on Leasing in November 1989, was to encourage a form of semiprivatization through the leasing of SOEs. Although this measure formalized the long-standing practice of forming cooperatives on the basis of leased state properties, Soviet reformers assigned a limited role to leasing. Officially, leasing was to be confined to small and medium-sized SOEs; the government planned to lease only 20 percent of state enterprises in 6 years.[31] This measure of semiprivatization was implemented more widely in the service sector and typically involved small firms with simple business operations. For example, 23,000 trade and catering stores (which produced 10.6 percent of the total output of the service sector) were leased out in 1990. In addition, 2,100 manufacturing firms (producing 4.6 percent of the gross output of the manufacturing sector), and 800 construction companies (representing about 3.6 percent of the share of the construction sector) were also leased out in 1990.[32] The accuracy of these figures is questionable, however, since some leased companies might have been double-counted as cooperatives, thus inflating the size of the nonstate sector. In any case, on the eve of the disintegration of the Soviet Union, leasing became the dominant form of semiprivatization, attracting about 9 million workers in various sectors by September 1991.[33]

The Soviet government did not contemplate the most thorough form of privatization—the sale of state-owned assets to private individuals—until the summer of 1990, after a full-scale program of privatizing the state sector was proposed in the ill-fated Shatalin Plan. Conservative economic planners advocated a plan that would limit full privatization to the service sector, with a small proportion of the SOEs in this sector to be put on the auction block. For example, as of October 1990, authorities in the Russian Republic, the Ukraine, Azerbaijan, and the republics of Central Asia were drafting plans to sell 21,100 retail outlets, 9,200 public catering facilities, and 12,800 household service businesses to private citizens and collectives.[34] But events soon overtook these plans, and the collapse of the Soviet Union made them irrelevant.

Separating genuine private firms from quasi-statal or quasi-private businesses presents a considerable challenge. This is an important issue because, if one accepts the official Soviet data on the size of the cooperatives, it would certainly appear that a dramatic development of the private sector had taken place during *perestroika,* while reality seems to contradict such a claim.

In the Soviet case, the cooperative sector, the largest component of the formal nonstate sector, was diverse and comprised genuine private, quasi-private, and quasi-statal firms. Careful examination of official Soviet sources, however, shows that genuine private firms constituted only a minority of the Soviet cooperatives, with the majority of the cooperatives being spinoff units (typically unprofitable) or affiliates of state enterprises. The USSR State Committee of Statistics (Goskomstat) claimed that about 80 percent of all operating cooperatives in 1989 were affiliated with state enterprises; 60 percent of the fixed assets of cooperatives were leased properties of state enterprises; state enterprises provided these cooperatives with more than 60 percent of their raw materials and other inputs; and these cooperatives accounted for 70 percent (about 28.2 billion rubles) of the gross output of all Soviet cooperatives.[35]

Separately, Western specialists questioned the operational independence and property ownership of Soviet cooperatives because, by most measures, an overwhelming majority of them seemed to be excessively dependent on the state. One study found that some Soviet cooperatives were no more than fronts, set up as "empty shells or accounting devices" by SOE managers, to parcel out overtime pay, evade taxes, and increase wages for enterprise employees.[36] Another study showed that 80 percent of all cooperatives either were physically established inside the state enterprises or operated under their aegis. The majority of the cooperatives were no more than subcontractors for state enterprises, producing for these enterprises and marketing through state-controlled distribution channels. In 1988, for instance, 45 percent of the services and 57 percent of the consumer goods produced by the cooperatives were sold to the state enterprises; in 1989, 83 percent were sold to the state; in the first quarter of 1990, the figure rose to 87 percent. In the construction sector, 97 percent of the cooperatives' work was done for the state.[37]

In some instances, nominally private cooperatives retained formal hierarchical links to state enterprises and even government ministries because their managers depended on the state for supplies, space, and even labor (as most of the employees in the cooperatives were moonlighters from the state sector). These managers also feared that they would be too vulnerable if they sought to operate independently in a market environment.[38] The strongest evidence reflecting the degree of co-optation of Soviet cooperatives by the state was that some economic ministries even included cooperative production within the state's economic planning. For example, the Ministry of Energy determined that, in its five-year plan for 1991–1995, 30 percent of its energy output would be produced by the cooperatives under the ministry's jurisdiction.[39]

The above data indicate that genuine private firms constituted a small minority of the Soviet cooperatives. The quasi-private cooperatives—apparently a minority as well—seemed to be those that leased assets from the state but otherwise operated with some autonomy, in terms of determining product-mix, obtaining their own inputs, and setting prices for their outputs. The remaining firms, approximately 60 percent, should be considered quasi-statal, since they both leased assets of the state and operated largely within the framework of the planned economic system. According to the Soviet Law on Cooperation, cooperatives that obtained their inputs from state-controlled sources at state-set prices were also required to sell their finished products at state-set prices. Because state bureaucracies had to supply cooperatives with resources needed to fulfill state orders, cooperatives were given incentives to become part of the state sector.[40]

Since most of the newly formed cooperatives were actually quasi-statal economic entities, the Soviet state sector had, in effect, co-opted most of the cooperatives by controlling their sources of inputs and limiting their operational freedom. This was the original intent of the reformers, who viewed the cooperative movement as merely a supplement to the state sector and not as its potential replacement. At the beginning of the movement, Prime Minister Ryzhkov said cooperatives were being "restored to help the state sector." Even as late as December 1989, he said, "With regard to private ownership, including ownership of means of production for individual labor activity, it could be of some considerable assistance to our economy. Its development must bring positive changes in those spheres where large enterprises are ineffectual."[41] Moreover, bureaucratic regulations favored the practice of finding "sponsoring" SOEs or ministries for cooperatives. This allowed the cooperatives to clear bureaucratic hurdles in registration and operation in exchange for greater control by these enterprises and ministries.[42]

The size of the work force in the cooperative sector is another complicating factor in determining just how "private" Soviet cooperatives were. Since moonlighters constituted a considerable proportion of the labor force, including them inflated the size of this sector. Available evidence suggests that at least half the employees of the cooperatives were moonlighters at the beginning of 1989, and this percentage was even higher (65 percent) a year earlier.[43] Full-time cooperative workers thus numbered about 2.6 million in the Soviet Union by the middle of 1990, or about 2 percent of the employees in the state sector.

In any case, if the cooperatives had developed as rapidly as the official Soviet data claimed, tangible improvements in the Soviet economy, such as a rising standard of living, reduced shortages of consumer goods, and higher growth rates, should have resulted. But in fact, the Soviet economy in the late 1980s reflected little improvement.

If the explosive growth of the private sector in China was the inevitable outcome of agricultural reforms, why were so few rural reforms implemented in the Soviet Union, and why was there no improvement in agricultural productivity during *perestroika*?

Some rural reforms were attempted under *perestroika*. That these reforms failed to lead to the birth of a viable private agricultural sector illustrates the difficulty of marketizing a highly developed communist system that is shackled by institutionalized dependency on the socialist welfare state.

Early reform efforts in agriculture involved breaking large rural work units into small ones to increase their accountability. But, whereas Chinese peasants quickly radicalized this limited reform with a ground-up decollectivization mass movement, no similar mass movement occurred in the Soviet Union. In August 1988, the government's superministry in charge of agriculture, the USSR State Agroindustrial Committee (Gosagroprom), recommended leases of up to 50 years in the agricultural sector to stimulate productivity. As a partial privatization measure, the Soviet program in fact offered more attractive terms than the Chinese household responsibility system, which limited leasing terms to 15 years (although they were renewable). This program, however, instantly encountered the same bureaucratic obstacles that the co-op movement experienced at the local level, with government officials and collective farm administrators resisting or showing little interest in implementing the reform.[44] An opinion poll of local elites showed that only a minority of collective and state farm chairmen thought leasing was the best method for reforming Soviet agriculture, while more than half expressed doubts about this program.[45] Lower-level opposition to leasing turned the implementation of the program into an exercise in bureaucratic "formalism." Collective and state farms ostensibly signed up "leases" while doing nothing of substance. On paper, nearly 33,000 farms (almost two-thirds of the state and collective farms in the Soviet Union) had fully adopted leasing programs in 1989, but the absence of improvement in productivity and the discovery of false statistics on leasing reported by local officials led one Goskomstat official to conclude that the overwhelming majority of the land leases were "paper leases."[46]

At the same time, collective and state farm workers were reluctant to participate in the program. In a survey of 5,000 students in an agricultural institute in late 1989, only 14 percent said that they would participate in a land lease program. Another poll of rural workers conducted in September 1989 revealed that only 30 percent were interested in various rural private-sector activities, such as leasing and cooperative or individual farming.[47] An *Izvestia* poll of rural residents in early 1990 showed that only 10–14 percent were actually ready to form private farms, and then only on the condition that a land law be passed first.[48] Other surveys also indicated widespread rural popular opposition to the private ownership of land. A survey of 1,400 farmers found that 80 percent thought "land should be national (or state) property" and should not be privatized. Another survey indicated that only 17 percent of collective and state farmers favored the sale and private ownership of land.[49]

This combination of lower-level bureaucratic opposition and mass indifference to the leasing program prompted Gorbachev to complain, in March 1989, that his rural reform had been met "with caution by collective farmers and workers who have lost . . . the habit of working hard, and have become accustomed to steady incomes regardless of end results."[50] Indeed, the contrast between the Soviet farmers' attitude toward rural reform initiatives and that of their Chinese counterparts was pronounced. From the outset, the majority of Chinese peasants—even in the absence of a government-sponsored leasing program—supported thorough decollectivization of agriculture. In a survey of peasants in Anhui in early 1979, 50 percent strongly supported decollectivization through the household responsibility system, with 30 percent holding a neutral position, and only 20 percent opposing it. After a year of experimenting with the process, 90 percent of the peasants supported complete decollectivization.[51]

Such vast attitudinal differences toward rural privatization were dramatically reflected in actual economic results. In the case of China, strong pressure from the peasantry pushed the ground-up decollectivization program to its completion in less than 4 years. This revolutionary institutional change, according to one study, accounted for most of the productivity gains in Chinese agriculture in the 1980s.[52] For the Soviet Union, privatization of agriculture made little progress. In August 1990, the USSR had only 29,547 individual farms, with an average size of 10.5 hectares. There were only 900 individual farms in the Russian Federation, while the three Baltic republics claimed 10,790 private farms with 73 percent of the total hectares. This dramatic difference prompted one Soviet agroeconomist to conclude that cultural values—particularly egalitarianism and prejudice against private property—in most of the Soviet Union were to blame for the slow progress in privatizing agriculture.[53]

Undeterred by the failure of the leasing program, the government introduced even more radical reform measures. In December 1990, the Yeltsin-led Russian Federation (RSFSR) government issued a land reform program to encourage agricultural semiprivatization. While placing a ten-year ban on land sales, the program permitted families to take over or lease government-owned land to set up private farms. In January 1991, Gorbachev signed a decree "giving away" 3–5 million hectares of "inefficiently used land" to peasants and small farmers. By May 1991, 20,144 legally independent peasant farms had been created in the Russian Federation. Altogether, however, these farms accounted for less than 0.5 percent of the agricultural land in the Russian Federation.[54]

In retrospect, the economic costs of the failure of privatization-oriented agricultural reforms were staggering. Official Soviet statistics showed that agriculture barely grew (1.1 percent per year) between 1986 and 1990. In 1990, gross agricultural output fell 2.3 percent; in 1991, it plunged another 7 percent.[55]

As the Soviet Union veered toward political and economic disintegration in 1990, a welcome burst of entrepreneurial activity took place at the grassroots level. In May 1990, the first privately run commodity exchange in the Soviet Union opened in Moscow, and the number of similar privately run exchanges soon rose to nearly 200 by mid-1991. Established without government approval, these were unregulated speculative markets.[56] By the end of 1991, the number of exchanges had grown to 400, but, according to one Soviet economist, they were exchanges "in name only, with half of them doing no actual trading."[57] The insignificant impact of these private commodity exchanges on market-oriented reforms was reaffirmed by a 1992 study showing that, of the 700 officially registered exchanges, only 4 or 5 dozen were actually functioning in 1992, and these played a small role in Russia's wholesale trade.[58]

Starting in late 1990, spontaneous privatization accelerated. Managerial elites in SOEs were the driving force behind this movement, and they persuaded employees to go along by promising various benefits. Some SOEs were converted into joint stock companies, with employees receiving a minority stake in the form of shares, and the management usually controlling a majority stake. More than 200 such management-led buy-outs were recorded by early 1991; most of them involved small- and medium-sized companies in industry and construction.[59] According to one top Russian official, state-owned property worth 2 billion rubles was thus privatized in 1991.[60]

At the center, after the conservatives joined forces to defeat the Shatalin Plan, "top-down" privatization remained on hold until mid-1991, when Gorbachev managed to rebuild a fragile alliance with the liberals. On the eve of the coup in August 1991, his government passed the Law on the Basic Principles of the Destatization and Privatization of Enterprises, which, for the first time, officially emphasized the privatization of the state sector as a main component of economic reform. At the same time, in republics where liberal forces had seized power, the new democratic governments began to push privatization. The Russian Parliament adopted a law on privatization in July 1991, and similar laws were also passed in the Baltics.

These efforts, however, came too late to revive the moribund Soviet economy. As of 1991, the state maintained its overwhelming dominance, controlling 92 percent of all productive capacities (47,000 industrial enterprises and 800,000 trade and service companies).[61] The gains of the private sector in the Soviet Union were simply too small to shore up the collapsing Soviet economy. During 1986–1990, Soviet gross industrial output grew 2.5 percent by the official account and only 0.9 percent by the CIA estimate. According to official figures, it fell 1.2 percent in 1990, and 7.8 percent in 1991.[62]

It is speculative to suggest that a more robust private sector might have helped ameliorate the Soviet economic failure during *perestroika,* but the fact that more than half of the net industrial growth in China six years after the initiation of reform came from the nonstate sector indicates that this could have been the case for the Soviet Union as well. However, there were no visible signs of a similar Big Surge on the eve of the collapse of the Soviet Union (six years after reform was launched). In any event, this nonoccurrence of a capitalist revolution during *perestroika* made the consolidation of democracy in the former Soviet Union more problematic.

The new political forces that were swept into power following the collapse of the Soviet Union at the end of 1991 clearly recognized the critical linkage between the development of the private sector through massive privatization and the consolidation of the fledgling Russian democracy. Indeed, Yeltsin's government staked much of the success of its radical economic reform on an unprecedented state-sponsored mass privatization program that attempted to restructure Russia's 226,657 SOEs—an effort that dwarfed similar programs in other postcommunist economies.[63]

After introducing the shock therapy stabilization program (characterized mainly by the liberalization of prices in the Russian case) in January 1992, the Russian government simultaneously launched a massive privatization program to create a private sector at breakneck speed. As experiences of privatization in Poland and the former East Germany indicated, it was a lengthy, cumbersome, and politically volatile task to transform state ownership into private ownership and create viable corporations from former SOEs. It is thus too early to assess the Russian experiment in mass privatization.[64] The program made uneven progress in different sectors (dramatic strides in the service sector, but a slow start in agriculture and industry in 1992) and did little to bolster a rapidly deteriorating economy. But two major differences in the development of the private sector under the aegis of the new democratic state in Russia since 1992 distinguished this experiment from the unsuccessful one under Gorbachev's rule.

The first and most important difference was the change in political leadership. Unlike Gorbachev's regime, the new government headed by Yeltsin was deeply committed to mass privatization of SOEs as the quickest way to build a private sector. Under the energetic leadership of Deputy Prime Minister Anatoly Chubais, the privatization program that the Russian government initiated at the beginning of 1992 made rapid gains in transferring a large portion of state-owned small enterprises (virtually all in the service sector) to Russia's emerging entrepreneurs. At the end of 1992, the government reported that more than 46,000 SOEs in the service sector had been privatized through auction and direct sale, with 28,000 of them sold to private individuals and the rest to their employees. Together, these newly privatized firms accounted for 36 percent of retail trade firms, 34.5 percent of wholesale firms, 21.7 percent of restaurants and public catering shops, and 40 percent of consumer service firms.[65]

In the privatization of large and medium SOEs, which was technically more complicated and politically more controversial than that of small SOEs (since this program would result in mass layoffs), the new government made little progress beyond issuing "privatization vouchers" to nearly every citizen. These vouchers allowed holders to participate in the purchase of stocks to be issued by large and medium SOEs slated for mass privatization.[66] By the middle of 1993, according to Chubais, the Russian government, relying on the voucher approach, "privatized" some 1,700 large enterprises employing about 2.4 million workers (roughly 10 percent of the Russian industrial work force).[67] Because the voucher approach itself was formalistic, involving no more than what might be called "paper privatization," which would have to be followed by the more painful and time-consuming process of enterprise restructuring, it remained to be seen whether this particular approach would be sufficient to create viable private corporations. In any case, the Russian government planned to privatize 10,000 large SOEs in 1993. Should this be accomplished, the state-sponsored privatization drive in Russia, Chubais announced at the beginning of 1993, would have reached "the stage of irreversibility."[68]

The second important difference was the obvious change in the psychology of the Russian labor force and their calculation of the costs and benefits of remaining in the disintegrating state sector or seeking alternative employment in the emerging private sector. As the state sector disintegrated with shocking speed and real income plummeted with high inflation, it was evident that the bankrupt state-socialist welfare institutions would soon collapse as well. For employees of the SOEs, this grim prospect lowered the perceived exit costs of abandoning the state sector. Simultaneously, higher pay offered by firms in the newly founded private sector also increased the benefits of exit.[69] Indeed, employment data from Russia for 1992 showed a rapid increase in the labor force in the private sector and a corresponding fast decline in the state sector. One researcher concluded that, in the middle of 1992, 7.5 percent of the Russian working population was employed in the nonstate sector (excluding collective farms). Of these workers, some 2 million were in cooperatives, 300,000 were self-employed, and another 1.2 million were employed in 60,000 small private firms.[70]

The progress in creating a private agricultural sector during 1992 was, however, quite slow. Across the former Soviet Union, the number of private farms doubled in 1992—to 470,000 covering some 12 million hectares. In Russia, there were 183,700 private farms in operation at the end of 1992, the average size being 43 hectares. These numbers, however, obscured the fact that private farming constituted a tiny portion of Russian agriculture, accounting for only 3 percent of the country's agricultural land and providing about 3.5 percent of the grain production in 1992.[71] Because the Russian peasantry depended on collective farming for all types of services, inputs, and production management, Yeltsin's government retained collective farming as the mainstay of Russian agriculture. According to Yeltsin's agriculture minister, Viktor N. Khlystun, even at the end of the transformation of Russia's agricultural sector half of its farms would be large collective farms,

20 percent would be smaller cooperative farms, 20 percent would be private farms, and the remaining 10 percent would be state farms.[72]

Explaining the Nonrevolution

The Initial Opening

The initial opening must accomplish a minimum number of tasks to generate the necessary momentum for change: it must create a conducive environment for the private sector and effect important decontrols of economic activities by the state through partial price and fiscal reforms. Empirical evidence suggests, however, that the initial economic opening in the Soviet Union (1985–1987) achieved few substantive economic results, although important legislation (the Law on Individual Labor Activities, the Law on State Enterprises, and the Law on Cooperation in the USSR) was passed during that period.

A crucial difference between the Chinese reformers and their Soviet counterparts in liberalizing the private sector was the *pragmatic-entrepreneurial* approach favored by the former and the *formal-legal* approach pursued by the latter. In China, the passage of operative laws and decrees, if any, usually followed the emergence of a grassroots economic movement, whereas in the Soviet Union, laws typically preceded the emergence of a similar movement. In China, reformers, intent upon harvesting the immediate gains from their measures, showed a greater flexibility in the legal formality of their initiatives. By comparison, Soviet reformers viewed the establishment of a legal framework as the primary instrument of reform because it would sanction the formation of economic entities contrary to state-socialist principles.

There were several disadvantages to the pragmatic-entrepreneurial approach, such as the lack of a consistent policy and legal protection to reduce long-term business risks. But these tended to be offset by the approach's high flexibility. The formal-legal approach, although reassuring once the basic legislative measures were enacted, was time-consuming and risked intense politicization, for controversial laws usually mobilized antireform forces. The legislative battle over the law on cooperatives dragged on for nearly two years in the Soviet Union, though it was unclear whether the mere passage of laws could create a sympathetic environment for the private sector.

The pragmatic-entrepreneurial approach might also be characterized as a *quiet* reform style, whereas the legal-formal approach might be considered a *noisy* reform style. Quiet reforms, being less politicizing, could be manipulated by the reformer to reduce open opposition. Deng's three No's edict on the private sector (no active promotion, no propaganda campaign, no crackdown) exemplified the quiet approach. The rapid development of the private sector in China thus took place, during much of the 1980s, with little fanfare. This sector grew fastest when media attention and legislative agenda were focused elsewhere.

In contrast, the formal-legal approach generated sweeping and dramatic proposals and engaged the public and the opposition. This approach raised public expectations with its promise of "fundamental" changes and galvanized an opposition that felt threatened. Thus, the war between supporters and opponents of the private sector in the Soviet Union was waged in the media, the legislature, the bureaucracy, and the marketplace. Eventually, the new private sector received little support from the public, which felt cheated by inflation and disappointed by the results, and it encountered fierce resistance from the mobilized conservative forces.

Before the Law on Cooperation in the USSR was formally enacted, its opponents in the Ministry of Finance, using their administrative power, proposed high income taxes on members of cooperatives, with rates at 60–90 percent for income over 500 rubles per month.[73] And, in December 1988, six months after the law was passed, an anticooperative coalition succeeded, in a resolution of the Council of Ministers, in curbing many cooperative business activities.[74] Ten months later, the same anticooperative forces imposed price controls on goods sold by cooperatives and banned trading activities that involved buying products from state-controlled sources and selling them on the open market.

In retrospect, the two main pre-1990 policies aimed at opening up the private sector (individual labor activities and cooperatives) were implemented in an economic environment inhospitable to the unfettered growth of the private sector. Between 1986 and 1989, reformers tackled individual issues in an incremental fashion by avoiding the central issue of privatizing state-owned industrial enterprises, which constituted the center of the Soviet economy. Most important was the passage of the Law on the State Enterprises. Another illustration of the ineffectiveness of the legalistic approach to economic reform, this initiative failed to improve productivity in the state enterprises but gave managers enough latitude to raise wages, thus directly contributing to explosive monetary growth and inflationary tendencies.[75]

Unlike Chinese reforms, the early Soviet economic reforms failed to create favorable conditions for the rapid emergence of the private sector. In China, decontrol of economic activities, fiscal decentralization, opening to the West, and partial price reform proceeded apace, whereas in the Soviet Union, these elements were absent. Although vital to the private sector, a wholesale market for producer goods failed to materialize because, unlike the Chinese, whose dual-track pricing diverted a large volume of producer goods from the state sector to the private, Soviet reformers launched no price reform.

Although the law on cooperatives required state enterprises and Gosnab (the state agency in charge of allocating producer goods) to make these inputs available to cooperatives, few SOEs and government agencies complied. Prime Minister Ryzhkov admitted in May 1988 that 84 percent of the cooperatives in Moscow had "considerable difficulties" in obtaining supplies.[76] This absence of a legal, privately controlled wholesale market for raw materials forced many cooperatives to obtain such materials illegally and at prices usually three times those paid by state enterprises.[77] To procure essential supplies, many cooperatives resorted to barter trade and even bribery, rendering themselves vulnerable to extortion by the local officials and managers of SOEs who acted as their "sponsors."[78] Government sources estimated that Soviet cooperatives paid more than 1 billion rubles in bribes in 1989 and 1.2 billion rubles in 1990.[79]

The passage of laws seldom guaranteed, by itself, the implementation of the policy embodied in them. A formal-legal approach failed because the Soviet government relied on those very mechanisms—local governments and economic bureaucracies—that had foiled earlier reform measures. Conservatives, with many chances to fight back, introduced restrictive amendments to the earlier measures or exercised administrative power to create obstacles to private entrepreneurs. These included restrictive registration, complex licensing procedures, and harassment in the form of tax audits and sanitation and safety inspections.[80]

Local authorities in the Soviet Union enjoyed wide discretionary powers of implementation, especially when the laws being implemented and enforced were ambiguous. Broad policy guidelines issued by the all-Union government were often translated into detailed, frequently unpublished, departmental directives that afforded local authorities opportunities to tamper with otherwise progressive legislation. One survey of cooperative operators in 1988 found that 1 of every 10 co-ops was denied registration by local officials.[81] Sometimes, government bureaucracies simply devised their own rules to restrain the growth of cooperatives, even when such rules were at odds with Soviet laws. *Moscow News* reported in January 1989 that some 800 departmental and local regulations, all in violation of the USSR Law on Cooperation, were being enforced across the country.[82] According to cooperative chairmen in 5 cities in the Soviet Union, they faced "inconsistencies in regulations governing cooperatives."[83]

The State Customs Control Main Administration's decision to set high tariffs on goods and equipment imported by cooperatives was another such example.[84] And, similarly, an administrative order issued by the USSR Ministry of Health in November 1988 prohibited the leasing of expensive medical equipment to cooperatives, effectively removing 40 percent of the cases from private clinics.[85] Taken together, restrictive regulations originating from various ministries and local authorities thwarted the purely formal-legal approach to developing the private sector.

Ironically, despite the proven ineffectiveness of the formal-legal approach in producing actual economic results, Soviet reformers adhered to it almost to the end of *perestroika*. The gap between reality and legislation widened as the Soviet economy plummeted toward collapse in 1990–1991. The new laws, resolutions, and decrees—the USSR Law on Ownership (March 1990), the Council of Ministers' resolution on joint stock companies (June 1990), the presidential decree establishing the USSR State Property Fund (August 1990)—were made irrelevant by the deteriorating political and economic situation.

The Nonactivation of Major Social Groups

The success of the private sector in China and its failure in the Soviet Union lay in a Big Push from below—the activation of a major social group that seized the economic opening to push its collective agenda. Such a Big Push led to the destruction of the social, economic, and political institutional frameworks that fettered private-sector activities through various elaborate control mechanisms; a powerful social force, constituting the "shock troops" of privatization, generated self-sustaining momentum for a mass privatization movement in China, but not in the Soviet Union.

In China, the peasant-initiated agricultural decollectivization, which Deng quietly endorsed, provided this Big Push in response to the initial rural opening. This Big Push, moreover, occurred in the center of the economy (agriculture) and swept aside most of the communist regime's rural political institutions and rendered its control mechanisms in much of the countryside ineffective, unleashing an army of hundreds of millions of peasants intent upon bettering their lives in the expanding private sector.

The Soviet Union experienced no similar Big Push, either from above or from below. The initial momentum was feeble, for the opening was created on the periphery of the economy (an underdeveloped service sector), and only in an incremental fashion. With the exception of a small number of individual entrepreneurs, many of whom were veterans of the prereform informal sector, no major social groups participated on a massive scale in the development of the private sector, and no major sector, neither the industrial nor the agricultural sector, was privatized or semiprivatized entirely in a *blitzkrieg* manner. No comparable shock wave of grassroots privatization swept through the Soviet Union. Meanwhile, however, the absence of the Big Push gave opponents of reform ample opportunities to regroup and marshall their forces to block further moves toward privatization with various bureaucratic strategies.

Why did mass activation of major social groups in response to the initial economic opening of *perestroika* fail to occur? Definitive answers are impossible, but plausible explanations can be advanced through an examination of the relationship between the size of the socialist welfare state and the autonomy, strength, and collective values of major social groups in the Soviet Union.

The Chinese socialist welfare state encompassed only about 20 percent of the total labor force, namely, those employed in state and quasi-state sectors. But the much larger Soviet socialist welfare state provided employment and income security, medical care, and other benefits and services for almost all Soviet workers and farmers.[86] As of 1988, about 97.46 percent of the total labor force (121.8 million out of 138.5 million) worked in the fully protected state sector, including collective farms.[87] Whereas in the Chinese socialist welfare state the peasantry received none of the benefits granted to state employees, in the Soviet socialist welfare state, generous benefits were offered to state employees, and the same benefits, slightly reduced, were given to workers on the state and collective farms. In 1987, for example, collective farmers received 2,003 rubles per person as wages for their work, in addition to 972 rubles per person paid out of the state's social consumption funds, which covered free medical care, pensions, and other services. Of the 58.1 million pensioners in the Soviet Union in 1987, 9.7 million were retired collective farm workers.[88]

A negative consequence of this all-embracing socialist welfare state and the state's monopoly in the labor market was the fostering of intense dependency of the Soviet labor force on the state and the raising of exit costs from this sector: the loss of lifetime employment, income security, access to subsidized housing, free health care, and other benefits. Looking back, one sees that the rapid development of the private sector under NEP took place because of the total *absence* of the socialist welfare state in the 1920s.

This might have resulted from a higher level of development in the Soviet Union, both compared with itself in the 1920s or compared with China in the late 1970s. The reach of the socialist welfare state was positively connected with the level of development, and the population's dependency on the state was greater in more developed communist states than in less developed ones. This factor perhaps explains why the obstacles to marketization, which requires the destruction or drastic curtailment of the socialist welfare state, tend to be greater in more developed communist states.

Another explanation can be sought in the political and technical complexities involved in privatizing industrialized, sophisticated, and developed planned economies. The private and quasi-private industrial sectors in China were developed basically *outside* the existing state-controlled industrial sector, in the less complex agrarian sector, and thus faced less opposition from the entrenched interests represented by managerial elites, political administrators, and industrial workers in the state sector. In contrast, as the experience of privatizing the industrial sector in Eastern European countries in the early 1990s shows, conversion from state ownership to private ownership in the industrial sector encountered greater resistance from similarly entrenched interests than the privatization of the agricultural and service sectors, where the technical requirements of privatization were less complex and workers and managers were more dispersed and less well organized.

The dominant values of a society and its social groups are maintained and reinforced by the structure of incentives and penalties of socioeconomic institutions. In a society with a developed socialist welfare state, the general public and specific groups are more likely to favor the welfare state and show prejudice against a market system, including private-sector activities. These value orientations may be another explanation for the nonactivation of major social groups in the development of the private sector in the Soviet Union during *perestroika*.[89]

The prevailing public attitude of a Soviet-type society toward the private sector was crucial. Favorable public opinion provided a more direct form of legitimization of mass participation in the private sector and injected a higher degree of confidence in private entrepreneurs than could be effected by official legislation. Conversely, a hostile public attitude toward the private sector and its participants served to demoralize and deter entrepreneurs, while providing conservatives with mass support in the suppression of the private sector. Was there a connection between public attitudes toward the private sector and the development of this sector during reform?

Opinion surveys from the Soviet Union make it possible to advance several propositions about the relationship between public views on the private sector and the nonactivation of major social groups. In the Gorbachev era, legal reforms and *glasnost* in the media had done much to legitimize, at least on paper, certain forms of private property and private entrepreneurship. But in reality, it was doubtful whether such positive political changes had contributed significantly to removing decades of popular prejudices against the private sector. The results of the public opinion polls conducted in the late 1980s and early 1990s indicated that the Soviet public was, on the whole, deeply divided and profoundly confused on the issue of privatization; available evidence suggests that favorable public attitudes toward the private sector did not emerge during *perestroika*.

The use of polling data to construct a general attitudinal profile for a country or a particular social group is prone to distortion and misinterpretation. Polling results depend on the wording of the questions posed. To overcome this problem, I will analyze polling data from several random large-scale surveys on similar issues phrased in different ways.

Many surveys from the Soviet Union suggested that there was a general public preference for "collective" ownership over "private" ownership. When asked what their preferred form of ownership (Table 4.3) was, more than 70 percent of those surveyed favored collective forms of ownership and

management, including leasing. About 30 percent of the respondents expressed a favorable opinion of private ownership of businesses, while 40
percent opposed it. Even cooperatives did not fare well with the public, despite their more collectivist organization, with only 35 percent of the respondents approving of them and 37 percent opposing them. A surprising finding
of the poll cited in Table 4.3 was the Soviet public's overall negative attitude
toward wholly owned foreign firms, with 37 percent of the respondents expressing disapproval of them. Another survey of 15,000 Soviet citizens in
1990 reflected a similar public attitude toward various forms of ownership.
Whereas 60 percent of the respondents showed support for leased state
firms, 40 percent said they disapproved of cooperatives and firms owned by
private individuals; half of the respondents opposed wholly owned foreign
firms.[90]

This negative public attitude toward private firms was reflected in employment preferences. A survey of residents of Moscow in 1990 found that
working for SOEs remained the most desirable employment (with 35 per-

Table 4.3   Soviet public attitude toward various forms of ownership (in
percentages)

Firm ownership	Approve	Disapprove	Indifferent	Don't know
Firms owned by collectives	72	8	10	11
Firms leased by collectives	72	9	8	11
Joint enterprises	71	10	7	12
Firms set up with investors' money	55	12	14	19
Cooperatives	36	34	15	15
Foreign-owned firms	35	37	8	20
Firms owned by individual citizens	31	42	9	18

Source: The All-Union Public Opinion Study Center, *Komsomolskaya pravda*, December
13, 1989, *Foreign Broadcast Information Service: Daily Reports—the Soviet Union*,
December 15, 1989, p. 45.

cent of the respondents choosing the state sector), whereas working for private (13 percent) and cooperative (7 percent) firms was less desirable.[91] As expected, this employment preference was translated into intense opposition to the use of hired labor by private employers. One survey, in October 1990, showed that half of the respondents opposed the use of hired labor by private entrepreneurs.[92] Another, in February 1990, found that 42 percent of the respondents were against using hired labor and 38 percent supported such a practice. The same survey also revealed that 27 percent of the respondents would not work for a private employer "under any circumstances," while 54 percent would, "but only for much higher pay."[93]

Preference for collective ownership, distrust of private firms, and unwillingness to work in the private sector were accompanied by a high level of public opposition to privatization. Indeed, the survey by Goskomstat in October 1990, after the announcement of the Shatalin Plan that put privatization at the top of the reform agenda, showed that 40 percent of the respondents opposed selling SOEs to private individuals and 33 percent supported this measure. Employees in state enterprises and collective and state farms tended to be far more negative about privatization than the population at large. The same poll found that employees in the state sector were the least supportive of privatization, as depicted in Table 4.4, with only 10 percent of the respondents expressing approval of the process. A small minority (10 percent) supported leasing SOEs to private individuals. Half of the state em-

Table 4.4   Attitude of state-sector employees toward privatization (in percentages)

Policy option	Support
Preserving the current ownership system of collective farms and state farms	50
Leaving state-owned enterprises as they are, but giving them more independence	40
Leasing land	20
Giving state-owned enterprises away to their employees without compensation to the state	10
Leasing state-owned enterprises to private individuals	10
Selling state-owned enterprises to private individuals	10

Source: Survey of 15,000 Soviet citizens employed in the state enterprises, collective and state farms, conducted by the Sociological Survey Bureau of Goskomstat, *Pravitelstvennyy vestnik,* no. 44 (October 1990), *Foreign Broadcast Information Service: Daily Reports—the Soviet Union,* November 15, 1990, pp. 41–42.

ployees wanted to preserve the ownership system of collective and state farms, and 40 percent indicated that SOEs should be left alone but given more independence.[94]

Another poll conducted by Goskomstat in early 1991 yielded similar results, with about 40 percent of workers saying that SOEs should "continue to be in state ownership" while a tiny minority (between 3.5 and 8.7 percent) supported various forms of privatization and semiprivatization, including turning SOEs into cooperatives, private enterprises, joint stock companies, foreign joint ventures, and leased enterprises.[95] This public wariness of the privatization of SOEs persisted even after radical economic reform was introduced by Yeltsin's government in Russia. A poll of 2,122 European Russians in October 1992 found that only 29 percent agreed that "it is all right to put many state enterprises up for sale," whereas 39 percent expressed disagreement and 31 percent said that they did not know.[96]

The weak support for privatization was accompanied by the public's negative perception of the most controversial private sector to emerge during reform—the cooperatives. Three different samples tracking the Soviet public attitude toward cooperatives between 1988 and 1990 revealed that (1) opponents of cooperatives (25 to 38 percent) consistently outnumbered their supporters (8 to 23 percent); (2) about half of the Soviet public held an ambivalent attitude toward this sector; and (3) the majority of the Soviet public (50 to 77 percent) tended to associate the growth of cooperatives with negative consequences such as inflation, crime, and social injustice. Only about a third of the respondents thought cooperatives would improve the economy.[97] Another poll showed similar negative public expectations of transition to a market economy, with about 40 to 50 percent of the respondents saying that they personally "feared most" the "social chaos, increase in crime and inflation" as market relations were introduced in the Soviet Union.[98]

Significantly, the lack of public support for the cooperatives did not appear to be the result of "ideological" bias against the private sector, as only a very small minority (20 percent) thought that the cooperatives would erode "the basis of socialism," and 37 percent thought that such an outcome was impossible.[99] As a group, members of the Soviet cooperatives were among the most disliked. A poll of Moscow residents in early 1990 found that co-op members were more disliked than the extremist right-wingers and communists; only neo-Nazis, homosexuals, nationalists, Stalinists, and supporters of military dictatorships were more disliked.[100]

To be sure, the general public in the Soviet Union consisted of diverse groups, and attitudes toward the private sector varied according to social groups. Opposition to the private sector was stronger among lower-status workers and farmers (beneficiaries of the protective socialist welfare state) than among higher-status and more skilled groups (principal victims of state-enforced egalitarianism under communism). One poll in 1990 found that only a small minority of pensioners (9.2 percent), state farm workers (9.9 percent), collective farmers (10.3 percent), and workers in SOEs (14.2 percent) were positive about private-sector activities.[101]

It is worth pointing out that the Soviet public did tend to show support for the more *vague* notions of marketization. In a 1990 poll, a higher percentage of respondents (from 30 percent of unskilled workers, to 38 percent of pensioners, to 71 percent of managerial staff and highly educated specialists) supported the "transition to a market economy."[102] Such support declined dramatically when they were asked to respond to the more *specific* forms of economic activities of the market, such as individual labor activities and cooperatives.[103] These results seem to confirm the proposition that lower-status groups, the vast majority of the productive forces in the Soviet Union and other communist states that already enjoyed the benefits of the socialist welfare state, were unlikely to be spontaneously activated in response to initial economic openings.[104] It is evident that the politically risky reduction or elimination of the institutions of the socialist welfare state would be necessary to reshape the attitudes of these groups.

Finally, although communism might have lost its appeal among much of the Soviet public, socialism apparently had not, and capitalism remained the least acceptable economic system. According to a poll of Moscow residents in late 1989, 61 percent held a positive view toward "socialism," while only 37 percent and 34 percent looked positively upon "communism" and "capitalism," respectively. The same poll found that only 17 percent viewed "socialism" negatively, while 38 percent had a negative view of "capitalism."[105] This indicates that the Soviet public looked favorably upon some features of socialism, especially its welfare-state benefits, and that a considerable percentage of the public might still believe in the "Third Way"—market-socialism—as a solution to their economic problems. At the elite level within the establishment, market-socialism still held sway. In a poll of 5,326 CPSU members, of which 892 were secretaries of party organizations, 66 percent said that they supported the development of a planned market economy.[106]

If the Soviet public attitudes toward the private sector fostered, at best, an ambivalent and, at worst, an inhospitable, psychological environment for the private sector during *perestroika,* did public attitudes and values of *specific groups* have a negative impact on the growth of the private sector in the Soviet Union? It would seem so, from a comparison of the level of development of the private sector (Table 4.2) and the research on the differences between public attitudes toward privatization in various Soviet republics by the American researcher Darrell Slider and his Soviet collaborators.[107] Specific private-sector activities grew much faster in republics where the people held positive attitudes toward privatization than in republics where such attitudes were less favorable.

Absence of a Takeover Coalition

The democratic breakthrough during *glasnost* derived much of its momentum from a political takeover coalition built by the liberal intelligentsia, disaffected industrial workers, radical reformers within the regime (typified by Yeltsin), and powerful nationalist forces on the periphery. Similarly, an informal economic takeover coalition in China accelerated the capitalist revolution and successfully defended its gains. Unfortunately, there was no similar economic takeover coalition during *perestroika* to impact significantly the growth of the private sector.

Given the various institutional, practical, and attitudinal obstacles to the private sector, the efforts by individual Soviet private entrepreneurs had been heroic and resourceful, but their overall gains were insignificant. One important explanation for the absence of a breakthrough to the market in the Soviet Union was that its leading entrepreneurial elements operated in isolation from other major social groups and failed to form a takeover coalition. Occasionally, Soviet entrepreneurs did receive support from the liberal press, but no evidence suggests that they were able to form an economic takeover coalition with the intelligentsia-dominated democratic forces. This media support was insufficient to offset the practical obstacles in the real world of economic activities, which, until the dissolution of the Soviet Union, remained in the firm grip of local governments and managerial elites of the planned economy.

Three factors militated against the formation of a takeover coalition in the development of the private sector in the Soviet Union. First, and most obvious, was the absence of foreign investors in private-sector activities, preventing Soviet private entrepreneurs from gaining access to capital, supplies, technology, and markets.

Second, the high level of politicization of economic reform in general and of privatization in particular precluded the formation of a coalition that would have included, of necessity, some elements of the old regime (such as the *nomenklatura*). Hurdles to coalition-building grew as the level of politicization rose. This politicization was manifested initially in the widely perceived dominance of private-sector activities by petty criminals, profiteers, and corrupt government and law-enforcement officials, popularly known as the Soviet mafia.[108] This negative public reaction to individual labor activities and cooperatives discouraged participation by other major social groups. The first wave of cooperatives and individual labor activities merely legalized the shadow economy and benefited those elements the public perceived as unsavory.

During the second wave of cooperatives, which mushroomed after the passage of the 1988 law and up to the collapse of the Soviet Union, the issue of *nomenklatura* privatization began to eclipse others as the most divisive aspect of privatization.[109] The liberal media scrutinized and attacked the efforts by the *nomenklatura,* who used their power to "steal" productive assets from the state sector in forming the so-called cooperatives and small private enterprises. But other social groups failed to join forces with the publicly detested elements of the *nomenklatura.* It appeared that the managerial elites of the Soviet *nomenklatura,* not the political administrators, or *apparatchiki,* were leading this spontaneous privatization drive.[110] One study of 586 cooperative managers in nine Soviet cities, carried out in early 1990, showed that 40 percent were enterprise managers and shop bosses, 34 percent were engineers and technicians, and only 8.5 percent of the cooperative chairmen were blue-collar workers.[111]

Moreover, these managerial elites failed to endear themselves to the ordinary Soviet workers because of the exclusionist manner in which they carried out the spontaneous privatization. Typically, they gained the lion's share of the benefits while excluding the majority of the work force from receiving similar gains, thus arousing resentment.[112] Soviet workers' animosity toward the managerial elites was also reflected in their specific opposition to turning their SOEs into either cooperatives or joint stock companies, since the managerial elites would dominate and benefit most from either of the proposed property forms. A study by Goskomstat in early 1991 found that only 3.5 percent of the workers supported reorganizing their enterprises into cooperatives, and 4.2 percent approved of transforming them into joint stock companies.[113]

Third, opposition from the ruling elites in local governments slowed the growth of the private sector during *perestroika.* A survey of officials of local soviet executive committees and law enforcement officers in 1988 revealed that 41 percent of the officials and 68 percent of the law enforcement officers favored tight control over cooperatives. The same survey showed that one-third of cooperative operators viewed the distrust and interference of local authorities as the main impediment to the development of cooperatives.[114] Western scholars and journalists also identified local government authorities as a principal obstacle to the development of the private sector, but they differed widely as to the reasons, with some citing lack of bureaucratic entrepreneurship and others blaming the ideological hostility of local elites.[115]

Three additional factors made local elites undesirable coalition members or deprived them of the motives to participate in such a coalition. Because local elites became primary targets of opposition attacks and public anger, they made unattractive coalition partners for private entrepreneurs. These elites, many of whom were categorized as *apparatchiki* rather than enterprise managers, did not benefit from the private-sector activities personally, so they lacked the financial incentives to support such activities.[116] Finally, unlike the decentralized Chinese fiscal system in the 1980s, which made local governments dependent on local revenues (especially from the fast-growing private sector), the Soviet fiscal system remained highly centralized during *perestroika*, a factor that did not *force* local governments to open up local revenue bases by encouraging private-sector growth. Initially, the Ministry of Finance monopolized the power to set the tax rates on the private sector; but even after February 1989, when republican governments gained such power, revenues from cooperatives were split between the central government and republican governments.[117]

The development of the Soviet private sector also suffered from the efforts of a loose *antitakeover* coalition consisting of government ministries, local authorities, official trade unions, and low-status groups (pensioners and collective and state farm workers). While the active opposition of the first two partners in this antitakeover coalition was well known, that of the last two deserves some mention here.[118] Official trade unions (representing workers in SOEs) were instrumental in drafting the additional restrictions on cooperatives imposed by the Council of Ministers in December 1988.[119] Certain low-income and low-status groups dependent on the socialist welfare state also opposed the private sector because they feared competition resulting from the rising income of private-sector participants. An all-Union opinion survey found that only 10 percent of pensioners and collective and state farm workers supported cooperatives, while 30 percent opposed them.[120] Another Union-wide survey in 1989 found a positive correlation between income-and-education status and attitude toward the private sector, with the poor and less educated more likely to oppose it.[121] Typically, they formed the basis of mass support for local ruling elites and central ministries in their efforts to block the private sector.

Absence of Favorable External Factors

Lacking essential internal stimuli to the development of the private sector, the Soviet Union also enjoyed few favorable external factors. Indeed, the contrast between the Soviet Union and China in this respect was pronounced. The following data reflect the insignificant presence of foreign economic influences in the Soviet Union during *perestroika*.

Foreign capital. Although foreign debt mounted under Gorbachev's rule (from $42 billion in 1988 to $86 billion in 1991 alone, mostly in government-backed loans), there were few indications that these funds were invested in productive capacities, or in the private sector, for they were largely used to service the debt and to finance essential imports.[122] During the same period, little private foreign investment flowed into the country in the late 1980s, and its impact was equally insignificant.

Private foreign direct investment, almost exclusively in the form of joint ventures with Soviet SOEs, began to trickle in shortly after the inauguration of *perestroika,* but only 315 joint ventures had been formed as of April 1989.[123] By March 1990, foreign investment in the Soviet Union totaled $300 million, with 1,500 joint ventures.[124] At the end of 1990, nearly 3,000 foreign joint ventures were registered in the Soviet Union; the total amount of investment reached 2 billion rubles. Of these joint ventures, about 40 percent were in the industrial sector, and most of the joint ventures were set up with German and American firms (246 and 218, respectively). One study suggested that only 20 percent of these firms had actually begun operating, although government figures reported that about 40 percent were functioning.[125] Their contribution to the Soviet GNP was a minuscule 0.2–0.3 percent a year, and their impact on the expansion of Soviet exports negligible. Government figures showed that, in 1990, joint ventures exported $63 million worth of products—only 0.27 percent of total Soviet exports.[126]

Foreign trade. The private sector was a minor player in Soviet foreign trade. In 1990, only 2,516 cooperatives were licensed to engage in foreign trade, and their exports for 1990 amounted to only $32 million.[127] In Russia, the cooperatives accounted for 0.06 percent (about $14 million) of the value of Russian exports, and 0.07 percent (about $18 million) of imports in 1990.[128]

The above indices of foreign economic influences—investment and trade—show that the Soviet private sector received negligible external support during *perestroika.* Several factors, ranging from the autarkic character of the Soviet economy to government policies, explain the absence of favorable foreign external influences on the development of the private sector in the Soviet Union.

(1) Government policies. Early government restrictions favoring the state monopoly on foreign trade severely limited private firms in commercial dealings with foreign businesses. Curbs were ostensibly lifted in April 1989, but in most cases the formal opening of foreign trade was not translated into genuine trade liberalization for the private sector. For example, because most Soviet cooperatives engaged in exporting scarce raw materials and importing lucrative items such as VCRs and used cars, the government issued regulations restricting such transactions and forcing cooperatives to trade with foreign businesses only through state-controlled trade organizations.[129]

The government was overcautious about attracting foreign investment. It imposed a 49 percent limit on ownership of equity by foreign investors (this restriction was removed in October 1990, when Gorbachev signed a decree permitting foreign investors to control up to 100 percent of equity). The high tax rates on foreign investment also made joint ventures in the Soviet

Union unattractive. Frequently, the Soviet SOEs that were partners with foreign firms tended to overvalue their capital contribution (such as land and buildings), thus reducing investment incentives.[130]

The government's reluctance to open the Soviet economy to the West paralleled the Soviet public's ambivalence. In a 1989 poll, only 35 percent of the respondents approved of foreign-owned firms, while 37 percent opposed them, with 20 percent undecided.[131] In another survey of 15,000 Soviet citizens in 1990, the Sociological Survey Bureau of Goskomstat reported that 50 percent opposed wholly owned foreign firms and only 10 percent supported them.[132] This public antipathy toward foreign investment continued unabated after the collapse of the Soviet Union. One poll of Russians in late 1991 found that, even amid political chaos and economic collapse, 40 percent of the respondents believed that foreign investment would lead to control by foreign influences.[133]

(2) Structural-institutional linkages with the world economy. Like the prereform Chinese economy, the Soviet economy prior to *perestroika* was notable for its autarkic character; China's exports made up about 4.6 percent of GNP in 1978; the external revenues, chiefly exports, accounted for less than 5 percent of the Soviet GNP in 1988.[134] But unlike the Chinese economy, which had been greatly internationalized since reform (with the exports/GNP ratio rising to nearly 17 percent by 1990 at the official exchange rate), the Soviet economy remained an autarkic one to the end of *perestroika*. Failure to shift the development strategy from an autarkic one to an outward-looking one was the primary cause of this situation. In addition, the Soviet economy in general, and the development of the private sector in particular, appeared to have suffered from weak and, in most cases, nonexistent institutional linkages with the world economy. Unlike the Chinese exports producers (many of which were private and foreign-funded firms) that targeted the competitive consumer markets in the West, the Soviet exports producers (exclusively state monopolies) relied either on the international commodity market for their major exports (precious metals and oil) or on the captive noncompetitive markets in Eastern Europe within the trade framework of the Council for Mutual Economic Assistance (CMEA), to which 55 percent of the Soviet exports in 1989 were directed.[135]

The Soviet Union's nonparticipation in such international economic institutions as the World Bank, the International Monetary Fund, and the General Agreement on Tariffs and Trade (GATT) denied it many benefits from these agencies. In contrast, China's participation in these institutions, excluding GATT, was of enormous value in the transformation of its economy in the 1980s. The World Bank alone provided China with $5.2 billion in soft loans between 1983 and 1990, in addition to technical expertise in economic restructuring.[136] Similarly, the West's restrictions on technology transfers and its trade sanctions against the Soviet Union, which persisted almost until the end of *perestroika*, hindered the internationalization of the Soviet economy.

The consequence of these negative factors, some attributable to the Soviet leadership and others to the economic legacies of the Cold War, was anemic growth of the private sector; this fragile component of society received little external support when it was most needed. Ironically, when such support was finally promised and was about to be delivered after the collapse of the Soviet Union in 1991, the absence of a healthy private sector inside the former Soviet Union vitiated the effectiveness of foreign aid, which went largely to state monopolies.

Accelerated Institutional Decay

The introduction of market forces in China helped accelerate the decaying process of the key institutions of the party-state and reduced institutional resistance to the growth of the private sector. Did a similar process take place in the Soviet Union under *perestroika?*

There were major differences between China and the Soviet Union. First, the institutional presence of the CPSU in economic planning and management in the Soviet Union was stronger, more penetrative and centralized than that of the CCP in China. Second, the *prior* institutional decay of the party-state in China was more advanced due to the Cultural Revolution, during which, according to one official account, 17.5 percent of government and party officials were subjected to investigation and persecution, and 75 percent of officials above the rank of vice-minister and vice provincial governor were also persecuted and investigated.[137] Although Leonid Brezhnev's long rule in the Soviet Union might have been dull, stagnant, and corrupt, it did not bring about the same kind of massive devastation to its institutional structure. The rapid destruction of the institutions of the party-state remained to be accomplished by Gorbachev's *glasnost*.

Third, compared with the CCP, the CPSU was more institutionalized, with a more educated membership and operative norms. Whereas the CCP prior to reform was a party predominantly staffed by less educated elements of society, the CPSU on the eve of *perestroika* was essentially a party of technocrats and relatively well educated *apparatchiki*. In 1983, 29.5 percent of CPSU members received a higher education, 43 percent a high-school education, 15.7 percent an incomplete high-school education, and 9.6 percent a primary education.[138] Moreover, the CPSU had a stronger institutional presence in the economic sector than the CCP. In 1981, while members of the CCP accounted for 9 percent of the total labor force and less than 5 percent of the rural labor force, members of the CPSU made up 13.7 percent of the total labor force in the Soviet Union.[139]

Finally, 73 percent of the CPSU's membership was concentrated in industry, agriculture, transportation, and retail sectors.[140] Solid institutional resistance to reform dictated that Soviet reformers first turn to mass political mobilization through *glasnost* in order to clear the way for *perestroika*, no matter how great the political risks. Indeed, as democratization quickened in the late 1980s, especially following the first competitive local elections, between late 1989 and early 1990, accelerated institutional decay of the party-state threatened institutional and political collapse. Although party organizations in Soviet enterprises retained power until mid-1990, they then collapsed into chaos.[141]

The slow growth of the private sector was linked to the relative strength of the political and economic institutions of the old regime in the early phases of *perestroika*. Why, then, did the accelerated decay of the same institutions fail to contribute to significant gains of the private sector in the Soviet Union?

One might point to the time lag between the destruction of old institutions and the construction of new ones, assuming that institutional decay must reach a certain point before a Big Surge in private-sector activities materializes. Such an argument implies that institutional decay of the party-state and of the planned economy is not necessarily *synchronized* with the advances in societal gains. The former usually precedes the latter. In China, the early signs of the Big Surge did not emerge until about four years after the initiation of reform, when the CCP's rural economic and political institutions had undergone severe decay. On the eve of the collapse of the Soviet Union, similarly, there were some encouraging signs that, with the breakdown of the central planning system and the socialist welfare state, private entrepreneurial energies were also being released in quantities.

One might also stress that accelerated institutional decay alone is a requisite *background* condition that merely provides an opportunity for a societal breakthrough. It does not automatically translate into resource gains for societal actors; these gains must be pursued aggressively. This implies that the absence of mass activation of major social groups in the production sphere (Soviet workers and peasants) was the primary reason for the failure of a marketization breakthrough despite accelerated institutional decay.

Moreover, if accelerated institutional decay of the state is not accompanied by a simultaneous transfer of resources from the state to society, this produces an institutional collapse of the state followed by anarchy—an apt description of the Soviet economy between the late 1980s and the early 1990s, when the institutions of the planned economy decayed rapidly while the private sector was too feeble to stabilize the economy.

There is an uneven rate of resource gain for societal forces in different areas, depending on the thrust of the dual-regime transition process. In the Soviet Union, the primary thrust of regime transition was democratization, and society's resource gains were chiefly political, not economic. Thus, even in regions where democratic forces eventually seized political power and effectively dismantled the key political institutions of the party-state toward the end of *perestroika*, dramatic gains in political resources were not accompanied by equivalent gains in economic resources. In fact, economic power remained in the hands of the elites who had controlled the planned economy. One study found that newly elected local governments dominated by democratic forces were, in nearly all cases, without economic resources or efficacious means of influencing economic decision-making.[142]

The differences between China and the Soviet Union illustrate why a society-led breakthrough in marketization in a dual-regime transition was more likely to occur in a less developed communist state than in a more developed one. Many of the same factors that contributed to the breakthrough to a market economy in China were either absent or of insignificant degrees in the Soviet Union under *perestroika*. Some of these factors, such as the mishandled initial opening of *perestroika*, the government's lack of commitment to substantive privatization of the state sector, and the lukewarm interest in attracting foreign investment, could be traced to the reformers' policy failures. In the Soviet Union, a high level of institutionalized dependency on the socialist welfare state, the absence of major social groups leading the marketization drive, the overcentralized economic planning system, the lower level of prior institutional decay, and the concomitant higher level of initial bureaucratic resistance to reform blocked a grassroots capitalist revolution such as occurred in China.

Several lessons emerge from the above comparison, and two deserve special emphasis. First, it is often easier to build a market system in sectors where the political and economic institutional reach of the old regime is relatively weak and narrow than in sectors where the penetration of the old regime is deep and wide. The vibrant Chinese private industrial sector was constructed essentially *outside*, rather than *from within*, the existing institutional frameworks of the planned economy. Second, the level of politicization of economic issues should be kept low in order to facilitate coalition-building. Unfortunately, in a dual-regime transition spearheaded by a democratizing breakthrough, a higher level of politicization proved unavoidable. This conclusion, however, does not imply that postcommunist authoritarian regimes are more capable of directing the transition to a market economy. If anything, the Chinese experience amply demonstrated that the regime's contribution to the marketizing breakthrough was minimal. Rather, autonomous social forces were chiefly responsible for the breakthrough, which the regime had neither planned nor anticipated.

The Self-Liberalization of China's Mass Media

5

In communist states where the top leadership launched economic reforms but attempted to maintain the party-state's monopoly of political power, as in China (since 1979) and Vietnam (since 1986), societal takeover could occur only through indirect—and primarily economic—means. In the absence of a political opening similar to Gorbachev's *glasnost,* the political activation of key social groups on a massive scale was unlikely; when it did occur, for example, in China during the three prodemocracy movements in 1979, 1986–1987, and 1989, it was met with government crackdowns. Thus, in a politically repressive environment, market forces became the principal means for societal actors gradually and subtly to influence the political process and alter the balance of power between the state and society. In regime transitions from communism, therefore, postcommunist authoritarian governments attempting to introduce market forces to revitalize the economy must face the political consequences of such a decision.

In other words, in a dual-regime transition, movement from communism to an authoritarian regime based on a market economy will inevitably create, as its spillover effects, favorable preconditions for the emergence of a polyarchy. The type of liberalization that results in this process should be characterized as *self-liberalization,* because it is not the outcome of a deliberate government policy, but the unintended consequence of market-oriented reforms.

No other example could more vividly illustrate this point than China's self-liberalization of the mass media in the 1980s, resulting from the convergence of two forces: the spillover effects from economic reform and the queue-jumping—early political mobilization—of the liberal intelligentsia. The paradox of the Deng era is that, although the regime tried to control the mass media (newspapers, magazines, book publishing, television, radio, and film) and resisted the liberalizing trends, the media experienced a remarkable degree of self-liberalization during the 1980s.

This self-liberalization was evident in: (1) the pluralization of permissible topics and the freedom with which they were treated; (2) increased criticisms of the government's policies and practices by the press; (3) the emergence of semiofficial publications such as the Shanghai-based *World Economic Herald* that served as a powerful forum for market-oriented reform and political democratization; and (4) the emergence of a resilient, well-integrated, and market-based network of publishing houses, privately operated printing facilities, distributors, and retailers.

Four factors were primarily responsible for this development: (a) the impact of market forces unleashed by the regime's economic reforms; (b) the foreign influence following China's opening to the West; (c) the effects of rapid economic development in the 1980s; and (d) the political activation of the Chinese intelligentsia with influence in the mass media.

The Chinese mass media since 1979 were constrained ideologically by the four cardinal principles laid down by Deng Xiaoping. The role of the mass media, in Deng's own words, was to "convincingly propagandize the four cardinal principles."[1] This meant the continuation of censorship agencies at all levels of government to keep newspapers, periodicals, television stations, and film studios under firm party control. In addition, the government periodically cracked down on unofficial publications, "pornographic" materials, and writings espousing "bourgeois liberalism." Between 1979 and 1991, it organized four large campaigns to purify the mass media. The first was launched shortly after Deng shut down the Democracy Wall in Beijing in 1979. Hundreds of unofficial publications were banned, the most famous of which was *Beijing Spring,* edited by Wei Jingsheng, a dissident who was sentenced to a fifteen-year prison term on charges of disseminating counter-revolutionary propaganda. The second round of attacks started in late 1983 with the "anti-spiritual-pollution" campaign. The four-month campaign also cracked down on pornography, literature, arts, and music that the regime deemed "low-taste."

The third assault on the mass media followed the student-led prodemocracy demonstrations between December 1986 and January 1987, which resulted in the downfall of Hu Yaobang and triggered the campaign against bourgeois liberalism. This campaign was characterized by an unprecedented ferocity. At Deng's behest, Liu Binyan, an investigative reporter renowned for exposing official corruption, was expelled from the Party. Between March 1987 and early 1988, the Party's propaganda department and the newly established State Press and Publications Administration (SPPA) organized a purge of newspapers and magazines. Consequently, 270 (15.4 percent of the total) newspapers were closed or forced to become "internal publications." The government also confiscated more than 10 million copies of "illegal publications."[2]

The fourth campaign against the mass media followed the Tiananmen Square massacre of June 1989. This crackdown surpassed the previous conservative counterattacks in scope, duration, and effect. The post-Tiananmen assault on the media included arrests of numerous dissidents, journalists, writers, and social scientists. Officials banned controversial films, confiscated millions of music and video cassettes, and shut down a large number of publications—from the influential *World Economic Herald* to popular tabloids. All publishing companies were subjected to reregistration. Within 1 year, the campaign had closed 12 percent of all newspapers, 13 percent of social science periodicals, and 7.6 percent of China's 534 publishing companies. The government also claimed to have seized 32 million copies of contraband books and 2.4 million music and video cassettes, banned more than 150 films, and raided and shut down 3,200 businesses engaged in the "illicit publishing business." More than 80,000 individuals were punished for media-related activities.[3]

This campaign continued in 1991. Official figures showed that, between the end of 1990 and March 1991, an additional 6.8 million copies of illegal publications were seized, including more than 3,000 titles of "pornographic materials" and 1,300 titles of "counterrevolutionary materials." The government closed more than 3,000 illegal publishing facilities and about 3,000 unlicensed private book retailers. It also confiscated 490,000 cassettes of banned music recordings and 50,000 contraband video tapes.[4]

Aside from its intermittent crusades against liberalizing trends in the media, the government's hardline stance was also evident in its vacillation on the drafting of China's first press law and its eventual refusal to pass such a law, despite pressure from Chinese journalists and leading liberals.

Long dissatisfied with the government's firm control of the media, Chinese intellectuals had been urging liberalization for some time. The extent of their unhappiness about the low credibility of the official media was reflected in an opinion survey conducted by the People's University in February 1988. Of the 200 leading professionals and cultural celebrities surveyed, 65 percent rejected the view that "the press enjoys a high credibility among the public." More than 90 percent agreed that "the press reflected too little the voices of the masses and provided too few opportunities for the masses to participate in the political process." About 60 percent agreed that "there is a huge distance between the content of the press coverage and the realities of people's lives and actual needs." Fifty-seven percent viewed the passage of the press law as the key to reforming the press.[5]

Formal legislative proposals for a press law had been announced in 1980 during the third session of the 5th People's National Congress, and they were repeatedly presented to the same body afterward, albeit with little result. In 1984, the prospects for the passage of a press law brightened when the legislative committee of the Congress announced that it had authorized the Committee on Education, Science, Culture, and Health to draft the press law.

Within the National People's Congress, support was building for the passage of the law. One poll showed that 58 percent of the delegates proposed that the Congress pass it as one of the basic laws of China.[6] Nothing happened for another three years, however. In 1987, Li Peng, the conservative prime minister, took over the State Council, which controlled the legislative agenda of the National People's Congress.[7] The State Council then decided to transfer the responsibility of drafting the press law, from the Committee on Education, Science, Culture, and Health to the State Press and Publications Administration, which was under the jurisdiction of the State Council. The Administration soon produced two different versions of the law.

In the meantime, journalists were increasing pressure for the passage of the law. In November 1985, the urgency for a press law was heightened by the filing of China's first libel case against one of the most influential magazines in the country, the Shanghai-based *Democracy and Law* (with a circulation of more than 2 million). In 1988, the court ruled for the plaintiff and penalized the magazine. After the suit was first reported, scores of libel cases were filed against the newspapers and magazines in Shanghai, with the majority of judgments against journalists.[8] Filing libel cases against investigative reporters became a favored retaliatory tactic of government officials whose misdeeds were being exposed in the press.[9]

The combination of Deng's deep personal misgivings about press freedom, the opposition of the hardliners and the bureaucracy in charge of censorship, and the crackdown on the mass media after Tiananmen in 1989 ended prospects for a press law. In the early 1990s, despite the revival of economic reform, there was no sign that the government was about to pass the press law. The number of libel suits filed against the media soared; most of them ended with the defeat of the defendants.[10] So, more than a decade after it was raised as a legislative issue, China's press law remained unwritten, and freedom of the press, consequently, remained legally unprotected.

In spite of the periodic campaigns against the mass media and the absence of legal protection for a free press, the Chinese media during 1979–1993 showed a remarkable degree of self-liberalization, with book publishing being the most liberalized, followed by journals and newspapers. Hundreds of thousands of copies of a history of the Cultural Revolution written by Yan Jiaqi, a leading political scientist who turned dissident leader in 1989, and Gao Gao were sold despite the government's initial attempts to ban it. Another book attacking the Chinese national character, entitled *The Ugly Chinese,* became a national bestseller. The investigative reporter Liu Binyan's disturbing tales of official corruption continued to appear in magazines and books even after he incurred the wrath of senior party officials, who attempted to ban his works. Despite the post-Tiananmen political repression and the government campaign against illicit publications launched between 1989 and 1991, numerous politically sensitive works were openly displayed and sold in private bookstores. These included a pirated Chinese translation of Boris Yeltsin's autobiography, *Against the Grain,* unauthorized, and, in most instances, sensational and damaging, biographies of Mao Zedong, Zhou Enlai, and other leaders of the old regime, and literary works by authors denounced by the government's propaganda machine after Tiananmen.[11]

Self-liberalization also manifested itself in the broadening of issues treated by the mass media. Discussions of privatization of state-owned assets, strengthening of the rule of law, democratic reforms, human rights, and other politically sensitive topics regularly appeared in Chinese newspapers and periodicals, even after the Tiananmen crackdown. Very often, the most daring publication was also the best-selling one. For example, *Shenzhen Youth,* a paper published nominally by the Youth League of the Shenzhen Economic Zone but actually run by a dozen radical young journalists, attained a nationwide circulation of more than one million because of its liberal editorials. In the summer of 1986, it first broached the taboo subject of Deng Xiaoping's retirement.

China's fledgling environmental movement similarly gained attention through the self-liberalized mass media. In 1989, opposition to the government's plan to build an environmentally controversial dam across the Yangtze in the Three Gorges area was openly voiced in the *World Economic Herald,* and a collection of essays criticizing the project appeared in a book published with private funds raised from well-known intellectuals and journalists. These efforts temporarily postponed the project.[12]

The media's self-liberalization made the government anxious. Blaming the pre-Tiananmen mass media for giving excessive coverage to privatization and a debate on Chinese culture spawned by the television series "River Elegy," the government feared "loss of control" in the media.[13] However, the self-liberalization of the media in China was restricted to certain subsectors, varying with the degrees of marketization in different sectors. Despite a loss of control in the print media to market forces, however, the government maintained, until the early 1990s, a tight grip on the electronic and screen media, as well as on most national and provincial newspapers run by party organizations.

Market Forces and Self-Liberalization

The principal momentum behind the self-liberalization of the Chinese mass media came from the transition from a planned economy to a market system. Marketization produced spillover effects with profound political implications for state-society relations in general and the process of state-to-society resource transfer in particular. The higher the level of marketization, the greater the degree of self-liberalization. Strong market forces reduced the effectiveness of government censorship of the media by multiplying the channels of production and dissemination. Increasing financial rewards encouraged entrepreneurs to publish materials the government wanted to ban. And, by causing a scarcity of these materials, the government unintentionally made them more attractive and profitable, mobilizing hundreds of thousands of ingenious private entrepreneurs, rather than a handful of intellectual dissidents, to devise brilliant stratagems to outwit government censors. Thus, the profit motive became an indispensable component of the pursuit of political freedom.

In China, the government's initial decontrol of the mass media was largely due to economic, not political, reasons. Unlike the inauguration of *glasnost* in the Soviet Union after 1986, the Chinese opening in the mass media in the early 1980s was aimed at reducing financial losses and not at freeing public discourse. The government slashed subsidies to media organs and allowed the introduction of market forces, including financial autonomy, management decentralization, deregulation, and diversification. At the end of 1984, all but a few periodicals had lost government support, thus forcing the magazine industry into a market environment.[14] Similar budget cuts brought about the financial independence of one-third of China's newspapers by 1992.[15] Consequently, most sectors of the Chinese media had experienced considerable penetration by market forces after a decade of economic reform.

Private and semiprivate distribution networks of printed materials rapidly gained market share at the expense of the state-controlled distribution system. By the late 1980s, private book vendors operated more than 40,000 small bookstores; collectively owned bookstores numbered 11,000, but the state-owned stores totaled about 9,000 (altogether, private and collective bookstores outnumbered the state concerns by 42,000, although state-owned stores were larger in size).[16] In 1979, state-owned Xinhua bookstores controlled 95 percent of the book retail market,[17] but by 1988, private and collective stores had gained control of nearly two-thirds of that market. The government-controlled postal system's monopoly on the distribution of newspapers and magazines fell to 42 percent by 1988 as private newsstand operators gained market dominance.[18]

Chinese publications diversified income sources and operations. Whereas the prereform Chinese press depended on government funding, media organs in the 1980s attained substantial financial independence through commercial advertising and a wide array of profitable services. Absent before reform, commercial advertising in China became a 6.7 billion yuan industry in 1992.[19] In 1990, commercial advertising revenues of 530 million yuan constituted a third of the press's income. China's print media had become the single largest outlet for commercial advertising, with a market share of 30.5 percent (compared with 26.1 percent for television networks and radio stations combined).[20]

Another structural change was the rapid institution of a privately operated supply system, which consisted of entrepreneurial agents who arranged deals between authors and government-owned but privately run publishing houses, private and semiprivate producers of newsprint, and operators of printing facilities. At the end of 1990, this system included 17,000 paper-manufacturing facilities and 8,800 printing factories in the quasi-private and private rural industrial sector.[21]

The Print Media

Generally speaking, the print media—diverse, decentralized, and penetrated by market forces—were the most self-liberalized sector in China in the 1980s. Book publishing and retailing was in turn the most self-liberalized part of the print media, and the process through which the private sector, through market forces, gained dominance in this industry illustrated the dynamics of societal takeover via economic means.

Prior to reform, state-owned publishing houses and bookstores virtually monopolized the book publishing and retail market. The government was the largest customer of Xinhua bookstores; it purchased books for its industrial enterprises, bureaucracies, schools, universities, and institutions. During the 1980s, however, the state's monopoly in this market was quickly broken, with fundamental changes in supply and demand. On the supply side, book publishing and retailing were marketized by competition from private bookstore operators who catered exclusively to private consumers, private-sector agents' penetration into government-owned publishing houses, and the rapid growth of book publishing. On the demand side, individual consumers replaced the government as the main customer of the industry. In 1977, government purchases of books exceeded those by private individuals, but by 1981, private individuals bought, in value, twice that of the government.[22] The entrepreneurship of private bookstore operators bested the state-owned bookstores, which were hobbled by bureaucratic and political restrictions that reduced their competitiveness.

For example, Xinhua bookstores were burdened by large inventories of unpopular books, mostly the works of Marx, Mao, and Chinese political leaders whom the public had little appetite for. In 1988, the Xinhua bookstores had 1.7 billion yuan worth of books in their inventories, amounting to almost 40 percent of their total sales that year. Despite this inventory-sales ratio, managers complained that nobody dared make the decision to dispose of these unsalable books.[23]

Moreover, government regulations banned Xinhua bookstores from selling books labeled "low-taste" or "pornographic," while these books were the bestsellers for private vendors, who ignored such restrictions. Xinhua bookstores were also required to maintain a minimum inventory of various types of books, regardless of their popularity. This bureaucratic requirement was not applicable to private booksellers, who kept inventory low and marketed whatever was popular.

Nor were state-owned bookstores helped by the new business freedom recently given to publishing houses. Typically, the publishing houses offered less popular books—about 90 percent of their products in terms of the number of published titles—to Xinhua bookstores for distribution. They marketed, through private retailers, the remaining 10 percent, which generated as much as 48 percent of their total revenues.

The balance sheet of Xinhua bookstores indicated their financial plight. In 1987, their revenues were 3.6 billion yuan, but they had only 130 million yuan in working capital. Many stores depended on bank loans. Unable to compete in the retail book business, some Xinhua bookstores in urban centers were converted into dance halls and restaurants, and others used most of their retail space to sell clothing, furniture, appliances, and toys. Some even rented their stores to private vendors and subsisted on rental income.[24] In contrast, profit-seeking private booksellers responded to market forces with flexibility, establishing a network that dominated the retail book market by the early 1990s. On the supply side, publishing houses were more willing to do business with private booksellers because they paid cash, whereas Xinhua bookstores purchased on credit. Private booksellers also performed the multiple role of book agents, wholesale distributors, and retail vendors. They paid higher fees to writers and translators and offered cash inducements—from several hundred yuan to 10 percent of the total sale—to publishing houses for government-issued "book numbers" (China's equivalent of ISBN, which served as a license to publish a book). Publishing houses could thus make a clean and quick profit without actually getting financially or materially involved in the process of publishing these books. Offers of money-filled "red envelopes" to printing factories got entrepreneurs' books printed first and distributed efficiently to the retail market.[25]

On the distribution side, the marketing power of private booksellers surpassed that of the Xinhua bookstores, according to a senior manager at Xinhua national headquarters. Private booksellers were capable of selling between 100,000 and hundreds of thousands of copies of the same book in a very short period, and they required as few as four months to purchase manuscripts from authors and get books on the market.[26] In Beijing, for instance, there were about 2,000 private street *shutan* (Chinese kiosks) in 1992; a typical *shutan* had about 60–100 books and magazines and more than a dozen newspapers on display. On an average day, a private *shutan* operator netted a profit of 150 yuan.[27] A large part of this profit derived from the high political and economic risks associated with operating private bookstores that served as the main conduit of illicit publications, whose suppliers routinely gave private book vendors commissions as high as 45 percent; in contrast, commissions paid by state-run book distributors and publishers never exceeded 20 percent.[28]

In the early 1980s, a rising budget deficit obliged the government to cut funds for publishing houses and tax them at 55 percent of their profits.[29] Making publishing houses responsible for employees' benefits and bonuses linked profitability with employee welfare. In the late 1980s, some previously government-run publishing houses were leased to individuals, usually in-house editors.[30] This policy motivated publishers to turn out the most profitable, rather than the most politically correct, works.

Although financial incentives were necessary, alone they were insufficient forces to self-liberalize the publishing industry. Rather, the government's 1984 deregulatory policy of permitting so-called cooperative publishing arrangements seems to have been the critical factor in self-liberalization. Cooperative publishing agreements were originally a response to the tendency of the profit-minded publishing houses to shun scholarly books and court bestsellers. The government permitted individual authors and publishing houses to enter into these agreements, in which they would share the costs of production. The bureaucrats did not, however, anticipate the private entrepreneur, who immediately saw the huge potential for profit-making in such arrangements.

Before the advent of this policy, publishing houses were responsible for the entire publishing process, from contracting authors, editing their works, finding printing factories, and marketing and distributing the products. They were also liable for financial and political risks. The private entrepreneurs capitalized on the new arrangements by taking over virtually all the functions of the publishing houses, becoming, in effect, the *de facto*, though unlicensed, publishers. They found authors, translators, or even pirated materials, and negotiated a nominal cooperative arrangement with publishing houses, paying a fixed fee or a share of proceeds for the use of government-issued book numbers or magazine identification numbers (which the publishing house had obtained free of charge from the local government agencies overseeing the publishing business). After purchasing a book number, a private entrepreneur would go to the local office of the State Administration of Commerce to receive a license to print. Entrepreneurs often paid the publisher to use its official name to make the book appear the legitimate product of the publisher.

The publishing concern would pocket the fee, while the private entrepreneur edited, designed covers, supplied illustrations, and contracted a printing factory. With the mushrooming of private and semiprivate printing factories in the countryside as part of China's rural industrialization, the printing facilities outside the government's control were easily accessible. After the books were printed, the private entrepreneurs would arrange shipping, marketing, and distribution (mainly to private vendors), thus gaining substantial control over every step in the publishing process. Even the shortage of newsprint resulting from the rapid growth of the print media did not slow the expansion of the private sector in the media. Private entrepreneurs had little difficulty in securing supplies because the government, in liberalizing the economy, had issued them licenses to buy and sell newsprint on the open market.

To understand how a government policy aimed at marketizing the economy could produce unintended consequences so devastating to its censorship of book publishing, let us review the complicated but fascinating connection between the price-liberalization of newsprint, the reforms of state-owned enterprises, and the self-liberalization of the book publishing industry.

In the mid-1980s, the government began the experiment of dual-pricing and self-marketing. Dual-pricing set two prices—one officially subsidized and the other a much higher market price—for the same goods, including newsprint. Self-marketing granted newsprint producers the right to sell a fixed portion of their products at market-determined prices without going through state-controlled distribution channels. This policy, intended to offer the producers incentives to increase output, worked to the disadvantage of the state sector because the manufacturers diverted scarce products to the open market at higher prices—typically from the government orders. In 1985, for instance, the official price for a ton of newsprint was 1,100 yuan; at this rate, the manufacturer could make a slim profit of 39.30 yuan per ton. Because the same manufacturer could get about 50 percent more on the open market, it was tempted to sell the newsprint on the market and, in fact, often did.[31]

In addition, the government directly controlled only the sixteen largest paper manufacturers in the country with its mandatory production quotas; the rest of the paper manufacturers were left to their own devices. With virtually no control over the tens of thousands of small-scale paper mills operated by private and semiprivate rural industrial firms, enormous production capacities were freed to cater to the private paper market.[32]

The impact of the limited price deregulation of the paper industry could be measured by the government's increasing inability both to find paper to print its books and to suppress the works it deemed harmful. In the first six months of 1985, for example, nearly one-sixth of the total paper produced within the government's plan was used to print what an official publication called "leisure books and unhealthy newspapers and magazines."[33] Under these astonishing circumstances, a privately controlled network of book publishing sprang into existence. Both the private entrepreneurs and the publishing houses benefited from this new arrangement, for the publishing houses assumed few financial or political risks, and the private entrepreneurs were able to produce in government-owned (and neglectfully watched) publishing houses.[34] The reach of this privately controlled commercial network could perhaps be estimated by the government's own admission, at the end of 1991, that it had shut down a major illegal publishing group that had established a distribution network in 27 of China's 30 provinces. This case involved 257 publishing houses, printing facilities, and bookstores. The ring was found to have produced 1.3 million copies of 230 different titles of "highly subversive antisocialist materials, pornographic and superstitious works."[35]

In the early 1990s, despite official campaigns and harsh penalties against illicit publications, high commercial returns continued to attract private entrepreneurs, who were even bolder than during the more relaxed mid-1980s. Rather than relying on cooperative publishing arrangements with official publishing houses, private entrepreneurs launched a new and more direct assault on state control of the print media. Without authorization, some bought the publishing permits of government-run publishing houses and newspapers to launch the first wave of private publishing houses and newspapers in China.[36] Others set up underground publishing houses or masqueraded their unlicensed publishing outfits as government-owned operations, fraudulently using the latter's names and trademarks.

Of the 108 illicit publications confiscated in Shandong Province in late 1991, 100 were published through such devices. This practice was made possible, in large part, by the proliferation of private printing facilities in China's rural industries and an extensive private book retailing network throughout the country. The director of the State Press and Publications Administration, the chief censorship official in charge of the crackdowns, admitted in late 1991 that it was difficult to cut off illegal publications at their source, because most "rural printing factories are left in a state of anarchy, and collective and private bookstores have become the major distribution channels of illegal publications."[37]

To be sure, the private invasion of the publishing industry constituted a necessary but not completely sufficient condition for political liberalization of the mass media. The immediate beneficiaries of the development of a marketized book publishing industry appeared to be mostly fans of *kungfu* novels and sexually explicit books. Nevertheless, this development provided at least one favorable condition for political liberalization in the mass media. Market forces eroded the government's control over the book publishing industry. Indeed, several politically controversial books that the government tried in vain to suppress were distributed in significant numbers, demonstrating the power of this market and its potential in future political liberalization.

Book publishing was the industry that experienced the highest level of pluralization and liberalization in China during reform. The magazine sector enjoyed the same gains, since most publishing houses also put out magazines. But what of the newspaper industry, a more important and influential sector of the print media?

The Chinese newspaper industry can be divided into two tiers: the party-controlled major dailies and the less regulated tabloid newspapers. Marketization in the newspaper sector during the 1980s was less pronounced than in the book publishing sector. Many semiofficial and unofficial newspapers came into existence during that decade. Most of them were directed at specific audiences and topics: health, culture, children, science, economy, and youth. They were typically affiliated with labor unions, women's organizations, the Youth League, research organizations, the judicial and law-enforcement agencies, and major state-owned enterprises, and there were no real privately owned or operated newspapers in China.[38] Moreover, because the Communist Party's propaganda departments at all levels still controlled the operations of most of the major newspapers (those published for cities, provinces, and the entire country), these papers had little freedom in news coverage.

The 1980s saw the influence and dominance of party-controlled newspapers decline dramatically relative to the development-driven growth of nonparty newspapers. Between 1980 and 1985, 1,008 newspapers were founded in China. Of these, only 103 were party controlled, while the overwhelming majority were specialized newspapers, evening papers, and other types over which the Communist Party organizations did not exercise direct editorial control.[39]

Although the Chinese newspaper industry as a whole experienced a threefold growth between 1981 and 1987 in its circulation per issue, market share for party-controlled papers, instead of rising, declined dramatically. In 1981, the ten largest party dailies, *People's Daily, Beijing Daily, Jiefang Daily, Tianjin Daily, Hebei Daily, Zhejiang Daily, Nanfang Daily, Xinhua Daily, Hunan Daily,* and *Heilongjiang Daily,* accounted for about 17 percent of the market share nationwide. In 1987, their share fell to about 6 percent.[40] This reveals only part of the story about the relentless pressures under which the party-controlled newspapers competed with the proliferation of nonparty newspapers. As a result of the new competition, the party-controlled newspapers reduced their propaganda content while increasing their human interest appeal and readability.

Even these figures obscure the extent of the decline of party-controlled dailies. Whereas nonparty papers enjoyed more editorial freedom and operational flexibility, party-controlled newspapers held a tremendous advantage in the steady supply of subsidized newsprint, for which most nonparty papers paid the higher market prices. Most important, party-controlled newspapers received huge indirect subsidies through government-paid subscriptions, which accounted for nearly 90 percent of the total circulation of party-controlled newspapers. About 90 percent of the subscribers to nonparty newspapers were private consumers. Without government subscriptions, the circulation of major party-controlled newspapers would have declined even further.[41]

Unlike party-operated newspapers, Chinese tabloids experienced rapid growth and followed the book publishing industry, with private entrepreneurs playing the dominant role in this often less-than-respectable business. Because most tabloids were not fully "legal," the government did not have precise data on their circulations, but there were abundant indications of the industry's vitality and its rapid ascendance in the media market. Most tabloids were published by nonparty newspapers and magazines, some were distributed through the postal system, but the majority were sold by private booksellers and newsstand operators.

The proliferation of tabloids, which focused on human interest and sensational stories, broke the monopoly of the major party newspapers. For example, prior to the 1980s, most cities and provinces had only one or two party newspapers, the exclusive channel of information in the print media. This situation quickly changed with the rise of tabloids. In 1981, the share of the officially licensed tabloids (excluding many tabloids without formal government approval) in the total newspaper circulation (per issue) was 22 percent, but this quickly tripled in three years, to 66 percent, mostly at the expense of the major party-controlled dailies.[42] The confluence of two forces—economic development and marketization—was propitious to the rise of these papers. As in the book publishing industry, the process of marketization facilitated the pluralization of the content of the newspapers.

Marketization in China's newspaper industry was manifested in the following trends during the 1980s. First, financial considerations compelled second-tier publications at city or county levels to increase their readability by popularizing their contents to attract subscribers and commercial advertising. Second, to avoid the rising costs and delays in distribution via a postal system already overburdened by the explosive growth of newspapers and magazines,[43] second-tier newspapers contracted private newsstand operators and hired their own delivery personnel. Third, those with printing facilities did jobs for other publishing companies, thus facilitating the production of books, many with contraband content, during the 1980s. In 1986, about 8 percent of the major newspapers, or 125, published tabloids, and 5 percent (83 in all) ran their own magazines.[44]

These new developments significantly marketized the newspaper industry: publishers now had a profit-motive, a deregulated but competitive business environment, diversification of operations and sources of income, and multiple distribution channels. As a result, they had, by the end of the 1980s, become less subject to political than market forces.

When an economic recession, triggered by the government-imposed austerity measures in the wake of the double-digit inflation of the late 1980s, hit China in 1988–1989, the newspaper and magazine industry went into a slump, with publications specializing in cultural and human interest stories experiencing circulation declines of 60–70 percent between 1988 and 1989 as private consumers reduced spending. Even the first-tier national newspapers saw their circulation decline by 30 percent. This drop was exacerbated by the cost of newsprint, which drove the prices of newspapers and periodicals up 100 to 300 percent in a year.[45]

The perils of the marketplace even more adversely affected the government-controlled major newspapers because of the state's limited ability to subsidize them. In the early 1990s, hampered by tight government censorship and buffeted by fierce competition from the tabloids, the major party newspapers saw their circulations plummet, advertising revenues shrink, and state subsidies dwindle. Official accounts showed that *Guangmin Ribao,* the party organ that targeted the intelligentsia as its main audience, lost nearly half its readers between 1986 and 1992 (from 1.5 million to 800,000).[46] The *People's Daily* lost 34 million yuan in 1992 alone. Even the Xinhua News Agency had seen its government subsidies reduced by 7 percent annually since 1987, with the prospect of their complete elimination.[47] Most party-controlled media organs reacted by imitating the money-making tactics of the tabloids: Xinhua issued calendars featuring scantily clad women, and national newspapers ranging from *Nongmin Ribao* (the *Peasant Daily*) to *Zhongguo Tiyubao (China Sports)* added "weekend editions" devoted largely to entertainment and sensationalist materials.[48]

The Electronic Media

Unlike the self-liberalized print media, the electronic and screen media in China experienced little marketization during the 1980s. Although the television, radio, and film industries saw similar hypergrowth and a slight relaxation of government control over their content, liberalization was not comparable to that in the print media. By the early 1990s, only a handful of movies—but not a single television program—had been produced for profit by private individuals using independently raised money.[49] On the whole, the government's censorship machine operated quite effectively during the 1980s in the television, radio, and film industries, banning any programs or movies it deemed threatening to its political control. The best example was the movie *Sun and Man,* based on Bai Hua's novella *Unrequited Love,* a powerful indictment of the communist regime's persecution of intellectuals.

A politically controversial television program such as "River Elegy" (1988), which was critical of China's Confucian heritage, inward-looking and authoritarian traditions, would not have been aired—only the personal intervention of Zhao Ziyang (then the Party's general secretary), who wanted to use the program to advance his own political agenda, saved it from the censors.[50]

The explanation for this striking difference between the print media and the electronic and screen media was the varying degrees of penetration by market forces in these sectors. The most prominent contrast between the print media and the electronic and screen media lay in the relatively low entry barrier for the former and the extremely high entry barrier for the latter. Generally speaking, entry barriers to potential competitors consist of three elements: initial capital requirements, technological threshold, and licensing procedures.

In the 1980s, although the government lifted many restrictions on book, newspaper, and magazine publishing as a result of market-oriented reforms, its licensing control in the electronic media remained unchanged. Because their enormous initial capital and technological requirements lay beyond the reach of most of China's emerging private entrepreneurs, the electronic media presented a nearly insurmountable entry barrier. Higher entry barriers blocked competition from the private sector, insulated the electronic media from market influences, and led to a lower degree of self-liberalization. The contrasting fates of a controversial movie, *Sun and Man,* and an equally controversial book, *1984,* dramatically illustrated this point. The former did not survive the censorship process; the latter, hardly affected by it, was sold openly as a work of "science fiction." This can be attributed to the structural differences between the two media sectors.

The book publishing industry was widely dispersed, with more than 500 publishing houses spread around the country. The costs of publishing a book were low, seldom exceeding tens of thousands of yuan. A license to set up a publishing company could be obtained from local government agencies. More than 60,000 bookstores, most privately owned, served as channels of distribution. The number of book titles published annually in China exceeded 65,900 in 1988, making the task of censorship impossible.

By comparison, the Chinese movie industry was heavily concentrated, with only 16 movie studios authorized to produce feature films. The average production cost of a feature film ranged from 700,000 yuan in the mid-1980s to 1.05 million yuan in 1991, thus forcing studios to seek government funding and forfeit whatever autonomy self-financing might have provided.[51] Licenses for setting up a movie studio had to be obtained from the State Council. There was only one channel of distribution for movies: the government-controlled Chinese Film Distribution Corporation. The number of feature films produced for 1988 was 158.[52]

Such factors attracted private entrepreneurs to book publishing, but discouraged them from venturing into the electronic and screen media sectors, thus allowing the censorship system to retain tight control. The government, however, had to pay dearly for its strict control of the electronic media. Highly censored television programs and films were so bad that they hardly attracted any audience. Li Ruihuan, a member of the Politburo Standing Committee in charge of propaganda, publicly complained in 1992 that China's television programs were filled with "garbage" and constituted "an insult to the audience." The Shanghai television industry, according to one official report, lost more than 100 million yuan each year on poor-quality programs that were produced but judged unworthy of broadcast.[53]

By 1993, therefore, even the electronic media—the last bastion of the state-controlled media—began to crack under the severe pressures from the newly unleashed market forces in another upsurge of China's continuing capitalist revolution. Notable developments included the establishment of financially autonomous television and radio stations that were spun off from unprofitable government stations. For example, Dongfang (Eastern) Television Station in Shanghai and Xihu Zhisheng (The Voice of the West Lake) in Hangzhou quickly became fierce rivals of the government-funded and controlled stations. Both had a much younger and smaller staff; both used innovative formats to compete for audience. Imitating American television programming, Dongfang Television introduced live news coverage of breaking stories, talk shows, call-in programs, celebrity interviews of many liberal intellectuals whom the hardliners had silenced after June 1989, and twenty-four-hour broadcasting. The adoption of live radio and television broadcast formats and the introduction of call-in programs were especially noteworthy because they rendered government censorship useless. Many callers to Dongfang Television complained about unsolved social problems (such as municipal services) and forced the city government to address them. The late-night programming of these start-up television and radio stations also expanded the scope of the permissible by featuring programs focused on such sensitive issues as sex, privacy, and other social concerns that had been largely kept out of the official electronic media.

The huge success of these experimental market-oriented television and radio stations encouraged others to follow suit. The State Press and Publications Administration revealed that in early 1993 it received dozens of applications from private interests wanting to set up similar stations. Confronted with the competitive pressures from these start-ups and embarrassed by the loss of audience, some government-funded television stations were forced to improve their programming. The Shanghai People's Television Station, the rival of Dongfang Television, launched a call-in program that had the mayor and deputy mayors of Shanghai taking calls from viewers, a significant step that granted the public direct, albeit limited, access to local politicians who were eager to enhance their own popularity.[54]

Similarly, a rising budget deficit and powerful market forces in the early

1990s compelled the Chinese authorities to begin opening the screen media. Strict official censorship in the 1980s and the post-Tiananmen crackdown on the media had resulted in huge economic costs. Between 1985 and 1990, film viewership declined by 26 percent.[55] Box-office revenues fell by 370 million yuan between 1991 and 1992. Thus, at the end of 1992, the government monopoly on the distribution of films finally ended. China's sixteen movie studios, all debtors, were granted the power to produce and distribute films and form joint ventures with overseas investors.

A significant reform measure was the decision to allow domestic distribution of some of the films jointly produced with overseas studios and directors. Typically, these touched on sensitive topics and were made by innovative young directors, the most famous being Zhang Yimou, who made *Judou* and *Raise the Red Lantern,* both Oscar nominees for best foreign-language films. With few exceptions, films produced by this new generation of directors were commercial successes in China. In 1992, more than thirty movies were produced with foreign participation, with another forty in progress. One source estimated that jointly produced films would soon capture as much as half of China's market.[56]

Foreign Influences and Self-Liberalization

In addition to market forces, an increase in foreign influence following Deng's open-door policy contributed to self-liberalization, especially in the electronic and screen media, which market forces alone were too weak to penetrate.

The principal means through which foreign influence penetrated the Chinese mass media included: (1) the expansion of foreign trade and business activities, especially the rapid growth of the tourist industry catering to overseas visitors; (2) developments in information and entertainment technology; and (3) the expansion of educational and cultural exchanges with the West. Together, these channels of penetration had reshaped the Chinese media industry by the early 1990s, making it more pluralistic in content and less subject to government censorship.

Eager for hard currency, the government singled out tourism early in China's open-door policy as a quick way to finance its development programs. Between 1980 and 1988, the tourist industry trebled its revenues. Tens of millions of overseas visitors, especially those Chinese-speaking tourists from Hong Kong, Singapore, and Taiwan, brought in and left behind a large number of books and magazines. There was no precise figure of how many foreign publications were brought into China "through the back door" during the 1980s, but at a minimal estimate of 2 books/magazines per visitor, with a total of 181 million overseas tourists (168 million of them being overseas Chinese and Chinese-speaking visitors from Hong Kong, Macao, and Taiwan) visiting China between 1982 and 1990, this figure could well be 360 million copies.[57] In this respect, although the Chinese-language publications from Taiwan and Hong Kong conceivably produced a greater impact on the masses on the mainland, the English and other Western language publications brought in by more than 10 million visitors from the West primarily influenced the Chinese elites who could read such literature in the original.

Foreign influence was further augmented by the government's policy of permitting the direct importation—"through the front door"—of major Western publications for sale in tourist hotels. Publications such as *Time*, *Newsweek*, the *Wall Street Journal*, the *Times of London*, *USA Today*, and *South China Morning Post* were sold in major tourist hotels. Closed-circuit televisions featuring Western entertainment and CNN news programs were installed in more than 700 tourist hotels. The influence of this direct infiltration by the Western mass media could be gauged by the government's decision to cut off CNN news programs and ban the sale of the above publications shortly after the Tiananmen Square crackdown in 1989.[58] The government also modified foreign investment laws to ban outsider investment in China's press, publishing, broadcasting, television, and film in a belated effort to limit foreign influence.[59]

The 1980s also saw an influx of foreign films and television programs, furthering the pluralization of content in this tightly controlled sector. Between 1979 and 1988, for example, film studios in Shanghai (mainly, the Shanghai Foreign Film Dubbing Studio) dubbed 4,702 copies of foreign feature films.[60] These became an important part of the industry, accounting for more than 10 percent of the market share in the late 1980s. In Beijing, foreign feature films gained a market share of 11.2 percent in 1988 and 12.3 percent in 1989.[61]

In addition to original language publications and movies, numerous foreign publications were translated into Chinese and widely distributed on the Chinese market in the 1980s. According to the Chinese Translators' Association, more than 28,500 books by foreign, mostly Western, authors (including more than 6,000 titles in literature) were translated into Chinese between 1978 and 1990. About 30 Chinese journals specialized in publishing translations of Western works, whereas during the 1950s, only two publishers were involved in this business. At the end of the 1980s, about 100 firms were engaged in publishing translations of foreign literature, and between 700 and 800 titles were translated and published each year in China in the early 1990s.[62]

Translations of Western works in the social sciences became available in significant quantities as well. Between 1979 and 1986, the Chinese Academy of Social Sciences (CASS) translated 2,750 books and articles from foreign sources.[63] The expansion of foreign influence in this sensitive area also facilitated the birth of political science as an academic discipline in China. From

1980 to 1987, more than 400 political science books were published, nearly 100 of them by well-known foreign writers, principally Western. *Political Science Abroad,* a journal published by the Institute of Political Science of the Chinese Academy of Social Sciences, was devoted to the publication of translations of foreign political science literature.[64]

How did this development influence Chinese readers, especially future Chinese elites? A 1990 study of Shanghai college students indicated that the scope and impact of the influx of Western ideas during the reform decade were substantial. Of the 1,862 students in 13 colleges in Shanghai, 56.6 percent said that they had read works in Western social sciences and philosophies; 43.2 percent had read Chinese translations of Sigmund Freud, Jean-Paul Sartre, and Max Weber; and 41.2 percent had read Chinese translations of Western literature.

The same study concluded that the students' values were markedly affected. For instance, 30.8 percent said that they identified with the theory of individual autonomy espoused by Existentialism; 26.9 percent identified with the ideas of democracy, liberty, and human rights in Western political theories; and about 41 percent said that China "may borrow" such Western political institutions as "checks and balances" and "parliamentary democracy."[65]

The importation of modern electronic technologies radically increased the dissemination of information to Chinese society in the 1980s. Ownership of home entertainment gadgetry skyrocketed in China, as depicted in Table 5.1. Although this table does not give the figure for the number of VCRs in Chinese urban families, it was estimated that about 7 percent of urban households had a VCR in 1991. In more developed urban areas such as Shanghai, Tianjin, Beijing, and Xiamen, more than 20 percent of the households had VCRs by 1991. In Guangzhou, the figure reached above 40 percent.[66] Nationwide, in 1989, more than 50,000 commercial "video clubs" for viewing prerecorded movies had been opened by private entrepreneurs and cultural clubs run by local governments. Estimated annual sales of VCRs exceeded 1 million after 1988 and were expected to rise to 3 million by the end of 1993.[67]

Foreign influences dominated this new media sector. Two-thirds of all prerecorded audio and video cassettes came from foreign sources, and nearly 90 percent of the video programs available in China in 1989 were imported.[68] By the early 1990s, foreign investors began to form joint ventures in the burgeoning Chinese cable television market. Wharf Holdings Ltd. of Hong Kong, for example, became the first foreign investor to receive permission to invest in this crucial market in early 1993, when it announced a plan to build a cable television system for the metropolitan Chengdu area in Sichuan Province.[69]

Because the entry barrier to the video market was relatively low, private

Table 5.1 The growth of the mass media in China, 1978–1991

	1978	1985	1988	1991
Television sets (million)	3.0	69.6	143.4	205.5
Television sets (per 100 people)	0.3	6.6	12.9	17.7
Radio receivers (million)	75.46	241.81	261.97	251.23[a]
Radio receivers (per 100 people)	7.8	22.8	23.6	22.0[a]
Cassette-players (million)	1.6	36.6	91.1	130.9
Cassette-players (per 100 people)	0.2	3.5	8.2	11.1
Titles of books published	14,987	45,603	65,961	90,156
Copies of books printed (billion)	3.77	6.67	6.22	6.20
Magazines published	930	4,705	5,865	6,109
Total printruns of magazines (billion)	0.76	2.56	2.55	2.08
Number of newspapers published[b]	69[c]	698	829	807
Total printruns of news-papers (billion)[b]	13.08	19.98	20.72	17.51

Sources: *Statistical Yearbook of China,* various years; *Digest of China's Statistical Data,*
1992, pp. 43, 112.
a. 1990 figure.
b. Only national and provincial newspapers are included here.
c. 1979 figure.

entrepreneurs quickly established a dominant presence in this new media sector, which, by the end of the 1980s, consisted of 500 registered studios that produced 600,000 prerecorded video cassettes (1,000 titles) in 1989. The rapid development and penetration by the private sector and the foreign influence in this industry frustrated government censors who repeatedly tried to monitor and control the content of the video programs.[70]

China's electronic links with the outside world were greatly expanded with the proliferation of satellite ground receiving stations in the 1980s. In 1985 the government permitted local television stations and educational and research institutions to install their own satellite ground receiving stations, and more than 16,000 were set up throughout China by the end of the decade, as shown in Table 5.2. Because it was impossible to monitor and control so many stations, employees at these stations were able to receive directly, watch, and even tape satellite-transmitted Western television programs. After the 1989 Tiananmen incident, the Ministries of State Security, of Public Security, and of Broadcasting, Film, and Television subjected all the ground stations to reregistration and penalized the unauthorized reception, dissemination, and recording of foreign television programs.[71]

Post-1989 developments in the electronic media in China, however, once again demonstrated the power of modern communications technology and the declining capacity of the state to enforce its rules and maintain its control over the flow of electronically disseminated information from foreign sources. The most compelling case here was the introduction of home satellite dishes to increasingly affluent Chinese consumers in the early 1990s. Using imported hi-tech components, Chinese manufacturers began to mass-produce home satellite dishes that sold in retail stores for 4,500 yuan (about $750) in 1992. A Beijing-based factory alone had the capacity to turn out 300,000 home satellite dishes a year.[72]

Table 5.2   The growth of television and radio broadcasting industries in China, 1980–1992

	1980	1982	1984	1986	1988	1990	1992
Television stations	38	47	93	292	422	509	591
Radio stations	106	118	167	278	461	635	812
Population reached by television broadcasting (percentage)[a]	—	57.3	64.7	71.4	75.4	79.4	—
Television ground satellite stations[b]	—	—	—	1,598	8,233	19,500	—

Sources: The Chinese Social Statistical Data, 1990, p. 255; *Statistical Yearbook of China, 1990,* p. 788; *Statistical Yearbook of China, 1991,* p. 760; *People's Daily,* February 20, 1993, p. 2.

a. Figures for 1982 and 1984 were obtained from *Almanac of China's Radio and Television, 1989* (Beijing: Beijing Broadcasting Institute Publishing Co., 1989), p. 332.

b. Excluding an estimated 4.5 million private home satellite dishes. *Almanac of China's Economy,* 1988 and 1989 (Beijing: Economic Management Publishing House). Figure for 1990 was obtained from *China Daily,* November 12, 1991, p. 1.

Despite government regulations banning private ownership of satellite dishes and the unauthorized reception of foreign satellite-transmitted programs, home satellite dishes first appeared in southern China, especially in Guangdong, and then gained popularity in other major urban centers such as Shanghai and Beijing. After a Hong Kong–based conglomerate (Hutchinson Whampoa, Ltd.) launched its Asiasat I satellite, in April 1990, to beam STAR (Satellite Television Asia Region) television programs directly to 38 countries in Asia and the Middle East (with a total population of 2.7 billion), owners of home satellite dishes in China were able to receive programs including Chinese-dubbed BBC news, American soap operas, English-language sports, films, and Music Television (MTV). One reliable official source estimated that more than 4.8 million households (as many as 25 million people) in China in 1992 could receive STAR television programs, despite the fact that the Ministry of Broadcast and Television had issued a document in 1991 explicitly banning the private reception of such programs.[73] Alarmed by this loss of control, the Chinese government attempted to ban the sale of the dishes, but to no avail. In most instances, retailers and private consumers simply ignored the ban.[74]

How should we assess the *political* impact of this penetration by foreign influences in the Chinese mass media? The infiltration of liberal Western ideas undermined official doctrines. Simultaneously, it legitimized liberal democratic values, giving ideological support to the fledgling prodemocracy movement among the urban intelligentsia. Supplying the intellectual ammunition with which the existing communist-authoritarian political system could be attacked, it furnished a vision for an alternate system of government. Larry Diamond observed that foreign influence could help foster "pluralism and autonomy in organizational life and the flow of information" and constitute "the social and cultural foundation for democracy . . . Because it is one step removed from the distribution of state power, it is less immediately threatening, thus somewhat more palatable, to authoritarian rulers than explicit demands for their withdrawal from power."[75]

Rapid Economic Growth and Self-Liberalization

As media technologies grew more diversified, sophisticated, and decentralized with the introduction of audio, video, and new telecommunications technologies such as cable television, fax machines, and cellular telephones, the regime became incapable of maintaining control over the information flow.[76] The proliferation of new, instantaneous communications technologies sped up the flow of information both within China and between China and the West. By 1991, for instance, government figures showed that more than 80,000 companies, institutions, and government "units" had fax machines, with projections of an additional 10,000 each year. This technology ultimately was made available to the Chinese public in post offices.[77]

At the same time, the political impact of the self-liberalization was magnified by the accelerated spread of television to urban and rural households. The controversial television series "River Elegy" (1988) could not have aroused a national debate over Chinese culture and development had television dissemination been at the level of the preceding decade.

The expansion of the reach of the mass media during the 1980s in general, and the unprecedented growth of the electronic media in particular, were catalysts for the self-liberalization of the Chinese mass media. In 1982, for example, barely more than half the population had access to television broadcasts (Table 5.2). In 1990, the figure rose to 80 percent. As the number of television stations grew from 38 in 1980 (about 1 for each province) to 591 in 1991, almost every urban household had a television set by the end of the decade. In rural areas in 1980 there was only 1 television set for every 250 households. By 1989, however, one-third of all rural households had a black and white television set and 3 percent had a color television set.[78] In urban areas, the early 1990s saw the advent of cable television in ordinary Chinese homes. Official sources showed that, at the beginning of 1993, 505 cable television companies had received government permission to operate, and more than 15 million households had cable television service.[79]

As Table 5.2 shows, by 1990 the Chinese electronic media (radio and television) were approaching the midway mark of the level reached by the more developed Soviet Union and several Eastern European countries in 1980; they had attained the same level as moderately developed communist states such as Romania and Bulgaria, although China's per capita GNP was less than a quarter of that of most Eastern European countries and the Soviet Union.[80]

Early Mobilization of the Intelligentsia

Penetration by private-sector forces, extensive marketization, and the foreign influence on the Chinese mass media during the 1980s coincided with the rising assertiveness of the Chinese intelligentsia. These developments had, by the early 1990s, profoundly changed the three aspects of the mass media—medium, message, and messenger.

Like the profit-seeking entrepreneurs who debilitated much of China's censorship system shortly after market forces were allowed to penetrate the mass media, the liberal intelligentsia seized the opportunity to maximize their political influence in this critical sector. They were primarily responsible for the periodic waves of political liberalization in the Chinese media that had shaken the regime since the late 1970s.

Altogether, there were five waves of "ground-up" liberalization of the mass media between 1978 and 1993. The first, known as the Democracy Wall movement (1978–1979), saw a brief flourishing of unofficial publications such as *Tansuo (Exploration)* and *Beijing Zichun (Beijing Spring)*; it coincided with an intraelite debate over the criteria of truth that precipitated the ideological defeat of holdovers from the Mao regime, headed by Hua Guofeng, and led to the rise of the pragmatist-reformist Deng regime at the end of 1978.

The second wave (1982–1983) featured a discussion of alienation in socialist societies and ended with the conservative backlash known as the "anti-spiritual-pollution campaign." During the third wave, 1985–1986, often called the "golden years of reform," there was a dramatic increase in the openness of political debate, especially over the issue of democratization as a means to overcome conservative resistance to economic reform. This wave differed from earlier debates, for it achieved a confluence between the ground-up and the top-down trends of liberalization in the media, with some key leaders, most notably the CCP's secretary general, Hu Yaobang, and its propaganda chief, Zhu Houze, apparently supporting the intelligentsia by placing the issue of democratization on the national agenda. This period ended with the hardliners' counterattack—the "anti-bourgeois-liberalism campaign"—against the student-led demonstrations that rocked China in December 1986 and January 1987. Both Hu and Zhu were purged.

The fourth wave of ground-up liberalization, between the summer of 1988 and the spring of 1989, ended with the Tiananmen Square massacre. Despite the political setback suffered by the liberal forces following the fall of Hu Yaobang and the launching of the antibourgeois liberalism campaign in early 1987, the intelligentsia had recovered and revived the trends of ground-up political liberalization in the Chinese media. At that time, three issues dominated the debate in the media concerning the future direction of reform: privatization, Chinese political culture and its Confucian heritage, and democratic and neoauthoritarian models of development. Although Zhao Ziyang, the moderate secretary general of the CCP, appeared to have played a role in securing the public release of the controversial television series "River Elegy," which criticized the Chinese Confucian heritage and blamed it for China's economic backwardness, liberal Chinese intellectuals were responsible for broaching some of the most sensitive topics in Chinese political discourse. This fourth wave peaked with the prodemocracy movement in the spring of 1989, when the government briefly lost control of its official media during the Tiananmen Square demonstrations in mid-May; it ended in June after the regime launched its post-Tiananmen assault on the media and the prodemocracy movement.

After the tragic setback of the prodemocracy movement in 1989, many leading intellectuals were jailed, exiled, or silenced. But, despite widespread pessimism about the prospects for democratization in China, the opposition movement that survived the post-Tiananmen crackdown demonstrated its resiliency by launching what appeared to be the fifth wave in late 1992. Like earlier waves of ground-up liberalization in the media, the fifth wave gathered momentum when the Chinese intelligentsia seized upon an economic opening, this time following Deng's tour of southern China in January 1992.

Ostensibly implementing Deng's call for combating hardline extremism, Chinese liberals produced books and articles attacking leftist extremism and demanding democratic reforms, media liberalization, and the protection of human rights.[81] *The Trends of History (Lishi Dechaoliu), Memoranda on Anti-Leftism (Fangzuo Beiwanglu),* and *The Disasters Caused by Leftism in China (Zhongguo Dezuohuo)* were the most notable examples. The first two were edited volumes containing essays by liberal intellectuals whose writings had been banned after Tiananmen; *The Disasters Caused by Leftism in China* was generated by a group of researchers with access to classified materials in the CCP's Office for the Study of Party History, the CCP's Research Office of the Party's Historical Documents, and the Chinese Academy of Social Sciences. It chronicled more than 200 instances of leftist extremism in the CCP's history: the slaughter of more than 10,000 individuals branded as members of the "AB League"—an anticommunist organization that had allegedly infiltrated the CCP—in the 1930s; the massacre of thousands of landlords and rich peasants in Hunan during the Cultural Revolution; the mistreatment of political prisoners in Beijing's notorious Qingcheng Prison.[82]

Unlike earlier waves of ground-up liberalization, the fifth wave was assisted by private-sector operators in the mass media and the inexorable forces of marketization unleashed in 1992. For instance, although the authorities quickly banned *The Trends of History* and *Memoranda on Anti-Leftism,* copies were sold in private bookstores; some of the essays by the most outspoken critics of the government were excerpted in tabloids and newspapers.[83] At the same time, China's beleaguered censors faced an unprecedented assault from resurgent purveyors of pornographic materials and "unauthorized" and often damaging biographies of former and current leaders of the Communist Party (37 titles were issued by 27 publishers in 1992). Further overwhelming China's decrepit censorship apparatus was the accelerated marketization of what remained of the official press through joint ventures with foreign investors and private-sector operators, the proliferation of tabloids, and the appearance of 2 new papers every 5 days and more than 400 new journals in 1992.[84]

During the five brief waves, Chinese intellectuals espoused three principal strategies to further political liberalization: takeover, attack on the periphery, and expositions of official corruption. A "takeover" by liberal-radical journalists of several newspapers and publications not directly affiliated with the Communist Party occurred in China during the 1980s. The Shanghai-based *World Economic Herald, Democracy and Law* (a monthly), and the Beijing-based *Science and Technology Daily, New Observer,* and *Chinese Youth* became the most vociferous advocates of reform during the 1980s. A "benign" Deng policy to rehabilitate the victims of Mao's Anti-rightist Campaign of 1957 produced an unintended boomerang effect against the regime. Because many of the former "Rightists" (a political label branded on mostly liberal intellectuals who criticized the CCP in 1957's Hundred Flowers Movement) were journalists, editors, and writers, they were allowed to return to their previous jobs as part of the rehabilitation program.

Years of persecution and hardship did not eradicate the fervor for political liberalization in at least some of the former Rightists. Liu Binyan, the investigative reporter, used his position as a senior reporter for the *People's Daily* to expose massive official corruption. Sun Changjiang, another former Rightist, transformed the *Science and Technology Daily* into a proreform forum. Ge Yang, yet another rehabilitated former Rightist, as editor of the *New Observer* advanced liberal causes. Qin Benli became editor-in-chief of the *World Economic Herald,* which played an activist proreform role unmatched by any other publication in China.[85] The generational change in the rank and file of the news organizations precipitated the rise of younger and more liberal journalists and editors, most evident in newly established papers. For instance, the average age of journalists at the *World Economic Herald* at its inception was 63 years, but this was soon reduced to 38 years upon the recruitment of 40 younger reporters and editors. More than half of the editorial board was staffed by people in their midthirties.[86]

Using these public forums, liberal journalists, writers, and social scientists adopted the tactic of "attacking on the periphery"—addressing sensitive political issues that lay in gray areas, and for which the regime had set no explicit restrictions. To use an apt analogy made by Qin Benli, this tactic was like hitting the ping-pong ball to the edge of the table. In his own words, this involved "pushing our coverage to the limit of the tolerance of the government while reducing the political risks for the paper to the lowest level."[87] The peripheral issues were, in fact, most fundamental: press freedom, private property, privatization, and humanism. But, because some of the regime's reform programs were rhetorically committed to these goals, public discussion entailed reduced political risk, absent a conservative crackdown.

Access to the public forum enabled liberals to expose official corruption and injustice, prominent features of Deng's postcommunist authoritarian regime. Always sensitive to exposure, the regime had formerly allowed journalists to write "internal memos" on official corruption and the abuse of power, to be seen only by senior party and government officials. During the reform decade, however, assertive journalists and editors, confronting cases of official corruption and injustice, brought them into the open in order to damage the regime's image.

*   *   *

The self-liberalization of the mass media in China illustrates the perils implicit in a regime transition that reformed an economic system without moving toward polyarchy. Once a communist regime embarks on economic reforms, it is extremely difficult, if not impossible, to control the spillover effects. Unintended consequences of economic-oriented policies result in the state's loss of resources to society and its declining ability to set the political agenda.

By the early 1990s, the transfer of media resources from the state to society had deprived the Communist Party of its monopoly on propaganda. The media had become, instead, an instrument shared by the state and society. A media infrastructure, capable of contributing to future political liberalization, had come into existence in China. The regime inaugurated its reform program at the end of the 1970s with full confidence in its ability to control the process of change in general, and the mass media in particular. But, after the crackdown of June 1989, government officials publicly lamented that "the erroneous guidance provided by the media and propaganda was one of the major reasons aggravating the [prodemocracy movement]."[88]

Two crucial questions—one theoretical and the other practical—remain to be addressed: (1) How well does the analytical framework of societal takeover explain the self-liberalization of the media? and (2) How solid were the resource gains for society?

The market-driven transformation in the Chinese mass media validated the logic of societal takeover during reform. Most of the factors central to this process were instrumental in transferring media resources from the state to society. The economic openings, whether created by market forces or government policy, enabled private entrepreneurs and liberal journalists to obtain resources and expand their influence, first in the print media and later in the electronic media. In this process, both groups were assisted by external sources that supplied books, magazines, music, video programs and films, television sets, VCRs, and satellite dishes.

Although private entrepreneurs and the liberal Chinese intelligentsia did not form any takeover coalition in name, the market forces introduced into the media by private entrepreneurs aided intellectuals in circumventing government censorship despite the intelligentsia's negligible contribution to the marketization process of the mass media. The marketized and modernized Chinese mass media magnified the impact of the ground-up liberalization launched by the intelligentsia. With each upsurge in the level of marketization in the mass media, successive waves of spontaneous liberalization exponentially increased, each producing a greater political impact than the previous wave. For example, the earlier waves of ground-up liberalization did not reach beyond Beijing, Shanghai, and a handful of major cities, but the later waves, especially between 1988 and 1989, shook the entire nation.

The self-liberalization of the mass media benefited, ironically but predictably, from the accelerated institutional decay of the state. The government-controlled media organs such as major party newspapers and state-owned Xinhua bookstores were noncompetitive and incapable of adapting to new market conditions. Their political influence in the mass media ebbed while the red ink in their financial books flowed. Similarly, rapid technological developments outstripped the state's capacity for rule-enforcement and rendered obsolete its traditional methods of information control. Censorship agencies, once a fearsome instrument of the party-state, were completely unable to combat hundreds of thousands of profit-seeking entrepreneurs whose extensive networks had undermined the economic foundations of the state's system of information control.

The Chinese government was aware of having lost control of the mass media. Waves of crackdowns and an ever-increasing number of official regulations imposed on the new mass media demonstrated the state's concerns and counteroffensive (it issued 22 documents devoted solely to the reregulation of the media between 1985 and 1989, with 11 in 1989 alone).[89] In the wake of the collapse of communism in Eastern Europe in late 1989, the government intensified its efforts to rein in the mass media, fearful that it was being undermined by "peaceful evolution"—its code word for Western cultural and ideological infiltration. This campaign escalated after the failed coup in Moscow in August 1991. One government publication, the *Beijing Daily,* declared on September 20 that it would be "suicidal if China did not resist the West's peaceful evolution."[90] Available current evidence in the early 1990s indicated that, although the state was successful in silencing liberal intellectuals through direct coercion, it failed to reverse market forces in the mass media.

Repeated campaigns against illegal publications found impregnable an increasingly complex, well-integrated, and rapidly growing media infrastructure which comprised tens of thousands of retail outlets, paper-manufacturing facilities, and printing factories in the quasi-private and private rural industrial sector. Too vast for the authorities to monitor and too deeply entrenched to be uprooted, it enabled unofficial publications to thrive in the 1990s, despite government crackdowns. Of 140 confiscated publications in Sha'anxi Province in late 1991, the authorities found that 129 were "illegal publications." In another spot check of 111 publications in Tianjin, also conducted in late 1991, the authorities found that 108 were "illegal."[91] In 1992, despite several intensive campaigns, millions of copies of "subversive publications" were found and confiscated, an indication of the government's failure to control underground publications.[92]

As the credibility of government-controlled and censored media organs remained low, the Chinese audience and readership continued to seek alternative sources of information, both foreign and domestic. A classified government document from late 1991 warned that official radio stations were losing their audience to hostile Western programs; it complained that "people in certain border areas have turned to foreign radio broadcast programs and stopped tuning to the Central People's Radio Broadcast programs."[93] In Guangzhou, for example, residents used highly visible outdoor television antennas to receive Hong Kong programs despite official bans, and Hong Kong television guides were sold on the streets.[94] An internal opinion survey of 3,000 journalists conducted by the Research Institute of the Media of the People's University in Beijing in 1991 revealed that 88 percent expressed dissatisfaction with the government's management of the media; 79 percent said that the credibility of the media and propaganda was "mediocre, fairly low, and very low among the people." Seventy-nine percent complained that "there is too much official restriction on news coverage in the media," and 68 percent said that the official news media "do not tell the truth on sensitive issues."[95] Portending new waves of intelligentsia-driven press liberalization should the political climate improve, this was an ominous sign for the government's role in the mass media.

This may suggest that the resource gains made by society in the mass media were both considerable and secure. However, they were unevenly distributed between the two main societal groups. The private entrepreneurs took the larger and more concrete share, and the intelligentsia, lacking direct control, relied on indirect assistance from the private entrepreneurs and occasional direct political support from a few top liberal elites, their patrons inside the ruling hierarchy.

What, then, are the long-term political implications of this combination of an intelligentsia capable of influencing public opinion and a mass media deeply penetrated by market forces? A semipluralistic media infrastructure had consolidated in China and should be viewed as favorable for future political liberalization. However, despite the contribution by the marketization process and the periodic queue-jumping by the intelligentsia, this dual process will not itself accomplish a rapid transition to democracy. The democratic breakthrough must occur first in the political sphere proper, when the top leadership shifts its priorities from economic development to democratization. In the event that a democratic breakthrough should occur in China after the completion of the capitalist revolution, the marketized media will facilitate the transition to and consolidation of new democratic institutions.

The Liberal Takeover of the Soviet Mass Media under *Glasnost*

6

U nlike the Chinese case, the opening of the Soviet media between 1985 and 1991 resulted from a regime-initiated program of political liberalization, which was quickly taken over by radical social forces. In the *glasnost* era, the forces responsible for the opening in the media were composed of three groups—reformers inside the regime, leading elements of the intelligentsia, and organized radical social movements. The ascendance and decline of the first group, the rise of the other two groups, and their takeover of the Soviet mass media offer a fascinating account of the radicalization of reform.

During the opening phase (1985–1987) the top reformers, chiefly Gorbachev and his supporters inside the CPSU, initiated changes by replacing conservative editors with liberal intellectuals, who proceeded to mobilize other members of the intelligentsia in advancing *glasnost*. During the second phase, the Big Surge (1988–1989), the liberals built up their own mass support base with a huge audience and immense popularity, while the reformers grew uneasy about the radicalization of the media. The newspapers, magazines, and television programs taken over by the liberals were gradually transformed into media institutions identified with *glasnost*. Mass support enabled the liberals to advance aggressively their own political agenda, even at the expense of their patrons inside the regime. Independent radical social movements began to emerge, penetrating the media with their own publications.

During the third phase (1990) liberal forces solidified their gains as part of the institutionalization of democratization under *glasnost,* and they began to defect from moderates to join the radical reformers who had splintered from the original reform coalition. These elements, coalescing into radical social and nationalist movements, formed a nascent takeover coalition and undermined the moderate reformers, forcing them to seek a temporary alliance with the conservatives.

The fourth phase (late 1990 and early 1991) was marked by this moderate-conservative coalition's unsuccessful counterattack against the liberal-dominated media. The liberal forces, having consolidated their gains, were impossible to dislodge, and the counterattack predictably fizzled out. The makeshift countertakeover coalition collapsed when confronted with strong resistance from the takeover coalition forces that had, by the middle of 1991, gained political power in many Soviet republics and local governments.

The failed coup in August 1991 marked the formal ascendance of the liberal media to supremacy, most prominently in Russia and the Baltics. The media's relationship with the new democratic government, however, was ambiguous and uneasy. The press thus continued its struggle for full autonomy, having gained political freedom but not economic independence.

The Takeover in Five Phases

The Initial Opening

The liberalization of the mass media was the defining characteristic of Gorbachev's *glasnost*. The remarkable speed with which the liberalization progressed was due to the convergence of liberal intellectuals and centrist reformers. The two groups shared an interest in opening the mass media, but they had different long-term reform agendas. Following the ascendance of the reformers to the top leadership of the regime, liberal intellectuals saw, in the initial reform opening, an opportunity to expand press freedom as the first step toward the democratization of the Soviet Union. Thus, in launching *glasnost,* Gorbachev merely tapped into the immense reservoir of political entrepreneurship of the intelligentsia—in the same way that Deng Xiaoping freed the immense entrepreneurship of the Chinese peasantry in initiating economic reform.

Meanwhile, the reformers, stymied in their economic reform, hoped to borrow the resources of this permanent counterelite to create some momentum of change and overcome opposition to *perestroika*. In early 1987, Gorbachev declared that *glasnost* should serve the interest of his economic *perestroika* and the Communist Party. "The main task of the press is to help the nation understand and assimilate the ideas of restructuring, to mobilize the masses to struggle for successful implementation of party plans . . . We need . . . *glasnost,* criticism, and self-criticism in order to implement major changes in all spheres of social life . . . but criticism should reflect the interests of the party."[1]

Thus, Soviet reformers formed an alliance with liberal intellectuals and provided them with "start-up capital" (access to government-controlled media). This instrumentalist approach to democratization had its drawbacks: temporary convergence of the two forces obscured the long-term conflict implicit in their goals; moderate reformers routinely overestimated their ability to control the newly mobilized social group and were seldom aware of the ramifications of this initiative.

Except for appointing liberals to key media positions and politically protecting them at the outset, the top reformers failed systematically to dismantle the institutions of censorship. Gorbachev did not seek the passage of the press law early during *glasnost* to institute legal protection of press freedom. He did not abolish censorship agencies such as Glavlit (the Chief Administration for the Protection of State Secrets in the Press). Also intact were other components of the Soviet censorship machine, such as Soyuzpechat (the All-Union Agency for the Distribution of Periodicals), Goskomizdat (the State Committee for Publishing Houses, Printing Plants, and the Book Trade), the Ministry of Culture, Gosteleradio (the State Committee for Television and Radio), and the Union of Journalists.

The principal force that destroyed the Soviet system of censorship came from the liberal intelligentsia. When the press law finally went into effect, in August 1990, the print media had already enjoyed, *de facto,* much of the freedom the new law was to provide. This development was in marked contrast with the stagnation of the Soviet private sector, despite an initial spate of legislation drafted to foster its growth. The contrast underscores that the direction and progress of reforms depend mostly on the ability of societal forces to seize the initial small opening and make a breakthrough.

The personal commitment of the top leaders was a necessary condition to political liberalization. Few authoritarian regimes inaugurated peaceful transitions when this was absent. In the Soviet case, Gorbachev demonstrated his personal commitment by appointing liberal writers and journalists to the editorships of major publications. His advisor Alexander Yakovlev, having gained control of the Propaganda Department of the CPSU Central Committee in July 1985, engineered a minitakeover of the Soviet print media in 1986, indicating a substantial expansion of *glasnost* following the 27th Congress of the CPSU in February–March 1986, a turning point in the evolution of Gorbachev's reforms. Yakovlev, more directly responsible for the execution of *glasnost* than Gorbachev, became its driving force during the early phases of press liberalization.[2]

Most of the new key media appointments were made in the summer of 1986. Yakovlev chose Vitaly Korotich, a liberal Ukrainian writer, as the chief editor of *Ogonek* in June 1986.[3] Yegor Yakovlev took over the editorship of *Moscow News* in August 1986. Grigoriy Baklanov was appointed editor of *Znamya,* and Sergey Zalygin, *Novy mir.* As the first party secretary of Moscow, Boris Yeltsin picked a liberal journalist, Mikhail Poltoranin, to be the editor-in-chief of *Moskovskaya pravda* in 1986. This minitakeover also occurred in other sectors of the mass media. In May 1986, Yakovlev nominated Yelem Klimov, a liberal film director, for the post of first secretary of the Board of the USSR Cinematographers Union. After taking office, Klimov released more than 30 previously banned films, including *Repentance* and *Road Checks*.[4]

Once these publications were taken over by liberals, they became powerful public forums for reform and rapidly gained popularity. Before Korotich assumed the editorship of *Ogonek*, it was a lackluster illustrated weekly, with a circulation of 230,000 in 1986. But this figure rose by 600 percent within a year, as Korotich transformed the paper into the flagship of *glasnost. Moscow News*, a weekly run by the Union of Soviet Societies for Friendship and Cultural Relations with Foreign Countries and Novosti Press Agency, had a tiny circulation of its Russian edition (125,000 in 1986); it doubled in the year after Yegor Yakovlev became editor, and would have risen higher had the Central Committee of the CPSU not limited its Russian edition.[5] The circulation of the weekly *Argumenty i fakty*, 1.4 million in 1985, rose to 3.5 million in 1987 and 32 million in 1989 after Vladislav Starkov was appointed editor in 1986, making it the largest publication in the Soviet Union.[6]

These liberal publications inspired the rest of the mass media to join the trend, resulting in a chain reaction of escalating liberalization. Consequently, the circulation of these liberal publications soared, while that of the first-tier, party-controlled press plummeted. This development forced other government-controlled publications, such as *Izvestia*, to become more open to keep their readership from defecting to the liberal press. Even the CPSU-controlled publications such as *Kommunist* and *Pravda* were compelled to relax editorial policies during the late 1980s.

During the initial stage of *glasnost*, the support of the top leaders enabled the liberal publications to test the limits and broaden the boundaries of the political opening. For instance, *Ogonek*'s Korotich claimed that Gorbachev had provided him with a phone to "call anyone."[7] Gorbachev's personal support for the initial opening was also evident in his memo to the Politburo in November 1985:

> We are particularly in need of objective information that depicts not what we would like to hear, but what really is . . . more concrete analysis of current developments, more fresh proposals . . . [There should be] room for criticism and self-criticism, especially for criticism from below. Only in this way and in such an atmosphere will we be able to avoid major miscalculations in our policy and practical work.[8]

At the same time, reformers attempted to restrain the repressive agencies of the state by selectively punishing lower-level officials who intimidated the press. The well-publicized case of the dismissal of a senior KGB officer in Voroshilovgrad in January 1987 for persecuting an investigative reporter was a deterrent to the brutal use of censorship.[9]

In other media sectors, the government began to take tentative steps toward opening. In April 1986, the Ministry of Culture decided to end censorship of 60 of the nation's 600 theaters.[10] Goskomizdat abolished mandatory internal reviews of manuscripts for publication in early 1988.[11] In 1987 a government commission was formed to review more than 6,000 banned books by Soviet and foreign authors. By March 1988, about 3,500 titles—of the 4,000 reviewed—were cleared for public release.[12] But these measures contributed marginally to *glasnost,* as most editors and journalists did not wait for instructions from above before printing material.

The relationship between Gorbachev and *glasnost* was full of contradictions and complexities. Gorbachev clearly had a narrow conception of *glasnost,* and one different from that of the liberal intelligentsia. Between 1985 and 1989, in his numerous meetings with editors and journalists, he repeatedly emphasized that *glasnost* was to serve his own political agenda, rather than that of the liberal intelligentsia. At one meeting in July 1987, Gorbachev announced the limits for *glasnost:* "*Glasnost* and democracy do not mean that everything is permitted. *Glasnost* is called upon to strengthen socialism and the spirit of our people, to strengthen morality . . . *Glasnost* also means criticism of shortcomings but it does not mean the undermining of socialism and our socialist values."[13]

Gorbachev's plan that *glasnost* would be managed and limited to suit his own agenda turned out to be a gross miscalculation. In the end, *glasnost* not only undermined socialism and socialist values, but directly contributed to the disintegration of the Soviet Union. Once the opening was created, the liberal intelligentsia imposed their own agenda on *glasnost,* transforming it from a regime-sponsored partial opening into a societally dominated process of full-fledged liberalization.

In the Soviet Union, large numbers of intellectuals who had resisted the old regime's attempts at domination constituted the mainstay of the pre-Gorbachev dissident movement.[14] They had been the driving force during the brief Thaw under Khrushchev in the late 1950s and early 1960s. Strategically positioned inside the media and capable of instant mobilization, they had access to considerable resources, including celebrity status and influence in the media. Unlike Gorbachev's *perestroika,* to which no major social groups responded aggressively and resourcefully, *glasnost* quickly generated its own momentum and was driven into the forbidden zone by the liberal intelligentsia.

Many leaders during the opening phase of *glasnost* were veterans of the Thaw, including Fyodor Burlatsky, a former speech writer for Khrushchev who became the political commentator for *Literaturnaya gazeta* and its editor-in-chief after 1990.[15] The poet Yevgeniy Yevtushenko, a major figure during the Thaw, was an outspoken champion of *glasnost.* Former junior associates of Alexander Tvardovsky, the liberal editor of *Novy mir* in the 1960s, also spearheaded *glasnost*. Vitaly Korotich, editor-in-chief of *Ogonek*, had worked under Tvardovsky at *Novy mir*. Several other writers and critics who had worked under Tvardovsky joined Korotich at *Ogonek* in 1986.[16]

The push from above, by itself, seldom provided the "liberating" momentum required for the rise of a self-sustaining social movement. A simultaneous response from below was needed for the Big Surge to materialize. Yevgeniy Yevtushenko claimed that *glasnost* was not a gift from above, but the result of many years of struggle by the Soviet intelligentsia despite official oppression.[17] The Soviet intellectuals' response to *glasnost* consisted of a frontal assault on the legitimating myth, existing institutions, and systemic failures of the communist system.

Loath to reopen historical wounds that would discredit the communist regime, Gorbachev did not completely endorse the renewed attack on Stalinism at the start of *glasnost*. At a meeting with Soviet writers, he reportedly said, "If we start trying to deal with the past, we will dissipate our energy."[18] His conservative colleague Yegor Ligachev shared Gorbachev's concern. Upon learning of Gorbachev's reference to Stalin's acts as "criminal" in the draft of his celebrated November 1987 speech commemorating the 70th anniversary of the bolshevik revolution, Ligachev bluntly warned him, "This would mean canceling our entire lives. We are opening the way for people to spit on our history."[19]

While the de-Stalinization campaign severely eroded the legitimacy of the communist regime, the newly liberalized press engaged in another campaign to expose official corruption, bureaucratic inefficiency, waste, and social problems illustrative of the failures of the system. Inevitably, the liberal press began to challenge the moderate reform program espoused by Gorbachev himself—by demanding rapid democratization and an end to the CPSU's monopoly of power.

Editors-in-chief of the liberal publications played an instrumental role in the dismantling of the Soviet censorship institutions. Under Yegor Yakovlev, *Moscow News* became the first Soviet publication to appear without a censor's approval stamp when it published the embarrassing story of Mathias Rust's landing in Red Square in 1987. With Korotich's support, *Ogonek* ran a powerful investigative series on the war in Afghanistan, which helped turn the Soviet public against the war. Ivan Laptev, editor-in-chief of *Izvestia*, transformed the newspaper of the USSR Supreme Soviet into a liberal publication that carried numerous articles critical of the government. For this reason, Laptev was replaced in May 1990, when the government found him too liberal and *Izvestia* was accused of serving "as a mouthpiece for the [opposition] Interregional Group of Deputies."[20]

These editors-in-chief also found strong supporters among the lower strata of the intelligentsia. Another aspect of societal *glasnost* was the contribution made by the junior members of the press to the elimination of censorship. *Ogonek*'s Korotich observed that when he took over the magazine, he was intrigued by the unrestrained conversations among his junior colleagues in the corridors. The same people who conversed fearlessly in the hallways, however, returned to their offices and produced the most boring magazine in the USSR. To bring this societal *glasnost* into the open, Korotich simply declared that he would not accept any articles that *Ogonek*'s staff would not talk about at home or in the hallways.[21]

Together, liberal editors and junior journalists escalated *glasnost* from below, producing fierce competition among liberal publications to be on the leading edge of the movement. The forbidden zone for the press, previously defended by self-imposed censorship and official coercion, rapidly shrank as journalists ended self-censorship, and the regime, restrained from overt repression by the need to project an aura of political openness, tolerated the media's transgressions. Thus, *Literaturnaya gazeta* published, with impunity, the first interview with Andrey Sakharov in January 1987, after the famous dissident was released from internal exile. Other major Soviet journals soon printed previously banned works: in March 1987, *Oktyabr'* published the poet Anna Akhmatova's "Requiem" collection; *Druzhba narodov* and *Neva* published previously banned anti-Stalinist works;[22] *Ogonek* prominently carried a long interview with the widow of Nikolai Bukharin and her letter to Gorbachev in November 1987, paving the way for her husband's eventual rehabilitation.[23]

Another force in societal *glasnost* was the traditional antiregime elements—Soviet dissidents outside the media establishment. Their principal contribution was the revival and proliferation of the unofficial press during *glasnost*. To build support for *glasnost* and seek reconciliation with the radical intelligentsia, Gorbachev granted amnesty to most political prisoners in 1987. This benign initiative produced unintended and undesirable consequences. Many former political prisoners, ultraradicals who had been punished for publishing *samizdat* materials (underground publications with small circulations), quickly resumed their trade after regaining freedom.

One of the first *samizdat* publications to appear was the magazine *Glasnost,* published by a former political prisoner, Sergey Grigoryants, in July 1987. Despite constant police harassment and attacks by *Pravda*, *Glasnost* prospered.[24] Other major *samizdat* publications included *Nashe delo* and *Grazhdanskiy referendum,* both published by former political prisoners. With a circulation of 60,000–100,000 in 1990, the 2 papers were used as the outlet of the radical Moscow Popular Front.[25] Similar *samizdat* publications proliferated all over the Soviet Union.

The rise of *samizdat* in the late 1980s was a useful indicator of the autonomous political mobilization of the radical forces during *glasnost*. In 1987, only 10–20 *samizdat* publications were distributed in the entire Soviet Union; by 1989, there were 548 *samizdat* publications in the Russian Federation alone.[26] The increase in political parties and organizations led to the mushrooming of unofficial publications, with the number of Russian-language *samizdat* materials reaching 700–1,000 in early 1991.[27] In 1989, reflecting the government's alarm at the spread of informal groups and their independent publications, *Pravda* warned that "certain independent publications are engaged not in concrete deeds and support for *perestroika* but . . . in the persistent propagation of anticommunist and anti-Soviet views."[28]

The Big Surge

The breakthrough in the print media led the initial opening. During the Big Surge phase (1988–1989), societal *glasnost* continued on a wide front and was characterized by the rapid increase in the market share by liberal publications. The initial media gains were consolidated in the Big Surge phase with phenomenal quantitative increases in the volume, coverage, and circulation of the liberal press. During this phase, the societal takeover in the media assumed four forms: (1) quantitative expansion; (2) institutionalization; (3) radicalization; and (4) extension to other media sectors.

Except for *Trud*, all conservative party-controlled publications lost circulation to liberal publications. *Pravda*'s circulation dropped from 11 million in 1986 to 3.2 million in 1991.[29] The circulation data for major Soviet publications in Table 6.1 indicates the radically changed structure of the print media and the circulation gains by liberal publications between 1987 and 1990.

As a group, the 5 largest conservative publications controlled by the government—*Pravda, Sovetskaya rossiya, Trud, Selskaya zhizn,* and *Sotsialisticheskaya industriya*—lost 2.6 million subscribers between 1987 and 1989. The 6 largest liberal publications—*Argumenty i fakty, Literaturnaya gazeta, Komsomolskaya pravda, Novy mir, Ogonek,* and *Moskovskie novosti*—gained 26 million subscribers in the same period. If the circulation of *Izvestia* were included in this group, the gains by the liberal media would be even more impressive.

After first gaining access to the media through the sponsorship of the top reformers, liberal editors gradually developed their own mass-based support and transformed their publications into *de facto* independent media institutions, regarded by the Soviet population as public forums and channels of direct political participation. Writing outspoken letters-to-the-editor for the liberal press became a favorite instrument for leading intellectuals and ordinary Soviet citizens in radicalizing *perestroika*. The call for the restoration of Alexander Solzhenitsyn's Soviet citizenship was first made in *Knizhnoe*

Table 6.1   The circulation of major Soviet publications, 1987–1990 (in millions of copies)[a]

Publication	1987	1988	1989	1990
Argumenty i fakty	3.50	9.50	20.45	31.50
Literaturnaya gazeta	3.10	3.80	6.27	4.23
Izvestia	8.0	10.43	10.13	9.48
Komsomolskaya pravda	17.0	17.60	17.59	20.35
Novy mir	0.49	1.15	1.56	2.37
Znamya	0.27	0.50	0.96	0.91
Ogonek	1.50	1.77	3.08	4.05
Moskovskie novosti	0.25	0.25	3.0	2.20
Pravda	11.10	10.70	9.65	6.48
Sovetskaya rossiya	4.55	5.25	4.22	3.01
Molodaya gvardiya	0.64	0.70	0.62	0.65
Krasnaya zvezda	—	—	1.37	1.08
Trud	18.10	18.70	19.84	20.0
Selskaya zhizn	8.74	7.47	6.59	5.77
Sotsialisticheskaya industriya	1.25	1.45	1.27	0.87

Sources: Calculated from data in *Moscow News,* no. 8, February 28, 1988, p. 2, and no. 47, November 26, 1989, p. 2.

a. The data for 1989–1990 are for subscription figures, which represented 90 percent of the total circulation. *Soyuz,* no. 35 (August 1990), *Foreign Broadcast Information Service: Daily Reports—the Soviet Union,* September 12, 1990, p. 58.

obozrenie—a weekly published by Goskomizdat—in August 1988 in a letter written by a well-known Soviet writer.[30]

Ogonek received about 1,000 letters from its readers each day. According to Korotich, the magazine was getting only about 20 letters a day when he became its editor in 1986.[31] People wrote to the magazine to complain about their poor living conditions and other social problems. "They're writing to me," Korotich said, "because they trust me more than their government. It's abnormal."[32] The power of influencing public opinion enjoyed by these new media institutions was illustrated by a comparison between Gorbachev and *Moscow News,* made by Eduard Sagalayev, the head of Soviet television news in 1989. Pointing to a white telephone on his desk, Sagalayev said that he could call Gorbachev any time if someone interfered with his reporting, but bringing the case to *Moscow News,* he added, would be even more powerful.[33]

Another indicator of the consolidation of the liberal gains in the media was their level of popularity. An opinion poll among 30,000 Soviet citizens found that liberal publications were the most popular: 60 percent chose *Ogonek* as the most popular Soviet publication; *Novy mir* and *Znamya* received 15 percent each.[34] Mass support enabled liberal publications to pursue more radical political goals, even at the risk of offending Gorbachev. Thus began the gradual process of the liberals' abandonment of Gorbachev's reform agenda. Concerned with such radicalization and its political consequences, Gorbachev in October 1989 summoned a group of editors-in-chief of leading liberal publications, including *Ogonek*'s Korotich, *Moscow News*'s Yakovlev, and *Argumenty i fakty*'s Starkov, and warned that they were pushing his *glasnost* too far and too fast. "When you read the newspapers," Gorbachev told the liberal editors, "you get the impression that you're standing up to your knees in gasoline. All it takes is a spark." He charged the liberal press with disseminating "irresponsible" and "negative" materials that increased society's depression and anxiety.[35] The unrelenting attack by the media on the key institutions of the party-state quickened the erosion of its legitimacy. Vadim A. Medvedev, a senior Politburo member who took over Alexander Yakovlev's responsibility in overseeing ideology and propaganda, warned Korotich in late 1989 that "people reading *Ogonek* will stop believing in socialism."[36]

Initially reticent in its coverage of the emerging proindependence movement in the Baltics, the liberal press became more vocal during the Big Surge phase. In late 1988 *Moscow News* became the first Moscow-based publication to criticize openly the central press's biased coverage of the emerging independence movement in the Baltics and urge fair reporting on those republics.[37] When the military crackdown took place in Lithuania in January 1991, the liberal press launched a chorus of condemnation of Gorbachev's policies. *Moscow News* called his actions "criminal." *Literaturnaya gazeta* extensively and objectively covered the situation in Lithuania to counter the distorted reportage by the official media, and it published its own statement denouncing the use of force. *Komsomolskaya pravda, Moskovsky komsomolets,* and the newly founded *Radio Rossiya,* controlled by the Russian Federation, attacked the government's crackdown.[38]

A merger occurred between liberal journalists and the independence movements in the Baltics and other republics with strong proindependence movements. The 250,000-strong People's Front of Latvia had its own weekly radio program and a weekly newspaper, *Atmoda,* with a printrun of 165,000 in both Russian and Latvian versions.[39] By 1990, a conservative official journal observed with alarm, "All parties, public movements, and people's fronts have begun to issue their own publications. They are especially numerous in Moscow, Leningrad, and the Baltic republics."[40]

Radicalization of *glasnost* spread to the electronic media, the news services, and the film industry during the Big Surge.[41] The liberal forces gained ground in the electronic media more slowly than in the print media because this sector had remained the stronghold of the propaganda apparatus of the party-state. In the Soviet Union, the electronic media were more centralized than the print media, and thus more subject to official censorship. Despite a slow start, however, liberalization accelerated in this sector during the Big Surge phase with unusual momentum. The single most powerful event in the electronic media, for instance, was the live televised sessions of the semi-openly elected Congress of People's Deputies, which captured the attention of the Soviet public.

A good example of a liberal-initiated opening in Soviet television was "Vzglyad," a weekly news magazine launched in October 1987 that aired on Friday nights on Central Television. A mixture of American and Soviet rock music, movie segments, investigative reporting, and serious discussion, "Vzglyad" was a popular program with an audience of 150 million. Its attacks on the old regime contributed to the electoral defeat of many party leaders in March 1989.[42]

Another example was "Television News Service" ("TSN"). The three 15-minute editions of daily news aired on Central Television in September 1989 as a result of the personal innovation of Alexander Gurnov, a liberal TV commentator. Modeled on American newscasts, it contained information-packed coverage of current events and directly competed with the government's main television evening news program, "Vremya," a 45-minute program reaching 150 million viewers in the mid-1980s.[43] "TSN" defended its independence fiercely. When the crackdown in Lithuania occurred in January 1991, the main moderator of "TSN" refused to read the government's version of the events and was dismissed. His replacement, who eventually read the official version, was also fired for using a "sarcastic tone."[44]

This partial liberal takeover of television broadcasting also occurred in republican and local television networks. The first edition of Leningrad television's innovative program "Fifth Wheel" went on the air in the spring of 1988, produced by a group of liberal journalists to challenge local party and government officials. A 2-hour program aired twice a week, "Fifth Wheel" exposed official corruption, social problems in the USSR, and the atrocities committed under Stalin. In the first 18 months of its existence, "Fifth Wheel" was severely censored by party propaganda officials, who deleted more than 20 segments from its programs. Like "Vzglyad," "Fifth Wheel" directly contributed to the overwhelming defeat of local *apparat-chiki,* including the first secretary of Leningrad, Yuri Solovyov, in the semi-open elections to the Soviet Congress of People's Deputies in March 1989. In retaliation, the provincial party committee decided to close down "Fifth Wheel" in May 1989. But, when the journalists informed the public of the news, a massive wave of popular protest against the Party's decision saved the program.[45]

The liberal takeover of television broadcasting on the periphery of the Soviet empire accelerated the rise of radical social movements, especially proindependence movements. "In the summer of 1988," wrote a veteran observer of the Soviet Union, "nationalist movements in the Baltic republics of Lithuania, Estonia, and Latvia were practically born on local television discussion shows. In Georgia, Armenia, Azerbaijan, and elsewhere, the spark of nationalism was spread by regional television."[46]

During the Big Surge phase, the state's monopoly of information flow broke down in news services. Interfax, the first unofficial news agency, was founded in September 1989. The Siberian Independent Information Agency (SiBIA) and the Vorkuta-based Northern Independent Agency were founded soon afterward.[47] Interfax was first started as a joint venture between the USSR Ministry of Radio and Television and an Italian firm, Interquadro. Using fax machines and reporters working for Gosteleradio, Interfax quickly established a reputation for independence and became a supplier of news for major Soviet *domestic* publications.

The Consolidation of Liberal Gains

The expansion of press freedom in the Soviet Union occurred without major institutional changes in the mass media. Such freedom, gained and broadened by the intelligentsia, remained legally unprotected prior to the passage of the press law, in late 1989. Periodically, the government imposed censorship on the mass media. The intervention of Vadim Medvedev stopped *Novy mir* from publishing works of Solzhenitsyn in October 1988.[48] In early December 1988, two Central Committee officials and Goskomizdat blocked *Knizhnoe obozrenie*'s plan to reprint Solzhenitsyn's *Matryona's House*. In early 1989, the weekly was again prevented by Glavlit from reprinting the same work.[49] Censorship by local party and government officials was more widespread. In 1988, authorities in Tajikistan, Uzbekistan, Kransnoyarsk Krai, and Kirgizia stopped the distribution of four documentary films, and the post-Yeltsin Moscow city government banned two documentaries, one of which depicted the plight of Soviet Afghan war veterans.[50]

With the rise of nationalist movements, the government began to resort to more subtle forms of censorship. In January 1989, the USSR Ministry of Internal Affairs issued the "Regulations on the Procedure for Representatives of the Mass Media to Be Admitted to, and to Remain in, Localities Where Measures to Ensure Public Order Are in Operation" to limit press access to large rallies, accidents, and other scenes of emergencies. Journalists had to obtain a pass from the Ministry of Internal Affairs to be admitted to such scenes.[51]

Thus, the passage of a law protecting press freedom became a top priority for the Soviet intelligentsia, who had demanded the passage of such a law at the early stages of *glasnost*. Gorbachev, however, remained lukewarm about the law, resulting in the delay of its passage for more than four years. Originally, according to the government's legislative plan, the press law was to be drafted and published by the end of 1986, and adopted by the Supreme Soviet in 1987.[52] The idea of a legal framework protecting press freedom was instantly resisted by the *apparatchiki.*

Gorbachev was conspicuously absent from the early legislative process, and he did not intervene personally to get the troubled bill out of its bureaucratic limbo between 1986 and 1988.[53] Even though Gorbachev and his chief aide, Alexander Yakovlev, wanted to use the press to advance their reform agenda, Vitaly Korotich complained in March 1990, "They won't fight for the [press] law."[54] When two drafts of the law eventually became known to the public in late 1988, the government favored a restrictive version drawn up by a group of *apparatchiki* headed by the conservative editor-in-chief of *Pravda,* Viktor Afanasiev. The competing version of the press law, which was rejected by the government, was written by three liberal Moscow jurists, Mikhail Fedotov, Vladimir Entin, and Yuri Baturin. To rally the press behind this alternative bill, some journalists first leaked the unofficial version to an Estonian Komsomol newspaper, *Molodezh' Estonii,* in October 1988.[55]

The new Congress of People's Deputies, elected in March 1989, breathed life into the legislative process of passing the press law. The People's Deputies, after comparing the two versions, found the government's draft so restrictive that they rejected it and chose, instead, the liberal, unofficial version.[56] The final draft was approved by the Supreme Soviet in late November 1989. The Law on the Press and Other Mass Media was adopted by the Supreme Soviet on June 12, 1990, and it went into effect on August 1, 1990. Although the Soviet press, especially the media organs dominated by liberals, already enjoyed most of the rights enshrined in the bill, this law represented a turning point in the evolution of *glasnost* by establishing a legal foundation for press freedom.

First, it explicitly banned prepublication censorship by the government. Second, it allowed any organization and adult individual to establish and operate publications and other forms of mass media, including radio and television stations. Third, as a precaution against government interference, the law deprived central and local authorities of the right to deny registration to any news organization. Finally, the law established journalists' right to request information from government agencies.[57]

By the end of 1990, the strength of the radical forces in the mass media had, in comparison with the early days of *glasnost,* increased tremendously. The passage of the press law had provided the media with legal protection, and the popularity and huge audience of their publications and programs offered mass support. Measured against the media organs controlled by the government, those dominated by the radical and nationalistic forces, though inferior in the electronic media, had gained a substantial advantage in the print media.

Immense resource gains thus permitted liberal forces to break away from Gorbachev and his moderate reform program. The defection by the liberal media paralleled a much larger defection by the liberal intelligentsia from their former benefactor, Gorbachev, to leaders such as Yeltsin, who championed a more radical political agenda in 1990. By 1991, most of the leading intellectuals who had supported Gorbachev at the beginning of reform, such as the sociologist Tatyana Zaslavskaya and the economist Nikolai Shmelev, had rallied around Yeltsin and become his advisors.[58]

After the press law formalized the legal existence of the independent press, a stampede ensued among the largest and most prestigious Soviet publications to break away from the government and register as independent news organizations. This development represented a direct and formal effort by forces of an emerging civil society to seize media resources from the state. On the day the new law became effective, Anatoly Ananiev, editor of the liberal monthly *Oktyabr'* of the RSFSR Writers' Union, registered his staff as the "founder" and owner of the monthly, turning it into an independent journal. *Ogonek* registered as an independent publication in August 1990, and *Moscow News* gained its independence using the same method a month later. After a well-publicized dispute with the USSR Writers' Union, *Literaturnaya gazeta* and *Znamya* broke away from the organization and registered with the RSFSR Ministry of the Mass Media, which was controlled by Yeltsin's supporters, as independent publications in September 1990. *Yunost, Druzhba narodev,* and *Inostrannaya literatura* followed the same route.

Argumenty i fakty, the largest Soviet weekly, became independent in October 1990. As a gesture signaling the evolution of the liberal-dominated publications from a collection of unorganized individual publications to a cohesive political force, *Moscow News* organized the first meeting of thirty independent newspapers and publications in the Soviet Union in late September 1990 to coordinate action and discuss plans for forming the USSR's first association of independent publications.[59]

This breakaway spread to other media sectors. Interfax tried to separate itself from Gosteleradio by registering as an independent news agency with the RSFSR Ministry of the Press and Information, causing a confrontation with Gosteleradio, which temporarily shut it down. Thanks to Yeltsin's intervention, Gosteleradio finally gave up its effort to take over Interfax, which resumed operation after a one-day shutdown.[60]

The dramatic dispersion of political power as part of the disintegration of the Soviet Union in 1990 facilitated the breakaway process in the media. Most liberal news organizations that had difficulty registering with the newly formed Goskompechat (the USSR State Committee for Publishing Houses, Printing Plants, and the Book Trade) successfully registered with the RSFSR Ministry of the Mass Media. In the breakaway republics, the proindependence governments seized the formerly government- and party-controlled press. In Latvia in 1990, the republican Supreme Soviet confiscated publications and publishing houses previously controlled and owned by the Communist Party.[61] Lithuania passed a liberal press law in February 1990, allowing private individuals to own and operate any mass medium.[62] The government of Landsbergis took over local radio and television stations from Gosteleradio in May 1990, with the republic's parliament as their owner.[63]

These developments were accompanied by the unprecedented proliferation of the independent press after the Law on the Press and Other Media went into effect. Legalized for the first time by the law, independent publications, especially former *samizdat* journals, mushroomed. Most of the independent press was operated by new political parties, popular fronts, and informal groups. In Moscow, 2,500 different publications were registered by May 1991.[64] In 1991, according to Mikhail Poltoranin, minister of the press and public information of the RSFSR, 1,700 new independent newspapers were registered in Russia, in addition to 1,800 new nonstate publishing houses.[65] In January 1991, 1,465 all-Union publications were registered, excluding those registered with the RSFSR Ministry of the Mass Media. Of these, 814 were government-controlled publications, and 498 were private.[66] This ended the party-state's monopoly in the mass media. Nationwide progress in institutionalizing press freedom was uneven, however. In some localities, principally in Central Asian republics, authorities refused to register new independent publications.[67]

The independence and the breakaway of the radicalized publications altered the balance of power between the state and societal forces in the dissemination of information. This development alarmed Gorbachev, especially when, in late 1990 and early 1991, he found himself and his policies under severe attack by the liberal media. At a session of the Supreme Soviet in January 1991, Gorbachev even suggested that the press law be suspended and that the Supreme Soviet assume control of television, radio, and all newspapers "to ensure that they include all points of view."[68] Several government agencies then prepared a package of amendments to the press law in order to limit press freedom, but the Soviet Parliament's Committee on Glasnost and the Rights and Appeals of Citizens rejected the proposals.[69]

The Conservative Countertakeover

Between late 1990 and the failed coup in August 1991, the makeshift anti-takeover coalition—formed in late 1990 and unraveled in the spring of 1991—and the coup leaders launched two separate attacks on the newly independent mass media. These two countertakeover attempts failed miserably in trying to regain the Soviet state's ability to control the runaway reform process. In the media, the same attempts to take back the resources from liberal forces also failed.

The success of the liberal press in resisting the conservative counterattack was, however, incomplete. Its resource gains were uneven, thus leaving areas of weakness that the government exploited in an attempt to reimpose control over society. In both China and the Soviet Union, the societal takeover of the mass media was one-dimensional. Each had its vulnerabilities. In China, societal forces acquired economic influences in the mass media, but were vulnerable to the regime's crackdowns. In the Soviet Union, liberal forces seized editorial control of most media outlets, but the government retained near total economic control over these outlets.

Despite the development of the private sector, which made possible non-official printing and publishing businesses, especially in the Baltics and Georgia after 1987, private book publishing concerns were quickly banned by a government keen on preserving its economic monopoly over publishing. In December 1988, the Council of Ministers amended the Law on Co-operation in the USSR to prohibit cooperatives from engaging in media business, although this amendment was repealed in December 1989.[70] The lack of a private and integrated network of publishing-related businesses diminished the impact of political liberalization.

In 1988, the government lifted restrictions on publishing books at the authors' expense. The lack of private publishing concerns and the state's monopoly of printing facilities meant that this liberalizing measure would produce marginal effects. During 1988, only 63 books were published at the authors' expense in the Soviet Union. In 1989, the number rose to 463, with a printrun of 3 million, accounting for about one-tenth of 1 percent of the books published that year. The main problem was a shortage of paper. The State Publishing Committee allocated 250 tons of paper for publishing vanity books, meaning that only authors who could procure paper supplies could get publishing houses to print their works. Conservative-controlled publishing houses also refused to take on such publishing and printing orders.[71]

In the Soviet Union, the government monopolized paper supplies through Gossnab (the State Committee for Material Supplies), printing facilities through Goskompechat, and distribution through Soyuzpechat. According to the RSFSR minister of the mass media, Mikhail Poltoranin, the CPSU Central Committee controlled 80 percent of the printing facilities in the Russian Federation that printed newspapers and magazines.[72]

The tactics the government employed in the countertakeover attempt between late 1990 and early 1991 show that it maximized its economic and technological advantages to compensate for its low political credibility. In the electronic media, the government kept the advantage of centralized power and monopoly over technological means of transmission.

Gosteleradio, which monopolized the television and radio industry, revived prereform censorship over television programming in late 1990. The Ministry of Communications had exclusive control of the communications satellites that transmitted television signals, and Gosteleradio owned all television facilities.[73] The government's advantage in the most important media sector allowed Gorbachev and his conservative allies to counterattack the defecting liberals. In November 1990, Leonid Kravchenko, the conservative general director of TASS, took over Gosteleradio and launched a systematic campaign of reversing liberalization in his jurisdiction.

He immediately banned the popular television program "Vzglyad," imposed strict censorship on all television news programs, and denied the RSFSR's Radio Rossiya—which Kravchenko described as an "enemy radio station"—access to Gosteleradio's main frequencies, thus reducing its coverage.[74] In Latvia, the central government allocated a special frequency to the pro-Soviet Intermovement as its propaganda tool.[75] The Soviet government maintained its monopoly of television until May 1991, when the growing power of the RSFSR government enabled it to establish Russian Television, which began to broadcast three times a day for a total of six hours on the second channel, which reached a smaller audience than the first channel. "Vesti," the news program of Russian Television, quickly surpassed its competitor, Central Television's "Vremya," in viewer popularity. A poll conducted by the All-Union Center for the Study of Public Opinion found that 57 percent of viewers preferred "Vesti," while 43 percent favored "Vremya."[76]

In addition to overt censorship, the antitakeover coalition resorted to economic strangulation against most liberal publications by cutting off paper supplies, increasing newsprint prices, imposing high distribution costs, and removing access to printing facilities. *Ogonek*'s Korotich noted, in October 1990, that "the government is trying to show that independence does not pay."[77] At that time, Soviet publications faced dwindling supplies of newsprint and skyrocketing costs. Even at state-subsidized prices, a ton of newsprint, which had cost 270 rubles in 1989, rose to 400 in 1990, and soared to 600 in 1991. On the black market, newsprint was sold at 3,000 rubles a ton in July 1990.[78] The newly independent publications, which had relied on government-subsidized newsprint, were caught unprepared by the twin scourge of inflation and shortage of newsprint. They viewed this as another thinly disguised government attempt to retake the media lost to liberal forces. Their fears were not groundless. For instance, a senior government official in charge of the allocation of newsprint in Gossnab complained in mid-1990, "The *Literaturnaya ucheba* magazine tells me they are going to print the Bible! And this at a time when we do not have enough paper to publish the materials of the coming 28th Congress of the CPSU!"[79]

The shortage of newsprint created serious problems for the liberal press.

When *Novy mir* wanted to increase its circulation for 1990 by offering its subscribers a free seven-volume collection of Solzhenitsyn's works, it failed to secure enough paper supplies. Although this marketing scheme succeeded in increasing its subscription by 1.15 million, the publication was unable to find the 5,000 extra tons of newsprint needed every year. The Izvestia Publishing House, which printed *Novy mir,* suspended its printing operation for that magazine and shut it down.[80] In 1991, the government decided to provide 70 percent of the newsprint for newspapers and magazines that it deemed unfriendly or unreliable, but to ensure a full supply for *Pravda* and other progovernment publications.[81] For example, in 1990, official publications received 95–97 percent of their paper supplies at prices 10–20 times lower than those charged the independent press.[82]

Another illustration of the enormous economic power the government deployed in countering the newly independent press was the shutdown of a radical newspaper, *Grazhdanskoye dostoinstvo,* which was founded in March 1989 by a new political party, the Constitutional Democrats. Having no access to private printing facilities or paper supplies, *Grazhdanskoye dostoinstvo* depended on Izvestia Publishers, a government-owned publishing house, to print its issues. Because of the paper's critical views of Gorbachev's policies, Izvestia Publishers stopped printing the 16-page weekly (circulation: 75,000) in late January 1991, citing insufficient printing capacity as the excuse, though the same publishing house increased its service to progovernment publications such as *Trud.*[83] Similar incidents occurred elsewhere. In November 1990, the first secretary of the Orel Oblast Party Committee directed a local publishing house to void its contract with an unofficial paper, *Golos demokrata,* effectively closing it down. Another unofficial publication in Uzbekistan, *Munosabat,* had its contract with an Uzbek publishing house broken in December 1990 as a result of interference by local CPSU officials.[84]

The government simultaneously increased the distribution costs for publications, imposing a heavier burden on independent journals that no longer had subsidies than on official publications which continued to receive such support. In the Soviet Union, although publishers determined the prices of publications, they depended on the post office, controlled by the Ministry of Communication, to deliver their publications and attract subscribers, because the Ministry also published the annual subscription catalog. Through Soyuzpechat, the sole distributor of newspapers and magazines, the Ministry of Communications started to charge higher prices for independent publications and lower rates for CPSU-controlled publications.[85]

In April 1991, the Ministry of Communications announced that Soyuzpechat would increase the rates for distribution of publications 300–350 percent. Newly independent publications with smaller circulations (under 200,000 for newspapers and 30,000 for magazines) were hit with even higher rates. This forced several independent newspapers in Moscow to renounce their status as all-Union publications because they could not afford the higher distribution costs. Moreover, through its kiosks, Soyuzpechat exercised monopolistic power of distribution to reduce the availability of liberal publications, using such tactics as placing copies of these publications under the counter and returning tens of thousands of "unsold" copies to their publishers. *Moscow News* saw its kiosk-distributed retail sales fall by 15,000 in Moscow in April 1991, and by 20,000 in May. Other independent liberal publications reported similar declines in retail sales.[86]

The government's monopolistic power, the distribution rate increases, and the rising shortage of newsprint contributed to a steep decline in most independent publications. Among the hardest hit were the former flagships of *glasnost: Ogonek* and *Literaturnaya gazeta. Ogonek*'s circulation plunged to 1.5 million in 1991 from 4.05 million in 1990, and *Literaturnaya gazeta*'s circulation fell to 1 million from 4.23 million in 1990.[87] In late 1991, the price of newsprint rose to 13,000 rubles per ton. Soaring newsprint and production costs forced *Komsomolskaya pravda* to publish on alternate days. *Ogonek,* a weekly, cut back its operation by publishing every other week.[88] Thus, even though overt repression might have been politically risky for the post-*glasnost* Soviet government, it could readily employ economic means to restrain the influence of the liberal media.

Despite the use of the economic means at their disposal, the conservative forces achieved only limited results, for they failed to regain the state's lost media resources. During the countertakeover phase, the liberal press was not silenced, not even when the countertakeover attempt culminated in the abortive coup in August 1991. A persuasive explanation for the complete failure of this attempt could be found in the new—and changed—balance of power between the state and society in the mass media.

Quantitatively, by late 1990 and early 1991, the liberal press had attained a decisive advantage over the conservative-controlled press. In May 1991, a member of the CPSU Politburo remarked, "Recently we calculated that a simultaneous salvo by the anti-CPSU press would be many times greater than the potential at our disposal."[89] In the electronic media, the government's previous monopoly was shattered by the emergence of independent radio stations, the Russian Television, and local and republican television stations seized by liberal forces.

Qualitatively, the liberal press enjoyed an even greater advantage, especially in its high credibility, thus further reducing the government's ability to influence public opinion. In the campaign for the Russian presidency, the government-controlled central media launched a blizzard of anti-Yeltsin propaganda, and the liberal press responded with their own effective promotion of Yeltsin. Given the low credibility of the government-controlled press, the anti-Yeltsin campaign appeared only to have backfired, and it ironically contributed to his landslide victory. Under the direction of Leonid Kravchek, Gosteleradio's chief, the Soviet Central Television prepared a series of anti-Yeltsin political programs to be aired on June 11, the day before the presidential election. These programs were not aired because Gorbachev told Kravchek that this series would only be counterproductive.[90]

The advantages of the liberal media were enhanced by the close cooperation among the various partners of the takeover coalition. The political and financial support provided by radical reformers such as Yeltsin, who had seized control of republican and local governments, was critical. The RSFSR Ministry of the Press assisted in the registration of many newly independent liberal publications that were denied registration by the all-Union authorities. In 1991, the government of the Russian Federation spent 780 million rubles in subsidies for recently established newspapers.[91]

The ultimate test of the process of democratization in the Soviet Union in general, and of the liberal takeover of the mass media in particular, was the attempted coup organized by the hardliners in August 1991. The short-lived coup did not offer the liberal media sufficient time to demonstrate its power. Many factors, such as Yeltsin's leadership, mass resistance in major cities, the ineptitude of the coup plotters, and the reluctance of the military to implement the plotters' orders, were mainly responsible for the quick collapse of the coup. But the liberal press made its valuable contribution to the defense of democratization at that critical juncture.

Between August 18 and 20, 1991, the State Committee for a State of Emergency (SCSE) banned all but eight publications. The liberal press, however, ingeniously improvised to thwart the hardliners' efforts to shut down the media. In the electronic media, Ekho Moskvy, an independent Moscow-based radio station that had attained fame by criticizing Gorbachev's crackdown in the Baltics in January 1991, continued broadcasting anticoup messages despite the KGB's repeated efforts to cut off its power supply. Its reporters set up shop in the Russian White House, Yeltsin's headquarters, and acted as the voice of the resistance. Another independent radio station, Mayak, resumed broadcasting on August 20, one day after it was shut down by the Emergency Committee. Other radio stations, such as Radio Russia and Radio 3-Anna, operated from inside the White House. Their radio frequencies were pasted on the streets of Moscow.[92] Liberal journalists at Central Television's "Vremya," which was tightly censored by the government, aired segments of pro-Yeltsin demonstrations in Moscow and Leningrad, and even relayed Yeltsin's call for a general strike.

In the print media, Izvestia published, on August 20, a slightly abridged version of Yeltsin's denunciation of the coup and call for a general strike. Thirty-six liberal publications, all banned by the Emergency Committee, made an ad hoc arrangement to continue publication during the coup. Some independent newspapers put out a joint edition called Obshchaya gazeta.

Moscow News published a limited-circulation issue, and *Nezavisamaya gazeta* produced a special issue by fax. Other banned newspapers also provided members of the "Memorial Society" with faxed copies of their special editions, which were then photocopied and distributed widely.[93]

The Formal Takeover: Press Freedom under the New Regime

The collapse of the coup was followed by a formal takeover of both political power and the remaining media resources by the now-triumphant takeover coalition. Yeltsin immediately issued a decree to seize the property of the CPSU, including its media organs. Of the 114 publishing houses and 81 printing plants previously owned by the CPSU, those located inside the RSFSR would be privatized.[94] TASS and the Novosti Agency were reorganized. Procoup publications, including *Glasnost* (a new CPSU publication), *Pravda, Sovetskaya rossiya, Rabochaya tribuna, Moskovskaya pravda,* and *Leninskoye znamya,* were suspended by Yeltsin's decree, though protest by the liberal press, ironically, saved these publications, which resumed operation quickly. Yegor Yakovlev, editor of *Moscow News,* was appointed by Gorbachev as the new head of Gosteleradio (later Ostankino Television and Radio). The journalists of *Izvestia* fired their conservative editor-in-chief, Yefimov, a supporter of the coup plotters, and seized control of the newspaper.

Does this formal takeover mark the ascendance of a fully autonomous civil society in the former Soviet Union? What is the relationship between the state and society under the new democratic regime in general and between the state and the newly independent press in particular?

Definitive answers to these two crucial questions must await the results of the ongoing transition to a market economy in the former Soviet Union. Tentatively, it can be argued that, given the one-dimensional (political) gains made by societal forces during *glasnost,* the formal assumption of power by the takeover coalition and the state-society relations under the new regime were marked by complex ambiguities, which were clearly reflected in the uncertainties and difficulties confronting the newly independent media.

Some of these problems were temporary and caused chiefly by the collapsing economy of the Soviet Union. It was estimated in early 1992 that 90 percent of Russia's newspapers and magazines were near bankruptcy.[95] Subscriptions fell drastically for the leading lights of liberal publications in the *glasnost* era. In 1992, the circulation of major Russian newspapers plunged an average of 33 percent.[96] The 16 largest magazines, all major liberal publications under *glasnost,* lost 7 million subscribers.[97] *Ogonek*'s subscriptions fell from 1.72 million in 1991 to 360,000 for 1993. The subscriptions of the Russian edition of *Moscow News* declined 74 percent, from 1.29 million in 1991 to 337,000 in 1992. The respected new publication *Nezavisimaya gazeta* saw its circulation in the Commonwealth of Independent States (CIS) fall from 71,000 in January 1992 to 26,000 in January 1993. *Komsomolskaya pravda*'s pressrun fell from 13.49 million in January 1992 to 1.9 million a year later.[98] Many newly independent publishing houses teetered on the verge of bankruptcy and faced a shrinking market. The plight of publishing houses prompted many leading Russian writers to call on President Yeltsin to intervene and "help save Russian literature and culture from death by free market."[99]

Between late 1991 and early 1992, 3 principal factors were behind the financial problems besetting the newly independent press. First, following the passage of the new press law, there was an explosion of new publications, overcrowding the media market. In early 1992, there were about 25,000 newspapers in Russia, with some 500 published in Moscow and 600 in St. Petersburg.[100] Second, the newly independent press was most adversely affected by the continuing fall in the production of paper and the resulting inflation of newsprint, as well as the runaway costs of production and distribution. In 1991, the production of pulp in Russia fell by 1 million tons, and that of newsprint, 400,000 tons.[101] Consequently, the price of a ton of newsprint reached 13,250 rubles in February 1992 and 25,000 rubles at the end of the year.[102] Finally, the rapid decrease in income for the population forced consumers to cut subscriptions.

There were, however, deep structural causes for these financial problems, traceable to the peculiarities of the dual-transition process and the non-market polyarchy, which exacerbated the temporary economic difficulties. The problems confronted by the mass media in Russia and other successor republics of the former Soviet Union resembled, in many striking ways, those experienced earlier by the mass media in Eastern Europe.[103]

One such structural factor was the state's continued economic monopoly in the news media. Alexander Klein, publishing manager of *Komsomolskaya pravda,* complained that the state retained monopolies in the production of newsprint, printing facilities, distribution, and transportation.[104] Consequently, lack of economic independence forced some newly independent publications to seek assistance from the state, thus risking their autonomy. Artyom Borovik, a well-known reporter who founded his own newspaper, *Top Secret,* specializing in investigative reporting, summarized the dilemma faced by the independent press in Russia when he planned to seek government assistance. "If you don't want to die, you have to get down on your knees and ask the state to include you in the small circle of publications it subsidizes."[105]

As a result of lobbying by the financially besieged news media, Yeltsin signed a decree in February 1992 to provide emergency relief to the press. It directed that Russia's paper-producing monopolies deliver at least 70 percent of their 1991 output at fixed prices to newspapers and magazines. The treasury was ordered to provide direct financial subsidies to the news media. The decree also gave those publications run by the state preferential tax treatment.[106]

The government allocated 9.2 billion rubles in subsidies for Russia's 25,000 publications in 1992. But most of the funds—5.5 billion rubles—would be spent on 120 major federal periodicals. It appeared that the Ministry of the Press and Information secretly selected the publications to aid.[107] For 1993, the government budgeted 30 billion rubles to subsidize the press.[108] In addition to granting subsidies to official publications, Yeltsin's government courted the most influential independent publications.

Izvestia, which had not sought government assistance, was given 900 million rubles in subsidies. Heavy money-losers such as *Trud* and *Komsomolskaya pravda* received about a billion rubles each. The new government declared that the subsidies and cheap newsprint supplies would be provided only to publications "put out in accordance with programs confirmed by the Ministry of the Press and Information," prompting the independent newspaper *Nezavisimaya gazeta* to claim that such subsidies were the result of "hysterical lobbying by large-circulation, government-sanctioned newspapers and magazines."[109] The lack of openness in selecting recipients of government aid and the apparent favoritism led *Moscow News* to charge that, with such selective granting of state subsidies, a "Palace Press" was being created by the government.[110]

In addition to the risk of compromising editorial independence through financial dependency on the state, the ambiguity of the new relationship between the government and the press was manifest in the former's efforts to increase its control in the mass media. In October 1991, as part of Yeltsin's decree on the mass media, the government formed a new agency—the State Inspectorate for the Defense of Freedom of the Press and the Media inside Russia's Ministry for the Mass Media. Despite its benign title, the agency actually resumed the administrative functions and took over the local offices of the now-defunct Glavlit, the chief censorship agency of the former Soviet Union. This development caused much anxiety among Russian journalists about the state's renewed attempts to curb their freedom.[111] Under the press law of the RSFSR (1991), the Ministry of Information of the Russian Federation was authorized to close a newspaper after issuing two warnings for what it considered editorial transgressions.

In 1992, the government maintained the state's near monopoly in the electronic media and took no measures to privatize the television and radio industries, as it had promised. On the contrary, it even blocked the attempted privatization of the state-owned television station in St. Petersburg. The government prevented the former Soviet news agency TASS from privatizing.

Instead, it merged TASS and part of Novosti into a gigantic official news agency, Itar-Tass, and formed a second official news agency, the Russian Information Agency (RIA).[112]

At the end of 1992, Yeltsin's government further centralized its control over the media. Yegor Yakovlev, a former champion of *glasnost,* was fired by Yeltsin in November as head of Ostankino Television and Radio, ostensibly because Yakovlev approved the broadcast of a documentary on ethnic conflicts in the Ossetian-Ingush area.[113] One Western analyst suggested, however, that Yakovlev, who attempted to turn the state-run Ostankino Television into an objective media organ close to Western professional standards, had fallen out of favor with Mikhail Poltoranin, the minister of information.[114]

In December 1992, Yeltsin ordered the establishment of the Russian Information Center, which centralized power over all the state-run media organs in Russia, including television and radio stations, news agencies, publications, and publishing houses. Yeltsin appointed his long-time aide Mikhail Poltoranin, who had just stepped down as the minister of information, to head the Center, which was ruled illegal by the Russian Constitutional Court in 1993. Yeltsin's moves alarmed the independent-minded liberals, who feared the concentration of media resources in one government bureaucracy. Yakovlev's replacement at Ostankino Television, Vyacheslav Bragin, a former CPSU careerist with no professional media experience, was viewed by most Russian journalists as a political hack.[115]

The state's direct and indirect control in the media inevitably compromised the latter's independence and integrity. In 1992, neither the newly independent publications, which continued to receive state subsidies, nor the state-run media organs succeeded in reaching a level of professional objectivity comparable to the prevailing Western standard. Rather, nearly all of them were deeply drawn into the postcollapse power struggle between the executive branch, headed by Yeltsin, and the legislative branch, which opposed many of Yeltsin's policies. In numerous instances, Yeltsin's political appointees in the media interfered in the editorial policies of state-run media agencies. One Western analyst reported that "both conservative and liberal Russian intellectuals seem to agree that the media have become less free since the democrats came to power in August 1991."[116]

In the hostile power struggle between the executive branch under Yeltsin and the Russian legislature, both sides fought over control of the mass media. In July 1992, the anti-Yeltsin forces in the Russian Supreme Soviet attempted—but failed—to establish a "Council for Monitoring the News Media," which would have the power to determine the size of government subsidies for individual publications. At about the same time, the chairman of the Russian Supreme Soviet, Ruslan Khasbulatov, also led an unsuccessful effort to seize *Izvestia,* which had taken a pro-Yeltsin position. In March 1993, at the height of the power struggle between the Congress of People's Deputies and Yeltsin's government, the legislative branch again tried to take control of the state-run media away from the executive branch. It passed a resolution to form "oversight councils" to keep watch on Itar-Tass and the Russian Information Agency.[117]

The increasing politicization of the media and declining press independence in Russia reduced media credibility. Opinion surveys showed a consistent decline in public trust in the central media organs. In a poll of 2,292 residents of European Russia in April 1992, 53 percent said that the Russian domestic media were not objective, and 32 percent viewed them as inaccurate.[118] The credibility of the print media, radio, and television in Russia remained low between June 1991 and early 1993—only 20–25 percent of the public said that they were "very trustworthy." State-controlled television and radio became the least trusted media organs in Russia in 1992. A poll of 2,122 European Russians in October 1992 found that only 6–9 percent thought that state-owned television and radio networks, including Russian Television, Ostankino Television, Radio Rossiya, and Ostankino Radio, were "very trustworthy."[119]

The most striking difference between the liberalization of the mass media in China and the Soviet Union centers on the different means used by autonomous social forces to seize a significant portion of the mass media. In China, market forces and foreign influence played a principal role in the self-liberalization of the mass media, while the contribution of the liberal intelligentsia was, though substantial at times, less important in terms of changing the basic media structure. In contrast, the Soviet liberal intelligentsia provided the primary momentum for the swift liberalization of the mass media during *glasnost,* whereas market forces and foreign influence made negligible contributions.

Moreover, compared with the Chinese mass media and communications industries, the Soviet media were very developed by the mid-1980s, as illustrated in Table 6.2. The source of liberalization, in the Soviet case at least, did not come from rapid economic development. However, the existing higher level of development in the Soviet media—together with an overall higher level of social mobilization—provided a favorable condition for the opening of this vital sector during *glasnost.*

In the Soviet Union, a developed mass media industry established extensive and well-functioning linkages within a highly modern society, by speeding up the flow of information and political mobilization of autonomous social groups. For instance, each Soviet family received about seven publications on subscription and from retailers in 1988—a very high figure.[120] Con-

Table 6.2   The level of development of the Soviet mass media, 1985 and 1987

Number of television broadcasting stations (1985)	6,736
Number of radio receivers per 100 people (1985)	57.1
Number of televisions per 100 people (1985)	28.5
Number of newspapers (1987)	8,000
Single printrun of newspapers (1987, million copies)	180
Number of magazines (1987)	1,500
Number of publishing houses (1987)	219
Number of printing factories (1987)	4,000
Titles of books and brochures published (1987)	80,000
Copies of books and brochures printed (1987, billion copies)	2.0

Sources: Sovetskaya rossiya, August 11, 1988, *Foreign Broadcast Information Service: Daily Reports—the Soviet Union,* 1988, p. 60; *USSR Facts and Figures Annual, 1986 and 1988* (Gulf Breeze, Fla.: Academic International Press); TASS, May 5, 1988, *Foreign Broadcast Information Service: Daily Reports—the Soviet Union,* May 10, 1988, p. 48; TASS, February 8, 1989, *Foreign Broadcast Information Service: Daily Reports—the Soviet Union,* February 9, 1989, p. 80.

versely, this wide and highly educated audience acted as a support base for the liberal-dominated mass media. In short, the combination of a better-educated population and a strong group of radical political entrepreneurs inside the Soviet media establishment made the societal takeover of this critical sector possible—and the political consequences of such a takeover costly for Gorbachev and his moderate reform project.

Conclusion

Three intriguing lessons, all with policy implications for would-be reformers, emerge from this study of the regime transitions from communism in China and the Soviet Union. First, despite the countries' differences in history, culture, and level of economic development, the transitions they underwent demonstrate that the reformer can seldom count on the existing institutions of the communist party-state to serve as the instruments of change. In both cases, the principal forces of change, whether economic or political, came from society. Instead of reinvigorating these institutions through adaptation, reform sapped their vitality, reduced their power, corrupted their integrity, and accelerated their decay. Indeed, the Chinese and Soviet reformers were forced to seek alternative organizational instruments and create new institutions to advance their programs.

Second, although most reformers' ability to manage change declines over time, there are opportunities early in the reform process to slow the rate of such decline and to mitigate its negative effects. The transition experiences in China and the Soviet Union show that such opportunities can be secured by the right sequencing of reform initiatives. A reformer's ability to manage change is likely to decrease more precipitously when the initial opening is created in the political process than when it originates in the economy. A societally driven capitalist revolution allows the reformer time to readjust strategies and rebuild alliances, whereas a democratizing societal revolution affords no such luxury. Empirically, autocratic ruling elites who begin with market-oriented reforms usually retain a greater ability to influence the course of change than elites who start with democratizing experiments. It is especially worth cautioning that flirting with democratizing reforms to improve economic performance is both risky and illusionary—risky for the reasons underscored above, illusionary because there is, in reality, little evidence to support this otherwise appealing proposition.

Third, a reformer's ability to manage change is inseparable from his ability to build and maintain support. The sources of support can be both domestic and external, economic and political. Externally, the introduction of favorable foreign economic and political resources into the two phases of the dual transition can affect the speed and costs of transition. In seeking foreign support, however, both societal forces and reformist elites should be realistic about its degree of availability. Forces of reform should not stake the success of their programs on external support because they have the least control over it. Indeed, a reformer who depends on foreign help for his political survival is never viable. The reformer's most critical task, therefore, is to build domestic support among major social groups and prevent the formation of a political takeover coalition.

In the event of the emergence of an economic takeover coalition, the reformer should actively seek to co-opt its moderate-conservative elements to help contain political radicals. Classic tactics of support-building include identifying loyal social groups with significant membership sizes but politically affordable demands; using government policies to benefit these groups; and incorporating the support of these groups into an institutional framework capable of providing the reformer with predictable support.[1] The Chinese and Soviet experiences recommend that the reformer ensure the exclusion of defection-prone groups with radical political agendas (such as ethnic groups and the intelligentsia) from the benefits of state-to-society resource transfer, which occurs in the early phase of the reform.

To prevent the emergence of a takeover coalition with a radical political agenda, a reformer may use the classic tactic of "divide and reform" through early negotiations with potential members of such coalitions and co-optation of their moderates. Negotiation with moderates in the opposition, however, is generally a more realistic option for regime transition in authoritarian states than in communist countries, because society in the former is more pluralized than in the latter. Reformers in authoritarian states can form moderate-dominated coalitions with well-known civic and business leaders controlling established social and economic organizations encompassing major groups, but reformers in communist states can rarely do so at the beginning of reform simply because there are so few such leaders and organizations prior to reform. When these leaders and organizations eventually emerge, they are characteristically radical and have revolutionary demands.

Reformers should thus pursue support-building with special vigor and timeliness—particularly when embarking on a risky reform sequence. The right sequence without accompanying support-building seldom automatically augments the manageability of reform. Belated support-building efforts following an ill-conceived sequence typically falter. Such manageability is most enhanced by the combination of the right sequence and timely support-building efforts.

*   *   *

All revolutions, whether social or political, routinely promise more than they can actually deliver, and the results they manage to deliver are ambiguous in the short-term and disappointing in the long-run. In this sense, the great societal revolutions in the ex-communist world were no exception. In the short-term, as noted, their achievements have been partial and, in many instances, fragile. A more immediate concern for the practically minded scholars of these countries, however, is whether the newly empowered societal groups can be relied on to employ responsibly and constructively their economic and political resources under a much weakened state.

Indeed, an intriguing aspect of regime transition in the former communist states is the considerable decline in the state's capacity *regardless of* the transitional route. Although this may be considered one of the many short-term transitional problems, the real cause of this *weak-state syndrome* is the rapid transfer of resources from the state to society, the institutional decay of the state, and the subsequent restructured relations between the state and society during the dual transition. Although postcommunist states may appear relatively robust in comparison with developing countries with even weaker state capacities, this syndrome is real and evident from the deteriorating ability of the postcommunist state to perform most of its critical functions, especially those related to resource extraction, regulation, law enforcement, and political mobilization. During the transitional process, all the ex-communist states experienced similar socioeconomic problems, such as widespread tax evasion, fraudulent business practices, ethnic and communal violence, explosion of social vices, and waves of crime that the government was unable to cope with. In a vicious cycle, these problems both contribute to and result from the weak-state syndrome.

The prospects of restrengthening the state after societal takeover are not bright, either. The oppression experienced under the old regime has caused the peoples of these countries to distrust the state and other forms of political authority. Attempts to revitalize the institutions of the state and enhance their authority are apt to arouse popular suspicions and fears about the restoration of autocracy, and thus encounter intense resistance. In most cases, the corruption of the core institutions of the state may be so advanced that no short-term solutions are available.

A weak state, when counterbalanced by a strong civil society, need not experience instability, ungovernability, paralysis, and decay. Strong societies are more capable of self-governance than weaker ones, and their institutions compensate for the temporarily enfeebled state institutions by performing some of the latter's functions. For transitional ex-communist societies, however, the weakening of the state does not automatically lead to the emergence of a strong civil society.

Despite the immense resource gains by societal actors, social institutions and the norms governing these entities remain fragile in most ex-communist states. A distinction needs to be made between a society that has regained macroautonomy through resource acquisition and the restoration of a civil society with well-established institutions and abiding norms. In ex-communist states, the societal revolution in the late 1980s and early 1990s clearly resulted in the strengthening of society at the expense of the state. It was the first and indispensable step toward the building of a civil society. This should not be confused, however, with the restoration of civil society in these countries, for civil society—by definition a society consisting of fully autonomous social institutions—hardly existed in these political systems prior to transition. Long periods of consolidation are required for the embryos of civil society to mature into functioning institutions.

The combination of a weak state and an underinstitutionalized society governed by weak, self-imposed norms and rules unavoidably creates social anomie, characterized by a prevalence of normless behavior across all groups. Left uncorrected, social anomie reinforces collective perceptions of disorder, insecurity, and loss of values after societal revolution. Sometimes, popular dissatisfaction with transitional social anomie brings back nostalgia for the more orderly and predictable ways of life under the old regimes. "Mao fever," which seized China in the late 1980s and early 1990s, was one such example. In Russia, Ukraine, and Belarus, a poll in early 1993 found that about 60 percent of those asked thought that "things were better under the old system." In an exit poll of voters in the critical elections for the Russian Parliament in December 1993, 55 percent of those polled responded that they were better off "under socialism, before *perestroika*"; 25 percent said that there was "not much difference."[2] The political implication of the persistence of the weak-state and underinstitutionalized society is more serious than temporary public longing for life under the old regime: it portends continuous breakdown of the polity and fracturing of society along both old (ethnic and subcultural) and new (socioeconomic) cleavages.

Inevitably, a comparison of regime transitions in China and the Soviet Union raises an important question: which route is the less costly exit from communism?

The regime transitions in China and the Soviet Union demonstrate that exits from communism along the authoritarian and democratic routes deliver significant benefits and incur high costs. For China, the capitalist revolution raised the standard of living rapidly, expanded civic and economic freedom of society substantially, and improved the country's status as a major world power dramatically. Although the capitalist revolution destroyed China's orthodox communism, it also temporarily saved its authoritarian rule. Under the material prosperity resulting from this revolution, China's postcommunist authoritarian regime gained a breathing space and, after the disintegration of the Soviet Union, even international recognition for its pragmatism and achievements—from such unlikely sources as Boris Yeltsin and the *Economist*.[3]

For the Soviet Union, the democratic-nationalist revolution led to the collapse of the Soviet empire, helped more than a dozen states to gain independence, and instituted new democratic governments in some of these states (the Baltics and Ukraine) and Russia itself. However, this revolution entailed immense political, social, and economic costs. Some former Soviet republics plunged into armed conflicts with each other; civil and political chaos plagued many others. The failure of *perestroika* led to a significant deterioration of the standard of living for the peoples of the former Soviet Union.

The fall in international standing of the former Soviet Union was even more dramatic. As the loser of the Cold War, the Soviet people saw, seven years after the initiation of *glasnost* and *perestroika*, the Soviet empire in Eastern Europe collapse, its rule in the peripheral states of the Soviet Union disintegrate, its economic status reduced to that of a developing country whose fiscal policies were subject to interference from multilateral lending agencies such as the World Bank and the International Monetary Fund, and the heart and soul of its power—Russia—faced with the real prospect of further disintegration.

This brief tabulation of the costs and benefits of the first phase of the dual transition in China and the Soviet Union suggests that the *up-front* transitional costs were greater for the Soviet Union than for China, although it remains to be seen which route will ultimately result in lower *total* transitional costs. As a reformer, Gorbachev was a clear failure, for he achieved virtually none of the goals of *glasnost* and *perestroika*. Under his rule, instead of improving, the Soviet economy deteriorated and ultimately collapsed; the communist rule he hoped to revitalize broke down completely; the Soviet Union's position as a world power, instead of gaining, fell precipitously; and the multinational Soviet empire he had attempted to preserve crumbled.

By comparison, in spite of his harsh rule, Deng may be considered a more skillful reformer who, though not having foreseen the potential for a capitalist revolution in his partial economic reforms, was pragmatic enough to embrace and defend it. As China's greatest modernizer, Deng will achieve a historical stature similar to that accorded to other Third World autocrats, such as South Korea's Park Chong Hee, Singapore's Lee Kuan Yew, and Chile's Augusto Pinochet—men who single-mindedly focused on rapid economic development as the top priority of their governments.

This book has focused on the dynamics of a capitalist revolution in China and a democratic-nationalist revolution in the former Soviet Union. Its analysis has been devoted almost exclusively to the first phase of the dual-transition process in the two countries, and has not yet addressed a speculative but important question: which route is more viable in establishing a democratic political system based on a market economy?

The answer, based on available evidence, is unfortunately ambiguous. Unique historical circumstances provided some of the Eastern European countries (principally Czechoslovakia, Hungary, Poland, and Slovenia) with a set of initial advantages that enhanced the viability of transition along the democratic double-breakthrough route. For other Eastern European countries lacking the same advantages, the prospects for dual transition were less clear. For the former Soviet Union, the same question has, in fact, received a definitive—and negative—answer. Strictly speaking, the transition process along this route broke down with the disintegration of the Soviet Union. For the successor states of the former Soviet Union, prospects for attaining democratic systems based on market economies are clearly mixed in the mid-1990s. Whereas the Baltic states, sharing some of the same initial advantages enjoyed by Hungary, Czechoslovakia, and Poland, seem to be moving more rapidly and viably toward that goal, the outlook for most other Soviet republics remains unclear and is made even more uncertain by four unsettling developments in Russia toward the end of 1993: the rapid political gains of the radical Right represented by the ultranationalist Liberal Democratic Party; the unexpected quick resurgence of the communists; the deep split among the reformist forces; and Yeltsin's shift toward soft authoritarianism at home and an increasingly imperialist foreign policy toward the breakaway former Soviet republics. For the ex-Soviet republics in Transcaucasia and Central Asia (with the possible exception of Armenia), this goal will not be reachable for a long time to come.

In contrast, the Chinese route has so far shown some promise of transforming a huge developing communist state via peaceful and evolutionary means. Compared with the failed Soviet model of reform under Gorbachev, the Chinese reform experience since 1979 has demonstrated substantial achievement in attaining some of the favorable socioeconomic structural conditions of a democratic political system. To the extent that the Chinese model resembles, in some key aspects, the classic route to a market-economy democracy—as followed both in Western European countries since the Industrial Revolution and in dozens of developing countries since World War II—historical cases of successful democratization of authoritarian states should brighten the prospects of the eventual establishment of democratic rule in China's coastal areas, where the capitalist revolution of the 1980s and early 1990s is more advanced. The ultimate—and most critical—test for the Chinese model is, however, whether its future leaders will be capable of redistributing the benefits of the country's ongoing capitalist revolution to its impoverished interiors, where the same revolution is less advanced, while holding on to the peripheral areas with large ethnic minorities—and the greatest potential for a nationalist revolution similar to that which dismembered the former Soviet Union.

Abbreviations / Notes / Acknowledgments / Index

Abbreviations

AWSJW	*Asian Wall Street Journal Weekly*
CD	*China Daily*
CD/BW	*China Daily: Business Weekly*
CDSP	*Current Digest of the Soviet Press*
CTW	*China Times Weekly*
DL	*Democracy and Law (Minzhu yu fazhi)*
FBIS-EEU	*Foreign Broadcast Information Service: Daily Reports—Eastern Europe*
FBIS-SOV	*Foreign Broadcast Information Service: Daily Reports—the Soviet Union*
FEER	*Far Eastern Economic Review*
JR	*Jingji Ribao (Economic Daily)*
LW	*Liaowang*
MN	*Moscow News*
NF	*News Front (Xinwen Zhanxian)*
NYT	*New York Times*
PD	*People's Daily* (overseas edition)
RFE/REEU	*Radio Free Europe: Report on Eastern Europe*
RFE/RL/RR	*Radio Free Europe and Radio Liberty: Research Report*
RL/RUSSR	*Radio Liberty: Report on the USSR*
WEH	*World Economic Herald (Shijie jingji daobao)*
WJ	*World Journal (Shijie Ribao)*
WSJ	*Wall Street Journal*
ZGTJNJ	*Zhongquo tongji nianjian (Statistical Yearbook of China)*

Notes

Introduction

1. Following the collapse of the Soviet Union in 1991, both Cuba and North Korea showed signs of opening up to the West by welcoming foreign investment, though neither regime announced any substantive plans for economic reform.
2. See Andrew C. Janos, "Social Science, Communism, and the Dynamics of Political Change," *World Politics,* vol. 44 (October 1991), pp. 81–112, and *The Strange Death of Soviet Communism,* a special issue of *National Interest,* no. 31 (Spring 1993).
3. The standard classification of a communist regime can be found in Stephen White, "What Is a Communist System?" *Studies in Comparative Communism,* vol. 16, no. 4 (Winter 1983), pp. 247–263.
4. The political origin of old regimes received serious attention from political scientists and economists specializing in comparative communist studies. See Richard Lowenthal, "Development versus Utopia in Communist Policy," in *Change in Communist Systems,* ed. Chalmers Johnson (Stanford: Stanford University Press, 1970), pp. 33–116; Janos Kornai, *The Socialist System: The Political Economy of Communism* (Princeton: Princeton University Press, 1992), pp. 21–26.
5. Samuel P. Huntington, "Democracy's Third Wave," *Journal of Democracy,* vol. 2, no. 2 (Spring 1991), pp. 31–32.
6. This definition is similar to the ones proposed by Robert Fishman, Guillermo O'Donnell, and Philippe Schmitter. See Fishman, "Rethinking State and Regime: Southern Europe's Transition to Democracy," *World Politics,* vol. 42, no. 3 (April 1990), p. 428; O'Donnell and Schmitter, *Transitions from Authoritarian Rule: Tentative Conclusions about Uncertain Democracies* (Baltimore: Johns Hopkins University Press, 1986), p. 73.
7. The definition of the state here is identical to the mainstream definition given by, for example, Theda Skocpol; see Skocpol, *States and Social Revolutions* (Cambridge: Cambridge University Press, 1979), p. 29.
8. Skocpol noted that a fundamental characteristic of the state was its extraction of

resources from society for its self-maintenance, but she overlooked the regime-state connection. See Skocpol, *States and Social Revolutions,* p. 29.

9. Samuel P. Huntington, *The Third Wave: Democratization in the Late Twentieth Century* (Norman, Okla.: University of Oklahoma Press, 1991), pp. 13–26.

10. For a more comprehensive comparative study of regime transition in communist states, see Gilbert Rozman, ed., *Dismantling Communism: Common Causes and Regional Variations* (Baltimore: Johns Hopkins University Press, 1992). For recent scholarly works on Chinese reform, see Harry Harding, *China's Second Revolution: Reform after Mao* (Washington, D.C.: The Brookings Institution, 1987); Ezra Vogel, *One Step Ahead in China: Guangdong under Reform* (Cambridge, Mass.: Harvard University Press, 1989); Nicholas Lardy, *Foreign Trade and Economic Reform in China, 1978–1990* (Cambridge: Cambridge University Press, 1992); Kenneth Lieberthal and Michel Oksenberg, *Policy-Making in China: Leaders, Structures, and Processes* (Princeton: Princeton University Press, 1988). For representative works on Gorbachev's reforms, see Stephen White, *Gorbachev and After* (New York: Cambridge University Press, 1991); Anders Aslund, *Gorbachev's Struggle for Economic Reform* (Ithaca: Cornell University Press, 1989); Vera Tolz, *The USSR's Emerging Multiparty System* (New York: Praeger, 1991); Geoffrey Hosking, *The Awakening of the Soviet Union* (Cambridge, Mass.: Harvard University Press, 1990); Ed A. Hewett and Victor H. Winston, eds., *Milestones in Glasnost and Perestroika* (Washington, D.C.: The Brookings Institution, 1991).

11. See Roderick MacFarquhar, "The Anatomy of Collapse," *New York Review of Books,* September 26, 1991, pp. 5–9.

12. Ibid.; Peter Ferdinand, "Russian and Soviet Shadows over China's Future?" *International Affairs,* vol. 68, no. 2 (1992), pp. 279–292. For a series of articles on Gorbachev's leadership and reform strategy, see George W. Breslauer, "Evaluating Gorbachev as Leader," *Soviet Economy,* vol. 5, no. 4 (1989), pp. 299–340; Peter Reddaway, "The Quality of Gorbachev's Leadership"; Archie Brown, "Gorbachev's Leadership: Another View"; and Andranik Migranyan, "Gorbachev's Leadership: A Soviet View," *Soviet Economy,* vol. 6, no. 2 (1990), pp. 125–159.

1.   Regime Transition in Communist States

1. Russell Bova, "Political Dynamics of the Post-Communist Transition," *World Politics,* vol. 44 (October 1991), pp. 113–138.

2. This view is shared by most specialists on communist states. See Geoffrey Hosking, "The Roots of Dissolution," *New York Review of Books,* January 16, 1992, p. 34; Grzegorz Ekiert, "Democratization Processes in East Central Europe: A Theoretical Reconsideration," *British Journal of Political Science,* vol. 21 (July 1991), pp. 285–313; and George Schopflin, "Post-Communism: Constructing New Democracies in Central Europe," *International Affairs,* vol. 67, no. 2 (Spring 1991), pp. 235–250. The historian Martin Malia emphasized the differences between the transition to democracy from an authoritarian regime and that from a totalitarian regime in "To the Stalin Mausoleum," *Daedalus* (Winter 1990), pp. 295–344.

3. See Alfred Stepan, ed., *Democratizing Brazil: Problems of Transition and Consolidation* (Oxford: Oxford University Press, 1989), pp. 143–296.

4. Although Tunisia seemed to have a huge state industrial sector which contributed 56 percent of the industrial output and employed 55 percent of the industrial labor force in 1982, this sector was actually quite small in Tunisia's predominantly agrarian economy and accounted for only 20 percent of total GDP and 25 percent of total employment. Mahmood Ali Ayub and Sven Olaf Hegstad, *Public Industrial Enterprises: Determinants of Performance* (Washington, D.C.: The World Bank, 1986), p. 77.

5. Stephan Haggard and Robert Kaufman, "Economic Adjustment and the Prospects for Democracy," in *The Politics of Economic Adjustment*, ed. Haggard and Kaufman (Princeton: Princeton University Press, 1992), pp. 319–350. Although the model used by Haggard and Kaufman is nearly the same as the one presented in Figure 1, they chose to treat regime transition from communist regimes and authoritarian regimes as an identical process, overlooking the differences between the two regimes in the degree of state intervention in the economy. Tsuyoshi Hasegawa presented a similar model in "The Connection between Political and Economic Reform in Communist Regimes," in *Dismantling Communism: Common Causes and Regional Variations*, ed. Gilbert Rozman (Baltimore: Johns Hopkins University Press, 1992), pp. 58–117.

6. Adam Przeworski, *Democracy and the Market: Political and Economic Reforms in Eastern Europe and Latin America* (Cambridge: Cambridge University Press, 1991), p. 140.

7. Robert Dahl, *Polyarchy* (New Haven: Yale University Press, 1971), p. 34. Guillermo O'Donnell and Philippe Schmitter, *Transitions from Authoritarian Rule: Tentative Conclusions about Uncertain Democracies* (Baltimore: Johns Hopkins University Press, 1986), p. 13.

8. Albert O. Hirschman, *Journeys toward Progress* (New York: The Twentieth Century Fund, 1963), pp. 261–264; Gabriel Almond, Scott Flanagan, and Robert Mundt, eds., *Crisis, Choice, and Change: Historical Studies of Political Development* (Boston: Little, Brown and Co., 1973).

9. See Samuel P. Huntington, *The Third Wave: Democratization in the Late Twentieth Century* (Norman, Okla.: University of Oklahoma Press, 1991), pp. 46–72; Charles Gillespie, "From Authoritarian Crises to Democratic Transitions," *Latin American Research Review*, vol. 22, no. 3 (1987), pp. 165–184.

10. Deng Xiaoping, *Deng Xiaoping tongzhi lungaige kaifang* (*Comrade Deng Xiaoping on Reform and Opening*, Beijing: People's Publishing House, 1989), p. 9.

11. Ronald J. Cima, "Vietnam's Economic Reform: Approaching the 1990s," *Asian Survey*, vol. 29, no. 8 (August 1989), p. 790; John H. Esterline, "Vietnam in 1987," *Asian Survey*, vol. 28, no. 1 (January 1988), p. 91.

12. Eduard Shevardnadze, *The Future Belongs to Freedom* (New York: The Free Press, 1991), p. 37.

13. Boris Yeltsin, *Against the Grain* (New York: Summit Books, 1990), p. 82.

14. Aristotle, *Politics*, ed. Ernest Barker (New York: Oxford University Press, 1962), p. 217.

15. Stephen White, "Economic Performance and Communist Legitimacy," *World Politics*, no. 3 (April 1986), pp. 462–482.

16. David Mason, Daniel Nelson, and Bohdan Szklarski, "Apathy and the Birth of Democracy: The Polish Struggle," *East European Politics and Societies*, vol. 5, no. 2 (Spring 1991), p. 211.

17. Ibid., pp. 212–215.

18. See Janos Kornai, *Contradictions and Dilemmas: Studies on the Socialist Economy and Society* (Cambridge, Mass.: MIT Press, 1986).

19. Shevardnadze, *The Future Belongs to Freedom*, p. 58; defense expenditures as a percentage of Soviet GNP were based on CIA estimates. See Ed A. Hewett, *Reforming the Soviet Union* (Washington, D.C.: The Brookings Institution, 1988), p. 67.

20. Aristotle, *Politics*, p. 217.

21. *Radio Free Europe Research*, vol. 14, no. 42, October 20, 1989, pp. 27–29; vol. 14, no. 48, November 30, 1989, pp. 11–25.

22. *Radio Free Europe Research*, vol. 14, no. 48, December 1, 1989, p. 19; Alfred Reisch, "Hungary in 1989: A Country in Transition," *RFE/REEU*, vol. 1, no. 1, January 5, 1990, p. 20.

23. *Deng Xiaoping lun dang de jianshe* (*Deng Xiaoping on the Development of the Party*, Beijing: People's Publishing House, 1990), p. 262.

24. *FEER*, October 26, 1989, p. 37.

25. For representative works on the East Asian NICs, see Robert Wade, *Governing the Market: Economic Theory and the Role of Government in East Asian Industrialization* (Princeton: Princeton University Press, 1990); Alice Amsden, *Asia's Next Giant: South Korea and Late Industrialization* (New York: Oxford University Press, 1989); Stephan Haggard, *Pathways from the Periphery: The Politics of Growth in the Newly Industrializing Countries* (Ithaca: Cornell University Press, 1990); Steven Schlossstein, *Asia's New Little Dragons: The Dynamic Emergence of Indonesia, Thailand, and Malaysia* (Chicago: Contemporary Books, 1991).

26. For the standard definition of a capitalist developmental state, see Chalmers Johnson, *MITI and the Japanese Miracle: The Growth of Industrial Policy, 1925–1975* (Stanford: Stanford University Press, 1982), pp. 19–34.

27. Barry Sautman, "Sirens of the Strongman: Neoauthoritarianism in Recent Chinese Political Thought," *China Quarterly*, no. 129 (March 1992), pp. 72–102.

28. *ZGTJNJ*, 1991, p. 21; estimate from data in *FEER*, April 22, 1993, p. 69, and Kevin Hewison, Richard Robison, and Garry Rodan, eds., *Southeast Asia in the 1990s: Authoritarianism, Democracy, and Capitalism* (London: Allen & Unwin, 1993), p. 215.

29. Dahl, *Polyarchy*, pp. 14–16 and 48–61.

30. Deng, *On the Development of the Party*, p. 251.

31. Stephen White, *Gorbachev and After* (New York: Cambridge University Press, 1991), pp. 24–26.

32. Andrew Nathan, *Chinese Democracy* (Berkeley: University of California Press, 1985), pp. 172–232, and Nathan, *China's Crisis* (New York: Columbia University Press, 1990), pp. 97–126 and 171–211. *FEER*, March 17, 1988, pp. 20–23; May 4, 1989, p. 15; October 26, 1989, pp. 37–38; October 24, 1991, pp. 16–17.

33. Victor Nee, "A Theory of Market Transition: From Redistribution to Markets

in State Socialism," *American Sociological Review,* vol. 54 (1989), pp. 663–681.

34. Amitai Etzioni, "Eastern Europe: The Wealth of Lessons," *Challenge* (July–August 1991), pp. 4–10; Adam Przeworski, "The Neoliberal Fallacy," *Journal of Democracy,* vol. 3, no. 3 (July 1992), pp. 45–59; Andreas Pickel, "Jump-Starting a Market Economy: A Critique of the Radical Strategy for Economic Reform in Light of the East German Experience," *Studies in Comparative Communism,* vol. 25, no. 2 (June 1992), pp. 177–191; Alice Amsden, "Beyond Shock Therapy: Why Eastern Europe's Recovery Starts in Washington," *American Prospect,* no. 13 (Spring 1993), pp. 87–98.

35. *Economist,* "Eastern Europe: The Old World's New World," March 13, 1993, p. 9.

36. Keith Bush, "Light at the End of the Tunnel?" *RFE/RL/RR,* May 14, 1993, p. 62.

37. Calculated from Amsden, "Beyond Shock Therapy," p. 89.

38. *NYT,* December 4, 1993, p. 6.

39. Niccolo Machiavelli, *The Prince* (New York: Random House, 1954), p. 35.

40. Albert Hirschman, "The Political Economy of Latin American Development: Seven Exercises in Retrospection," *Latin American Research Review,* vol. 22, no. 3 (1987), pp. 28–29.

41. David McQuaid, "The Parliamentary Elections: A Postmortem," *RFE/REEU,* vol. 2, no. 45, November 8, 1991, pp. 15–21.

42. *Economist,* November 2, 1991, p. 4.

43. *Economist,* December 14, 1991, p. 56.

44. Vladimir Kusin, "The Birth Pangs of Democratic Politics," and Anna Sabbat-Swidlicka, "Mazowiecki's Year in Review," *RFE/REEU,* vol. 2, no. 1, January 4, 1991, pp. 45–49 and pp. 25–31; Kjell Engelbrekt, "Cracks in the Union of Democratic Forces," *RFE/REEU,* vol. 2, no. 20, May 17, 1991, pp. 1–5; Jiri Pehe, "The Realignment of Political Forces," *RFE/REEU,* vol. 2, no. 21, May 24, 1991, pp. 1–5.

45. Vera Tolz, "Political Parties in Russia," *RFE/RL/RR,* vol. 1, no. 1, January 3, 1992, p. 13.

46. *WSJ,* December 19, 1991, A11; *NYT,* December 28, 1991, p. 1.

47. Huntington, *The Third Wave,* pp. 208–279; Karen L. Remmer, "The Political Impact of Economic Crisis in Latin America in the 1980s," *American Political Science Review,* vol. 85, no. 3 (September 1991), pp. 777–800.

48. Stephan Haggard and Robert Kaufman, "Economic Adjustment in New Democracies," in *Fragile Coalitions: The Politics of Economic Adjustment,* ed. Joan M. Nelson (New Brunswick, N.J.: Transaction Books, 1989), pp. 57–77; Remmer, "Democracy and Economic Crisis: The Latin American Experience," *World Politics,* vol. 42, no. 3 (April 1990), pp. 315–335.

49. The coalitions that overthrew the old regimes in these countries were clearly too large to maintain over time, according to Riker's size principle. See William Riker, *A Theory of Political Coalitions* (New Haven: Yale University Press, 1962).

50. Voytek Zubek, "The Threshold of Poland's Transition: The 1989 Electoral Campaign as the Last Act of a United Solidarity," *Studies in Comparative Com-*

munism, vol. 26, no. 4 (December 1991), pp. 355–376; Krzysztof Jasiewicz, "From Solidarity to Fragmentation," *Journal of Democracy,* vol. 3, no. 2 (April 1992), pp. 55–69.

51. See *Economist,* February 1, 1992, pp. 52–53; Anna Sabbat-Swidlicka, "Poland: Weak Government, Fractious Sejm, Isolated President," *RFE/RL/RR,* vol. 1, no. 15, April 10, 1992, pp. 1–7; Louisa Vinton, "Poland: Government Crisis Ends, Budget Crisis Begins," *RFE/RL/RR,* vol. 1, no. 3, January 17, 1992, pp. 14–21.

52. *NYT,* April 6, 1992, A5; *WSJ,* April 7, 1992, A13.

53. Riina Kionka, "Plea for Special Powers Topples Estonian Government," *RFE/RL/RR,* vol. 1, no. 7, February 14, 1992, pp. 31–34; Jan Obrman, "President Havel's Diminishing Political Influence," *RFE/RL/RR,* vol. 1, no. 11, March 13, 1992, pp. 18–23.

54. Janos Kornai, "Socialist Transformation and Privatization: Shifting from a Socialist System," *East European Politics and Societies,* vol. 4, no. 2 (Spring 1990), pp. 273–275; for a study of the formation of the bourgeoisie under communist rule in Hungary, see Ivan Szelenyi, *Socialist Entrepreneurs* (Madison: University of Wisconsin Press, 1988).

55. David Stark, "Privatization in Hungary: From Plan to Market or from Plan to Clan?" *East European Politics and Societies,* vol. 4, no. 3 (Fall 1990), pp. 351–392; Simon Johnson and Heidi Kroll, "Managerial Strategies for Spontaneous Privatization," *Soviet Economy,* vol. 7, no. 4 (October–December 1991), pp. 281–316; Gerd Schwartz, "Privatization: Possible Lessons from the Hungarian Case," *World Development,* vol. 19, no. 12 (1991), pp. 1731–1736.

56. Barrington Moore, Jr., *Social Origins of Dictatorship and Democracy: Lord and Peasant in the Making of the Modern World* (Boston: Beacon Press, 1966).

57. *NYT,* February 23, 1992, E4.

58. *NYT,* March 31, 1992, A7.

59. Jiri Pehe, "Opinion Polls on Economic Reform," *RFE/REEU,* vol. 2, no. 4, January 25, 1991, pp. 4–6; *Gazeta Wyborcza* (Warsaw), February 15, 1990, quoted in *FBIS-EEU,* March 1, 1990, p. 48; *Gazeta Wyborcza,* April 20, 1990, *FBIS-EEU,* April 26, 1990, p. 53; *BTA* (Sofia radio station), February 13, 1990, *FBIS-EEU,* February 16, 1990, p. 7.

60. Michael Deis and Jill Chin, "Czech and Slovak Views on Economic Reform," *RFE/RL/RR,* vol. 1, no. 23, June 5, 1992, p. 64.

61. According to a poll of 1,440 Soviet citizens in May 1990 conducted by the All-Union Center for the Study of Public Opinion, quoted in V. Kosmarskii et al., "Attitudes of the Population toward the Prospect of Making the Transition to a Market," *Soviet Review* (July–August 1991), p. 25.

62. Media and Opinion Research Department, RFE/RL Research Institute, *RFE/RL/RR,* vol. 1, no. 21, May 22, 1992, pp. 62–63.

63. *WSJ,* March 20, 1992, A6.

64. Janos Kornai, "An Emotional Bulletin on Economic Transformation," (Budapest: HVG RT, 1989), quoted in Karoly Okolcsanyi, "Janos Kornai's Recipe for Economic Recovery," *RFE/REEU,* vol. 1, no. 6, February 9, 1990, pp. 18–21.

65. Nelson, "The Politics of Economic Transformation," pp. 442–447; Haggard and Kaufman, "Economic Adjustment and the Prospects for Democracy," pp. 336–338; Przeworski, *Democracy and the Market,* pp. 180–187.

66. Samuel P. Huntington, *Political Order in Changing Societies* (New Haven: Yale University Press, 1968), pp. 346–362; Dahl, *Polyarchy*, pp. 33–47; Dankwart A. Rustow, "Transitions to Democracy: Toward a Dynamic Model," *Comparative Politics*, vol. 2 (April 1970), pp. 337–363.

67. Albert O. Hirschman, "The Case against 'One Thing at a Time,'" *World Development*, vol. 18, no. 8, p. 121.

68. Peter Reddaway, "The End of the Empire," *New York Review of Books*, November 7, 1991, p. 53.

69. *Itar-Tass*, January 12, 1993, *FBIS-SOV*, January 12, 1993, p. 15; *Il Giornale*, October 18, 1992, *FBIS-SOV*, October 22, 1992, p. 33.

70. *Interfax*, December 21, 1992, pp. 6–7.

71. *AWSJW*, August 24, 1992, p. 2.

72. See Table 3.1.

73. *Economist*, March 13, 1993, p. 10.

74. Prabhu Pingali and Vo-Tong Xuan, "Vietnam: Decollectivization and Rice Productivity Growth," *Economic Development and Cultural Change*, vol. 40, no. 4 (July 1992), p. 712.

75. Melanie Beresford, "The Political Economy of Dismantling the 'Bureaucratic Centralism and Subsidy System' in Vietnam," in *Southeast Asia in the 1990s*, ed. Kevin Hewison, Richard Robison, and Garry Rodan (London: Allen & Unwin, 1993), p. 222.

76. Bartlomiej Kaminski, *The Collapse of State Socialism: The Case of Poland* (Princeton: Princeton University Press, 1991), p. 179.

77. Janos Kornai, "The Hungarian Reform Process: Visions, Hopes, and Reality," in *Remaking the Economic Institutions of Socialism*, ed. David Stark and Victor Nee (Stanford: Stanford University Press, 1989), p. 36.

78. *Economist*, January 23, 1993, pp. 21–23.

2. Explaining the Tocqueville Paradox

1. Author's estimate, see Table 3.1; the quasi-private sector here refers to economic entities controlled jointly by groups of individuals and local communities.

2. *PD*, February 20, 1993, p. 2.

3. *CTW*, no. 75, June 6–12, 1993, p. 48.

4. *CD*, January 6, 1992, p. 4.

5. *CTW*, no. 75, June 6–12, 1993, p. 48.

6. Alexis de Tocqueville, *The Old Regime and the French Revolution* (New York: Anchor Books, 1955), pp. 176–177.

7. Ibid.

8. Edmund Burke, *Reflections on the Revolution in France* (New York: Penguin Books, 1984), p. 106.

9. Ibid.

10. Samuel P. Huntington, *Political Order in Changing Societies* (New Haven: Yale University Press, 1968), pp. 362–380.

11. Albert O. Hirschman, *Journeys toward Progress* (New York: The Twentieth Century Fund, 1963), pp. 276–297.

12. Classified CCP document issued by the Politburo on February 20, 1992, excerpted in *WJ*, March 2, 1992, p. 3.

13. Huntington, *Political Order in Changing Societies*, p. 344.

14. For in-depth analyses of the role of individual leadership see Dankwart A. Rustow, ed., *Philosophers and Kings: Studies in Leadership*, especially chapters on Ataturk and Bismarck (New York: George Braziller, 1970); for a study of coalition-building during the Meiji Restoration, see James White, "State Building and Modernization: The Meiji Restoration," in *Crisis, Choice, and Change: Historical Studies of Political Development*, ed. Gabriel Almond, Scott Flanagan, and Robert Mundt (Boston: Little, Brown and Co., 1973), pp. 499–559; for an excellent study of historical cases of state-guided reforms, see Ellen Kay Trimberger, *Revolution from Above: Military Bureaucrats and Development in Japan, Turkey, Egypt, and Peru* (New Brunswick, N.J.: Transaction Books, 1978).

15. Wlodzimierz Brus, "The East European Reforms: What Happened to Them?" *Soviet Studies* (April 1979), pp. 257–258.

16. Samuel P. Huntington, "One Soul at a Time: Political Science and Political Reform," *American Political Science Review*, vol. 82, no. 1 (March 1988), p. 4; Hirschman, *Journeys toward Progress*, pp. 251–267.

17. Guillermo O'Donnell and Philippe Schmitter, *Transitions from Authoritarian Rule: Tentative Conclusions* (Baltimore: Johns Hopkins University Press, 1986), p. 26. Judith Sedaitis and Jim Butterfield compiled several fascinating studies detailing the rise of autonomous social movements in the Soviet Union during *perestroika*. See Sedaitis and Butterfield, eds., *Perestroika from Below: Social Movements in the Soviet Union* (Boulder, Colo.: Westview Press, 1991).

18. Stephen K. Ma, "Chinese Bureaucracy and Post-Mao Reforms," *Asian Survey* (November 1990), p. 1039. Before 1978, only 12.8 percent of party members attained a level of education of senior high school or above. Stanley Rosen, "The Chinese Communist Party and Chinese Society," *Australian Journal of Chinese Affairs*, no. 24 (July 1990), p. 58.

19. Andrew Walder, *Communist Neo-Traditionalism: Work and Authority in Chinese Industry* (Berkeley: University of California Press, 1986), addressed the issue of the organized dependency of Chinese industrial workers.

20. Timothy Garton Ash, *The Uses of Adversity: Essays on the Fate of Central Europe* (New York: Vintage Books, 1989).

21. Vladimir Tismaneanu, *Reinventing Politics: Eastern Europe from Stalin to Havel* (New York: The Free Press, 1992), pp. 113–174; Robert Zuzowski, *Political Dissent and Opposition in Poland: The Workers' Defense Committee "KOR"* (Westport, Conn.: Praeger, 1992); Janine Wedel, ed., *The Unplanned Society: Poland during and after Communism* (New York: Columbia University Press, 1992).

22. Donna Bahry and Brian D. Silver, "Soviet Citizen Participation on the Eve of Democratization," *American Political Science Review*, vol. 84, no. 3 (September 1990), pp. 821–847.

23. Ash, *The Uses of Adversity;* Abraham Brumberg, ed., *Poland: Genesis of a Revolution* (New York: Vintage Books, 1983); Peter Reddaway, "Dissent in the Soviet Union," *Problems of Communism* (November–December 1983), pp. 1–15;

Vladimir Shlapentokh, *Soviet Intellectuals and Political Power: The Post-Stalin Era* (Princeton: Princeton University Press, 1990).

24. See Merle Goldman, *China's Intellectuals: Advise and Dissent* (Cambridge, Mass.: Harvard University Press, 1981).

25. The Soviet intelligentsia, for example, was the driving force behind the mushrooming of informal groups in the late 1980s. Vladimir Brovkin, "Revolution from Below: Informal Political Associations in Russia, 1988–1989," *Soviet Studies,* vol. 42, no. 2 (April 1990).

26. Jeffrey W. Hahn, "Continuity and Change in Russian Political Culture," *British Journal of Political Science,* no. 21 (September 1991), pp. 393–421; Min Qi, *Zhongguo zhengzhi wenhua* (*Chinese Political Culture,* Kunmin: Yunnan People's Publishing House, 1989).

27. Vladimir G. Kostakov, Abram Bergson, and Jerry Hough, "Labor Problems in Light of *Perestroika,*" *Soviet Economy,* vol. 4, no. 1 (1988), pp. 95–101.

28. Min, *Chinese Political Culture,* pp. 179 and 190.

29. Rada Nikolaev, "Results of the National Elections," *RFE/REEU,* vol. 1, no. 26, June 29, 1990, pp. 1–4.

30. Michael Shafir, "Romanian Local Elections Herald New Political Map," *RFE/RL/RR,* vol. 1, no. 11, March 13, 1992, pp. 24–31.

31. Some of the best examples of coalition-building can be found in Ezra Vogel's study of reform in Guangdong Province, *One Step Ahead in China: Guangdong under Reform* (Cambridge, Mass.: Harvard University Press, 1989).

32. See Alfred Stepan, *Rethinking Military Politics* (Princeton: Princeton University Press, 1988), p. 7.

33. *PD,* May 11, 1992, p. 1; *ZGTJNJ, 1991,* p. 737.

34. Huntington, *The Third Wave,* pp. 85–100; Laurence Whitehead, "International Aspects of Democratization," in *Transitions from Authoritarian Rule: Comparative Perspectives,* ed. Guillermo O'Donnell et al. (Baltimore: Johns Hopkins University Press, 1988), pp. 3–46.

35. Larry Diamond, "Promoting Democracy," *Foreign Policy,* no. 87 (Summer 1992), pp. 25–46; O'Donnell and Schmitter reached the same conclusion in *Transitions from Authoritarian Rule: Tentative Conclusions,* p. 20.

36. *NYT,* November 12, 1991, C18.

37. *NYT,* February 20, 1992, C3.

38. *Economist,* March 13, 1993, p. 10.

39. For a case study of the impact of external economic forces on China's economic reform in the 1980s, see Nicholas Lardy, *Foreign Trade and Economic Reform in China, 1978–1990* (Cambridge: Cambridge University Press, 1990).

40. *PD,* April 21, 1992, p. 1. This figure represents the invested amount and is smaller than the $121.5 billion in approved foreign investment contracts. See *CD,* April 22, 1992, p. 1, *PD,* September 16, 1991, p. 1.

41. *ZGTJNJ, 1991,* p. 851; *PD,* September 20, 1991, p. 1; *PD,* February 20, 1993, p. 2; *WJ,* December 31, 1992, p. 16.

42. The trade ratio for 1978 is calculated from data in *ZGTJNJ, 1991,* p. 31; the figure for 1992 is from *PD,* June 26, 1993, p. 6. According to Dwight Perkins, the average ratio between exports and GNP for very large countries in the per capita income range of $600 to $2,000 was about 12 percent, Perkins, "Reform-

ing China's Economic System," *Journal of Economic Literature,* vol. 26 (June 1988), p. 635; for the Soviet Union, the comparable ratio was less than 5 percent in 1990, *Business in the USSR* (May 1991), p. 52; the ratio for the United States came from *Economist,* July 4, 1992, p. 26. However, calculating the ratio between exports and GNP presents a major problem for China because of the disputed size of its real GNP; see Lardy, *Foreign Trade and Economic Reform in China,* pp. 150–155.

43. *WJ,* September 16, 1991, p. 10.

44. *Outlook,* April 27, 1992, p. 16.

45. *Fortune,* April 5, 1993, p. 98; *AWSJW,* March 15, 1993, p. 11.

46. *Outlook,* March 16, 1992, p. 31.

47. *Financial Times,* June 7, 1993, p. 11.

48. Thomas Remington, "Regime Transition in Communist Systems: The Soviet Case," *Soviet Economy,* vol. 6, no. 2 (1990), p. 161.

49. Timothy Colton, "The Politics of Democratization: The Moscow Election of 1990," *Soviet Economy,* vol. 4, no. 6 (1990), pp. 285–344.

50. See Paul Gregory, "The Impact of *Perestroika* on the Soviet Planned Economy: Results of a Survey of Moscow Economic Officials," *Soviet Studies,* vol. 43, no. 5 (1991), pp. 859–873.

51. *FEER,* October 5, 1989, pp. 24–26.

52. Robert Delfs, "Saying No to Peking," *FEER,* April 4, 1991, pp. 21–28. The rapid gain in local fiscal autonomy at the expense of the central government was reflected in the fact that between 1979 and 1988 the central government incurred a net budget deficit of 74.7 billion yuan, whereas local governments had a budget surplus of nearly 10 billion yuan. General Planning Department, Ministry of Finance, *China Financial Statistics (1950–1988)* (Beijing: Financial and Economic Publishing House, 1989), p. 149.

53. Quoted in David Remnick, "Dead Souls," *New York Review of Books,* December 19, 1991, p. 74.

54. Stephen M. Meyer, "How the Threat (and the Coup) Collapsed: The Politicization of the Soviet Military," *International Security,* vol. 6, no. 3 (Winter 1991/1992), pp. 5–38.

55. *NYT,* July 27, 1991, A7. The primary reasons cited for those who left the CPSU were the following: (1) lack of faith in the CPSU as a leading force in society—26 percent; (2) absence of any real benefit from their participation in party work— 26 percent; (3) unwillingness to associate with unworthy people—25 percent; (4) disagreement with the policy of *perestroika*—17 percent; (5) loss of faith in socialism—14 percent; (6) unwillingness to answer for the mistakes of the past—13 percent. *Pravda,* February 26, 1991, *FBIS-SOV,* March 7, 1991, p. 46.

56. Vladisklav Romanov, "Politics and the Provinces—A View from the Ukraine," *Russia and the World,* no. 20 (1991), p. 21.

57. *MN,* no. 17, April 21–27, 1991, p. 7.

58. *MN,* no. 30, July 28–August 3, 1991, p. 6.

59. *LW,* no. 1 (1990), p. 12.

60. *FEER,* February 4, 1993, p. 27.

61. Samuel P. Huntington was one of the first to observe the connection between

dramatic social change and increasing incidence of corruption, see Huntington, *Political Order in Changing Societies*, pp. 59–71; also see Ben Slay, "Financial Scandals and the Evolution of the Banking System," *RFE/REE*, vol. 2, no. 39, September 27, 1991, pp. 21–27. For an analysis of official corruption in China, see Connie Squires Meaney, "Market Reform and Disintegrative Corruption in Urban China," and Jean Oi, "Partial Market Reform and Corruption in Rural China," in *Reform and Reaction in Post-Mao China: The Road to Tiananmen*, ed. Richard Baum (New York: Routledge, 1991), pp. 104–161.

62. *WJ*, October 22, 1991, p. 10; *WJ*, March 28, 1992, p. 11.

63. *Outlook*, January 9, 1989, p. 7.

64. Min, *Chinese Political Culture*, p. 98.

65. *WJ*, January 25, 1992, p. 10.

66. Friedrick A. Hayek, *The Road to Serfdom* (Chicago: University of Chicago Press, 1944); Dahl, *Polyarchy;* Charles E. Lindblom, *Politics and Markets* (New York: Basic Books, 1977); Milton Friedman, *Capitalism and Freedom* (Chicago: University of Chicago Press, 1962); Peter L. Berger, *The Capitalist Revolution* (New York: Basic Books, 1986).

67. Janos Kornai, "The Hungarian Reform Process: Visions, Hopes, and Reality," and Ivan Szelenyi, "Eastern Europe in an Epoch of Transition: Toward a Socialist Mixed Economy?" in *Remaking the Economic Institutions of Socialism*, ed. Stark and Nee, pp. 32–94 and 208–232; Wlodzimierz Brus, "Political Pluralism and Markets in Communist Systems," in *Pluralism in the Soviet Union*, ed. Susan Gross Solomon (New York: St. Martin's Press, 1982), pp. 108–130.

68. See Daniel Deudney and G. John Ikenberry, "The International Sources of Soviet Change," *International Security*, vol. 6, no. 3 (Winter 1991/1992), pp. 74–118.

69. The upsurge of political and social activities following decompression was similarly common in transition from authoritarian regimes. See O'Donnell and Schmitter, *Transitions from Authoritarian Rule: Tentative Conclusions*, pp. 53–56.

70. *ZGTJNJ, 1991*, p. 396.

71. Calculated from *ZGTJNJ, 1991,* pp. 378 and 396.

72. See Table 3.1.

73. *Outlook*, August 5, 1991, p. 14.

74. The State Statistical Bureau, *Zhongguo shanye waijin tongji zhiliao, 1952–1988* (*Chinese Commerce and Foreign Economic Relations Statistical Data,* Beijing: Chinese Statistical Publishing House, 1990), pp. 537 and 539.

75. In a poll in 1987, 33.67 percent of industrial workers, 39.32 percent of the cadres, and 26.56 percent of the peasants said that they did not understand or tolerate the 1986–1987 democracy movement. Min, *Chinese Political Culture*, p. 125.

76. *MN*, no. 14, April 9–16, 1989, p. 8.

77. See Anna A. Temkina, "The Workers' Movement in Leningrad, 1986–1991," *Soviet Studies*, vol. 44, no. 2 (1992), pp. 209–236; I. G. Shablinskii, "Where Is Our Labor Movement Going?" *Soviet Review* (November–December 1991), pp. 44–61.

78. Vera Tolz, *The USSR's Emerging Multiparty System* (New York: Praeger, 1990), pp. 10–45.

79. Tolz, "Informal Groups and Soviet Politics," *RL/RUSSR*, vol. 1, no. 47, November 24, 1989, p. 4.

80. *MN*, no. 7, February 25–March 4, 1990, p. 9.

81. Ibid., p. 6.

82. See Tolz, *The USSR's Emerging Multiparty System*, pp. 36–45; Brovkin, "Revolution from Below," pp. 233–257.

83. See Jan Arveds Trapans, ed., *Toward Independence: The Baltic Popular Movements* (Boulder, Colo.: Westview Press, 1991).

84. In a major speech made to CCP propagandists in May 1987, Zhao Ziyang effectively ended the conservatives' attempts to broaden the antibourgeois liberalization campaign into the economic arena. He received Deng's strong support. For a full text of Zhao's speech, see *PD*, July 10, 1987, pp. 1–2.

85. Estimate based on data in *ZGTJNJ, 1991*, pp. 26, 47, 315, 375, 379, and 395.

86. According to official figures, by the end of 1990 China had 73,857 free markets for consumer goods and 3,000 markets for "small industrial products." *CD*, September 13, 1991, p. 4.

87. *ZGTJNJ, 1991*, pp. 31 and 615. In 1986, this ratio was 11.1 percent; since 1987, the ratio has never fallen below 12.2 percent.

88. For a summary of the political mobilization of the labor force in the Soviet Union, see Peter Rutland, "Labor Unrest and Movements in 1989 and 1990," *Soviet Economy*, vol. 6, no. 3 (1990), pp. 345–384; Elizabeth Teague, "Embryos of People's Power," *RL/RUSSR*, vol. 1, no. 32, August 11, 1989, pp. 1–4.

89. Alexander Rahr, "Inside the Interregional Group," *RL/RUSSR*, vol. 2, no. 43, October 26, 1990, p. 1.

90. For a list of newly formed political parties and their founding dates, see *New Outlook* (Fall 1990), pp. 29–38; Eberhard Schneider, "The New Political Forces in Russia, Ukraine, and Belorussia," *RL/RUSSR*, vol. 3, no. 50, December 13, 1991, pp. 10–18.

91. *Outlook*, April 27, 1992, p. 16; *PD*, May 16, 1992, p. 1. The total value of assets held by state industrial firms amounted to 1,730 billion yuan in 1991, according to *CD*, July 26, 1991, p. 3.

92. Official data, reprinted in *WJ*, September 11, 1991, p. 10.

93. Poll conducted by the Soviet Center for Public Opinion and Market Research in thirty-three cities and seventeen rural districts in the Soviet Union, *MN*, no. 31, July 28–August 3, 1991, p. 6.

94. Dawn Mann, "Nongovernment by Decree," *RL/RUSSR*, vol. 2, no. 35, August 31, 1990, pp. 1–4.

95. *MN*, no. 18, May 5–12, 1991, p. 5.

96. Alexander Rahr, "The CPSU Strikes Back," *RL/RUSSR*, vol. 3, no. 8, February 22, 1991, pp. 1–3.

97. *PD*, December 24, 1991, p. 3.

98. UPI dispatch, December 7, 1989.

99. *CD*, January 22, 1992, p. 3; *CD*, December 30, 1991, p. 1.

100. For an account of the campaign, see Michael E. Urban, "Boris El'tsin, Democratic Russia, and the Campaign for the Russian Presidency," *Soviet Studies*, vol. 44, no. 2 (1992), pp. 187–207.

101. Elizabeth Perry and Ellen Fuller, for example, noted the "exclusivity" of the student movement in 1989; see Perry and Fuller, "China's Long March to Democracy," *World Policy Journal* (Fall 1991), pp. 663–685.

102. See Table 3.1.

3. China's Capitalist Revolution

1. For a review of privatization in Eastern Europe and the former Soviet Union, see *RFE/RL/RR*, vol. 1, no. 17, April 24, 1992. For articles on the subject, see David Lipton and Jeffrey Sachs, "Privatization in Eastern Europe: The Case of Poland," *Brookings Papers on Economic Activity*, no. 2 (1990), pp. 293–314; Janos Kornai, "Socialist Transformation and Privatization: Shifting from a Socialist System," *East European Politics and Society*, vol. 4, no. 2 (Spring 1990), pp. 255–304; Igor Filatotchev, Trevor Buck, and Mike Wright, "Privatization and Buy-Outs in the USSR," *Soviet Studies*, vol. 44, no. 2 (1992), pp. 265–282.

2. Janos Kornai, *The Road to a Free Economy* (New York: Norton, 1990); Gertrude E. Schroeder, "Property Rights Issues in Economic Reforms in Socialist Countries," *Studies in Comparative Communism*, vol. 21, no. 2 (Summer 1988), pp. 175–188.

3. See *Guanyu jingji guanli tizhi gaige zongti shexiang de chubu yijian* (*Some Preliminary Views on a Comprehensive Program for Reforming the Economic System*, the Office of the Economic Systems Reform Group of the Finance Commission of the State's Council, December 3, 1979); *Shinian jingji tizhi gaige* (*Ten Years of Economic Systems Reform in China*, Beijing: Jingji Guanli Publishing Co. and Gaige Publishing Co., 1988), pp. 826–834; *Jingji tizhi gaige dehuigu hejinghou gaige dejibeng silu* (*A Review of the Economic Systems Reform and Basic Thoughts on Future Reforms*, the Office of the Research Group on Economic Systems Reform, the State Council, April 23, 1987), in *Ten Years of Economic Systems Reform*, pp. 835–841.

4. *CD,* January 6, 1992, p. 4.

5. *Zhongguo xiangzhen qiye nianjian, 1990* (*Yearbook of China's Rural Industries,* Beijing: Nongye Publishing Co., 1991), pp. 4 and 125–127.

6. *LW,* no. 52, December 30, 1991, p. 6.

7. Liu Wenpu, Zhang Houyi, and Qing Shaoxiang, "Guanyu nongchun siying jingji fazhan de lilun fengxi" ("A Theoretical Analysis of the Development of the Rural Private Economy"), *Zhongguo shehui kexue* (*Social Sciences in China*), no. 6 (1989), pp. 63–75.

8. *Outlook,* April 27, 1992, p. 16.

9. *PD,* December 24, 1991, p. 3.

10. *LW,* no. 52, December 30, 1991, p. 6.

11. *LW,* no. 26 (1991), p. 19; *JR,* October 21, 1989, p. 2.

12. *ZGTJNJ, 1991,* pp. 15–16, 95, and 377.

13. *Almanac of China's Economy, 1988,* section 11, p. 158; *Almanac of China's Economy, 1989,* section 10, p. 153.

14. *LW,* no. 50, December 16, 1991, p. 7; *Outlook,* August 5, 1991, p. 14.

15. *WJ,* August 31, 1991, p. 11.

16. Calculated using the data given in Tables 3.1 and 3.3.

17. *PD*, February 19, 1991, p. 3.

18. *PD*, January 16, 1991, p. 1.

19. *Zhongguo tongji zhaiyao, 1992 (Digest of China's Statistical Data)*, p. 93.

20. *PD*, December 11, 1991, p. 3; *Outlook*, January 6, 1992, p. 17.

21. Robert F. Ash, "The Evolution of Agricultural Policy," *China Quarterly*, no. 116 (December 1988), pp. 529–555.

22. This program was spelled out in "Zhonggong zhongyang guanyu jiakuai nongye fazhan ruogan wenti de jueding chao'an" ("The Resolution of the Central Committee of the CCP on Accelerating Agricultural Development and Other Issues—Draft") and "Nongchun renmin gongshe gongzhuo tiaole shixing chao'an" ("Working Regulations for Rural People's Communes—Draft"); also see Lu Xueyi, *Liancan chengbao zherenzhi yanjiu (Studies of the Yield-Based Contract Responsibility System*, Shanghai: Shanghai People's Publishing Co., 1984).

23. Ibid.

24. Lu, *Studies of the Yield-Based Responsibility System*, pp. 64–71.

25. Ibid., pp. 75 and 84.

26. *Zhongguo nongchun tongji nianjian, 1985 (Statistical Yearbook of Rural China, 1985)*, p. 3.

27. *WEH*, February 15, 1988, p. 2.

28. Ibid.

29. *Outlook*, June 20, 1988, pp. 3–5.

30. *Zhongguo gongchandang zhizheng sishi nian (The Chinese Communist Party's Four Decades in Power, 1949–1989*, Beijing: Zhonggong Dangshi Ziliao Publishing Co., 1989), pp. 446 and 545.

31. *WEH*, September 19, 1988, p. 6.

32. *Outlook*, December 15, 1986; "On Finding Employment for Urban Youth," issued by the Central Committee and the State Council on August 24, 1979.

33. "Guowuyuan guanyu chengzhen fei nongye geti jingji ruogan zhengcexing guiding" ("The State Council's Supplementary Regulations on Several Policy Regulations on Urban Nonagricultural Private Economy"), April 13, 1983, *Zhongyao jingji fagui ziliao xuanbian, 1977–1986 (Selection of the Central Government's Laws and Regulations on the Economy*, Beijing: Zhongguo Jingji Publishing Co., 1987), p. 25.

34. *JR*, October 21, 1989, p. 3.

35. *WJ*, August 31, 1991, p. 11.

36. "Guowuyuan guanyu chengzhen laodongzhe hezuo jingyingde ruogan guiding" ("The State Council's Regulations on Urban Laborers' Cooperative Economic Activities"), *Zhongyao jingji fagui ziliao xuanbian, 1977–1986 (Selection of the Central Government's Laws and Regulations on the Economy*, Beijing: Zhongguo Jingji Publishing Co., 1987), p. 23.

37. Jia Ting and Wang Kaicheng, "Siying qiyezhu jieceng zaizhongguo de quqi he fazhan" ("The Rise and Development of a Class of Private Business Owners in China"), *Shehuixue Yanjiu (Sociological Studies)*, no. 6 (1988), pp. 89–100.

38. Gao Shangquan, "Shinian laide zhongguo jingji tizhi gaige" ("Chinese Economic System Reform in the Last Decade"), *Almanac of China's Economy*,

1989, section 2, p. 40; *PD,* September 10, 1990, p. 3; *CD,* October 26, 1991, p. 4.

39. *Xinguancha (New Observer),* September 10, 1988, p. 2.

40. Zhu Qingfang, "Chengxiang chabie yu nongchun shehui wenti" ("The Urban-Rural Gap and Rural Social Problems"), *Shehuixue Yanjiu (Sociological Studies),* no. 2 (1989), p. 26.

41. *Jingji Nianjiu (Economic Research),* no. 3 (1992), p. 35.

42. *Chinese Social Statistics, 1990* (Beijing: Zhongguo Tongji Publishers, 1990), p. 127.

43. Calculated from *Chinese Social Statistics, 1990,* p. 127, and *Chinese Social Statistics, 1985,* p. 291.

44. Stanley Rosen, "The Chinese Communist Party and Chinese Society: Popular Attitudes toward Party Membership and the Party's Image," *Australian Journal of Chinese Affairs,* no. 24 (July 1990), p. 57.

45. John Burns, "China's Nomenklatura System," *Problems of Communism* (September–October 1987), pp. 36–50.

46. Calculated from the data given in *ZGTJNJ, 1990,* p. 89, and Rosen, "The Chinese Communist Party and Chinese Society," pp. 55–57.

47. *Outlook,* November 3, 1986, p. 6.

48. *Outlook,* February 15, 1988, p. 10; *LW,* October 30, 1989, p. 16.

49. *Outlook,* February 15, 1988, p. 11.

50. *Almanac of China's Economy, 1988,* section 11, p. 158; *Almanac of China's Economy, 1989,* section 10, p. 153.

51. *CD,* June 26, 1992, p. 4; *PD,* February 19, 1991, p. 1.

52. Min Qi, *Zhongguo zhengzhi wenhua (Chinese Political Culture,* Kunmin: Yunnan People's Publishing House, 1989), pp. 33–35 and 68.

53. *PD,* July 18, 1986, p. 4.

54. *Outlook,* August 1, 1988, p. 6.

55. The Office for Public Opinion Survey and Sociological Studies of the Chinese Research Institute for Economic Systems Reform, *Gaige deshehui xinli: Bianqian yuxuanze (The Sociopsychology of Reform: Change and Choice,* Chengdu: Sichuan People's Publishing House, 1988), pp. 13–16.

56. *LW,* no. 52, December 30, 1991, pp. 6–7.

57. For a case study of the role of local political elites in the development of China's private sector, see Yia-Liang Liu, "Reform from Below: The Private Economy and Local Politics in the Rural Industrialization of Wenzhou," *China Quarterly,* no. 130 (June 1992), pp. 293–316.

58. Jia Ting, Wang Dekuan, and Tang Baoling, "Dui Liaoning siren qiye de diaocha yu sikao" ("An Investigation of and Some Thoughts on Private Firms in Liaoning"), *Shehuixue Yanjiu (Sociological Studies),* no. 5 (1987), pp. 39–45.

59. See Jean Oi, "Fiscal Reform and the Economic Foundations of Local State Corporatism in China," *World Politics,* vol. 45, no. 1 (October 1992), pp. 99–126.

60. *PD,* June 24, 1992, p. 2.

61. Zeng Guangcan, "A Review of Nine Years of Economic Reform in Guangdong," *Gaige (Reform),* no. 2 (1988), pp. 115–121.

62. *PD,* May 25, 1992, p. 1.

63. *LW,* no. 52, December 30, 1991, p. 6.
64. *PD,* December 24, 1991, p. 3.
65. *LW,* July 1, 1991, pp. 19–20.
66. *WEH,* January 30, 1984, p. 6.
67. *WJ,* September 16, 1991, p. 10.
68. *CD,* May 4, 1992, p. 4.
69. *Outlook,* March 19, 1990, p. 9.
70. *CD/BW,* April 21, 1992, p. 1; *PD,* September 24, 1991, p. 1.
71. *PD,* September 24, 1991, p. 1; *PD,* May 7, 1993, p. 1.
72. *WJ,* November 25, 1991, p. 10.
73. *CD,* May 4, 1992, p. 4.
74. *PD,* February 25, 1991, p. 1; *PD,* October 26, 1991, p. 3.
75. *PD,* May 21, 1993, p. 1.
76. *WJ,* June 28, 1992, p. 6.
77. Nicholas Lardy reached the same conclusion in "Chinese Foreign Trade," *China Quarterly,* no. 131 (September 1992), pp. 691–720.
78. See John Kao, "The Worldwide Web of Chinese Business," *Harvard Business Review* (March–April 1993), pp. 24–34; *Economist,* July 18, 1992, pp. 21–24.
79. *Economist,* July 18, 1992, p. 21.
80. *Zhongguo shangye waijing tongji ziliao, 1952–1988 (Statistical Data of Chinese Commerce and Foreign Trade),* pp. 548–549; *ZGTJNJ, 1991,* p. 630.
81. *WEH,* April 25, 1988, p. 14.
82. *JR,* October 21, 1989, p. 3.
83. There are about 20 million members of the CCP in the countryside; official statistics show that the total number of rural laborers in 1988 was about 400 million. The percentage of rural laborers who were members of the Party at the end of the 1980s was about 5 percent. *ZGTJNJ, 1990,* p. 330.
84. Jia and Wang, "The Rise and Development of a Class of Private Business Owners in China," p. 22.
85. Yu Taihou, "Siying jingji fazhan de lishi qushi—Shengyan siying jingji diaocha" ("The Historical Trend in the Development of the Private Economy—An Investigation of the Private Economy in Shengyan"), *Shehuixue Jikan (Social Science Journal),* nos. 2 and 3 (1989), p. 121.
86. Lin Qingsong, "Private Enterprises: Their Emergence, Rapid Growth, and Problems," in *China's Rural Industry: Structure, Development, and Reform,* ed. William Byrd and Lin Qingsong (New York: Oxford University Press, 1990), p. 180.
87. Zhang Musheng and Bai Ruobing, "Guanyu dangqian nongchun 'gugong' jingying de shijian yu lilun" ("On the Current Practice and Theory of Business Operations. Based on Hired Labor in the Countryside"), *Countryside, Economy, and Society,* vol. 3 (Beijing: Zhishi Publishing Co., 1985), p. 183.
88. Lin, "Private Enterprises: Their Emergence, Rapid Growth, and Problems," p. 177.
89. Zhou Qiren and Hu Zhuanjun, "Zhongguo xiangzheng qiye de zichan xingcheng, yinjin tezheng jiqi hongguan xiaoying" ("The Formation and Inflow of Capital and Their Macroeconomic Effect in China's Rural Industries"), *Social Sciences in China,* no. 6 (1987), pp. 41–66.

90. Liu Wenpu, Zhang Houyi, and Qing Shaoxiang, "Guanyu nongchun siying jingji fazhan de lilun fengxi" ("A Theoretical Analysis of the Development of the Rural Private Economy"), *Social Sciences in China*, no. 6 (1989), pp. 63–75.

91. Victor Nee, "Social Inequalities in Reforming State Socialism: Between Redistribution and Markets in China," *American Sociological Review*, vol. 56 (June 1991), pp. 267–282.

92. See Tian Jiyun's article on rural reform, *PD*, December 24, 1991, p. 3.

93. Calculated from the figures given in Rosen, "The Chinese Communist Party and Chinese Society," pp. 54–57.

94. Dai Zhou and Kang Nungcheng, *Nongchun zhengdang wenti wenda* (*Questions and Answers on the Rectification of the Party in the Countryside*, Beijing: Hongqi Publishing House, 1986), pp. 6 and 56.

95. Ibid., pp. 10–11.

96. Survey of 465 peasants done in July 1987 by a private polling group, used in Min, *Chinese Political Culture*, p. 102.

97. *WJ*, May 3, 1992, p. 6.

98. *WJ*, November 25, 1991, p. 10.

99. *CD*, January 21, 1992, p. 4.

100. *PD*, December 24, 1991, p. 3.

101. *LW*, no. 26, July 1, 1991, p. 19.

102. A government newspaper reported in late 1991 that about 80 percent of private businesses, 40 percent of collective firms, and 20 percent of SOEs engaged in tax evasion. *WJ*, October 3, 1991, p. 10.

103. In a poll of 900 entrepreneurs in a city in East China, 86 percent of the respondents said that their main reason for falsely registering their businesses as "collectively owned" was to gain "a sense of security" and "cut through government red tape." *LW*, no. 26 (1991), p. 20.

104. *WJ*, November 29, 1991, p. 10.

105. *WJ*, October 13, 1991, p. 6.

106. *CD*, March 28, 1992, p. 4; *WJ*, August 11, 1991, p. 10.

107. *WJ*, May 17, 1992, p. 6.

108. *WJ*, February 4, 1993, p. 17.

109. *WJ*, February 25, 1993, p. 37; *WSJ*, January 14, 1993, A12.

110. *PD*, November 21, 1991, p. 4; *CD*, November 9, 1991, p. 4.

111. *Min Piao (Hong Kong)*, story reprinted in *WJ*, November 4, 1991, p. 10; *Min Piao*, story reprinted in *WJ*, November 11, 1991, p. 11; *WJ*, August 30, 1991, p. 10.

4. The Private Sector under *Perestroika*

1. TASS, September 17, 1985, *FBIS-SOV*, September 18, 1985, T1.

2. Gregory Grossman, "The 'Second Economy' of the USSR," *Problems of Communism*, vol. 26, no. 5 (September–October 1977), pp. 25–40.

3. *Rabochaya tribuna*, July 14, 1990, *FBIS-SOV*, July 18, 1990, pp. 60–61.

4. *Rabochaya tribuna*, November 2, 1990, *FBIS-SOV*, November 7, 1990, p. 57.

5. See Stephen White, *Gorbachev in Power* (Cambridge: Cambridge University

Press, 1991), ch. 2; Anders Aslund, *Gorbachev's Struggle for Economic Reform* (Ithaca: Cornell University Press, 1989), chs. 3–5. In terms of decollectivizing agriculture, the policy option of leasing farm land to peasants was not seriously considered until 1989. Karen M. Brooks, "Soviet Agriculture's Halting Reforms," *Problems of Communism*, no. 2 (March–April 1990), pp. 29–41.

6. The Soviet government did not officially lift restrictions on moonlighting until October 1988. *Izvestia*, October 3, 1988, *FBIS-SOV*, October 4, 1988, p. 65.

7. Anton Gurevich, "Obstacles to Individual Labor," *RL/RUSSR*, vol. 31, no. 31, July 14, 1987, pp. 1–4.

8. Moscow Domestic Service, April 30, 1987, *FBIS-SOV*, May 5, 1987, S1.

9. *Izvestia*, June 2, 1986, *FBIS-SOV*, June 26, 1986, S1.

10. Aslund, *Gorbachev's Struggle for Economic Reform*, pp. 154–163.

11. Karin Plokker, "The Development of Individual and Cooperative Labour Activity in the Soviet Union," *Soviet Studies*, vol. 42, no. 3 (July 1990), p. 422.

12. *MN*, no. 22, June 5–12, 1988, p. 11.

13. *Voprosy ekonomiki*, no. 11 (1989), p. 130, quoted in Anthony Jones and William Moskoff, *Ko-ops: The Rebirth of Entrepreneurship in the Soviet Union* (Bloomington: Indiana University Press, 1991), p. 100.

14. *Ekonomika i zhizn*, no. 32 (1990), quoted in John Tedstrom, "Economic Slide Continues," *RL/RUSSR*, vol. 2, no. 37, September 14, 1990, p. 11.

15. *Selskaya zhizn*, March 12, 1989, *FBIS-SOV*, March 23, 1989, p. 81; for an account of the NEP, see Alan Ball, *Russia's Last Capitalists: The Nepmen, 1921–1929* (Berkeley: University of California Press, 1987).

16. *Pravda*, June 30, 1987, *CDSP*, vol. 29, no. 27, August 15, 1987, p. 11.

17. *Pravda*, November 25, 1987, *CDSP*, vol. 29, no. 48, December 30, 1987, p. 10.

18. Ibid.; also see Anthony Jones and William Moskoff, "New Cooperatives in the USSR," *Problems of Communism*, no. 6 (November–December 1989), pp. 27–39.

19. *Ekonomika i zhizn*, no. 49 (1990), *FBIS-SOV*, December 12, 1990, p. 53.

20. Ibid.

21. *MN*, no. 12, April 1–8, 1990, p. 10; *Ekonomika i zhizn*, no. 49 (December 1990), *FBIS-SOV*, December 12, 1990, p. 53.

22. *MN*, no. 12, April 1–8, 1990, p. 10.

23. *Commersant*, March 4, 1991, p. 14.

24. *Izvestia*, March 3, 1990, *FBIS-SOV*, March 8, 1990, p. 76.

25. Darrell Slider, Vladimir Magun, and Vladimir Gimpelson, "Public Opinion on Privatization: Republican Differences," *Soviet Economy*, vol. 7, no. 3 (1991), p. 271.

26. *Sotsialisticheskaya industriya*, February 21, 1989, *FBIS-SOV*, March 6, 1989, p. 94; *Izvestia*, July 11, 1989, *FBIS-SOV*, August 24, 1989, p. 80. Darrell Slider also identified the role of regional governments as a primary factor for the variations in the growth of the private sector. See Slider, "Embattled Entrepreneurs," p. 810.

27. *MN*, no. 12, April 1–8, 1990, p. 10.

28. *NYT*, July 14, 1991, A1 and A8.

29. *Commersant*, February 18, 1991.

30. *Economist*, January 4, 1992, p. 40; *Argumenty i fakty*, no. 43 (November 1991), p. 5, *CDSP*, vol. 43, no. 44, December 4, 1991, p. 24.

31. *Izvestia,* January 17, 1990, *FBIS-SOV,* January 22, 1990, pp. 115–117.
32. *Ekonomika i zhizn,* no. 49 (1990), *FBIS-SOV,* December 12, 1990, p. 53.
33. *Argumenty i fakty,* no. 43 (November 1991), p. 5, *CDSP,* vol. 43, no. 44, December 4, 1991, p. 24.
34. *Ekonomika i zhizn,* no. 49 (December 1990), *FBIS-SOV,* December 12, 1990, pp. 53–54.
35. *MN,* no. 12, April 1–8, 1990, p. 10.
36. Michael Burawoy and Kathryn Hendley, "Between *Perestroika* and Privatization: Divided Strategies and Political Crisis in a Soviet Enterprise," *Soviet Studies,* vol. 44, no. 3 (1992), pp. 371–402.
37. Jones and Moskoff, *Ko-ops,* pp. 20–23.
38. Simon Johnson and Heidi Kroll, "Managerial Strategies for Spontaneous Privatization," *Soviet Economy,* vol. 7, no. 4 (1991), pp. 299–303.
39. Jones and Moskoff, *Ko-ops,* p. 41.
40. *Sotsialisticheskaya industriya,* February 21, 1989, *FBIS-SOV,* March 6, 1989, pp. 93–96; John Tedstrom, "Soviet Cooperatives: A Difficult Road to Legitimacy," *RL/RUSSR,* vol. 32, no. 23, June 8, 1988, pp. 1–9; *Pravda,* September 14, 1989, *FBIS-SOV,* October 2, 1989, p. 91.
41. *MN,* no. 12, April 1–8, 1990, p. 10; *Pravda,* December 12, 1989, *FBIS-SOV,* December 29, 1989, p. 44.
42. John Tedstrom, "The Status of Soviet Cooperatives," *RL/RUSSR,* vol. 1, no. 34, August 25, 1989, p. 13.
43. Ibid., p. 14.
44. John Tedstrom, "Recent Trends in the Soviet Economy: A Balance Sheet on the Reforms," *RL/RUSSR,* vol. 1, no. 5, February 3, 1989, p. 14.
45. Stephen Wegren, "Dilemmas of Agrarian Reform in the Soviet Union," *Soviet Studies,* vol. 44, no. 1 (1992), p. 15.
46. Ibid., p. 16.
47. Ibid., p. 17.
48. Hedrick Smith, *The New Russians* (New York: Random House, 1990), p. 231.
49. Wegren, "Dilemmas of Agrarian Reform," p. 20.
50. Quoted in ibid., p. 17.
51. Chen Yizi, "Nongchuan de shunguan, Zhongguo de xiwang" ("The Dawn in the Countryside and China's Hope"), in *Nongchuan, jingji, shehui (Countryside, Economy, and Society),* vol. 1, ed. The Research Group on China's Rural Development Issues (Beijing: Zhishi Publishing House, 1985), p. 34.
52. Justin Yifu Lin, "Rural Reform and Agricultural Growth in China," *American Economic Review,* vol. 82, no. 1 (March 1992), pp. 34–51.
53. Sergei Strokov, "Back to the Land," *Business in the USSR* (February 1991), pp. 19–21.
54. Don Van Atta, "First Results of the 'Stolypin' Land Reform in the RSFSR," *RL/RUSSR,* vol. 3, no. 29, July 19, 1991, p. 21.
55. Keith Bush, "The Disastrous Last Year of the USSR," *RFE/RL/RR,* vol. 1, no. 12, March 20, 1992, p. 40.
56. Alla Romanova, "Exchange Fever on a Non-Existent Market," *Business in the USSR* (May 1991), pp. 24–26.
57. Vladimir Capelik, "Yeltsin's Economic Reform: A Pessimistic Appraisal," *RFE/RL/RR,* vol. 1, no. 4, January 24, 1992, p. 28.

58. Stefan Zhurek, "Commodity Exchanges in Russia: Success or Failure," *RFE/RL/RR*, vol. 2, no. 6, February 5, 1993, p. 41.
59. Sergei Shatolov, "Ownership Changes in the Soviet Union—Opinion from Moscow," *Transition* (World Bank newsletter), vol. 2, no. 4 (April 1991), p. 5.
60. *NYT*, February 8, 1992, p. 4.
61. Shatolov, "Ownership Changes in the Soviet Union," p. 4.
62. Bush, "The Disastrous Last Year of the USSR," p. 40.
63. *Interfax*, September 17, 1992, *FBIS-SOV*, September 18, 1992, p. 21.
64. For a skeptical view on mass privatization, see Stephen Cohen and Andrew Schwartz, "Privatization in the Former Soviet Empire: The Tunnel at the End of the Light," *American Prospect*, no. 13 (Spring 1993), pp. 99–108.
65. *Izvestia*, January 27, 1993, *CDSP*, vol. 45, no. 4, February 24, 1993, p. 33.
66. Ibid.
67. *WSJ*, June 16, 1993, A12.
68. *NYT*, February 25, 1993, A3.
69. Official figures released by the USSR at the end of 1991 showed that wages of workers in the cooperatives and joint ventures were at least one-third higher than those of workers in SOEs. Vladimir Gimpelson, "Changing Work Attitude in Russia's New Private Sector," *RFE/RL/RR*, vol. 2, no. 6, February 5, 1993, p. 39.
70. Gimpelson, "Changing Work Attitude in Russia's New Private Sector," p. 37.
71. *Izvestia*, February 2, 1993, *CDSP*, vol. 45, no. 5, March 3, 1993, p. 22; *NYT*, October 6, 1992, A10.
72. *NYT*, October 6, 1992, A10.
73. The Ministry of Finance's tax proposal was eventually rejected by the Supreme Soviet in May 1988. John Tedstrom, "New Draft Law on Income Taxes," *RL/RUSSR*, vol. 1, no. 21, May 26, 1989, pp. 8–10.
74. For the text of the resolution, see *Izvestia*, December 31, 1988, *FBIS-SOV*, January 3, 1989, pp. 54–56.
75. See Aslund, *Gorbachev's Struggle for Economic Reform*, pp. 104–108; also see James H. Noren, "The Soviet Economic Crisis: Another Perspective," *Soviet Economy*, vol. 6, no. 1 (1990), pp. 3–55.
76. Quoted in Tedstrom, "Soviet Cooperatives: A Difficult Road to Legitimacy," p. 6.
77. *Sotsialisticheskaya industriya*, February 21, 1989, *FBIS-SOV*, March 6, 1989, p. 94.
78. Ibid.
79. The figure for 1989 was given by Leonid Abalkin. See *Rabochaya tribuna*, July 14, 1990, *FBIS-SOV*, July 18, 1990, pp. 60–61; *NYT*, July 14, 1991, A1 and A8.
80. Tedstrom, "Soviet Cooperatives: A Difficult Road to Legitimacy."
81. *Izvestia*, December 22, 1988, *CDSP*, vol. 40, no. 51, January 18, 1989, p. 10.
82. *Izvestia*, July 11, 1989, *FBIS-SOV*, August 24, 1989, p. 80; *Izvestia*, January 20, 1990, *FBIS-SOV*, June 21, 1990, p. 108.
83. Slider, "Embattled Entrepreneurs," p. 817.
84. *Izvestia*, November 27, 1989, *FBIS-SOV*, December 6, 1989, p. 118.
85. Margot Jacobs, "Are the Restrictions on Medical Cooperatives Justified?" *RL/RUSSR*, vol. 1, no. 13, March 31, 1989, pp. 9–12.

86. For instance, workers on state farms earned an average of 192 rubles per person every month in 1987; the same figure for workers on collective farms was 167 rubles. Alan Pollard, ed., *USSR Facts and Figures Annual, 1990* (Gulf Breeze, Fla.: Academic International Press, 1990), pp. 122–123.

87. D. J. Peterson, "New Data Published on Employment and Unemployment in the USSR," *RL/RUSSR*, vol. 2, no. 1, January 5, 1990, p. 4.

88. Pollard, *USSR Facts and Figures Annual, 1990*, pp. 123–124.

89. Several Western and Soviet scholars cautioned against stereotyping the Russians as nonentrepreneurial. See Robert Shiller, Maxim Boycko, and Vladimir Korobov, "Hunting for Homo Sovieticus: Situational versus Attitudinal Factors in Economic Behavior," *Brookings Papers on Economic Activity*, no. 1 (1992), pp. 127–194. Their study had some problems, such as the small sample size of respondents (about 130) from Western countries and the use of the telephone to conduct the survey in Russia.

90. *Pravitelstvennyy vestnik*, no. 44 (October 1990), *FBIS-SOV*, November 15, 1990, pp. 41–42.

91. IMA-Press Agency poll of 801 residents of Moscow, *MN*, no. 20, May 27–June 3, 1990, p. 10.

92. Survey of 15,000 Soviet citizens by the Sociological Survey Bureau of Goskomstat, *Pravitelstvennyy vestnik*, no. 44 (October 1990), *FBIS-SOV*, November 15, 1990, pp. 41–42.

93. Survey of 2,597 people by the All-Union Center for the Study of Public Opinions, *Izvestia*, February 27, 1990, *FBIS-SOV*, March 21, 1990, p. 80.

94. Survey of 15,000 Soviet citizens by Goskomstat, *FBIS-SOV*, November 15, 1990, pp. 41–42.

95. Igor Filatotchev, Trevor Buck, and Mike Wright, "Privatization and Buy-Outs in the USSR," *Soviet Studies*, vol. 44, no. 2 (1992), p. 272.

96. Mary Cline, "Attitudes toward Economic Reform in Russia," *RFE/RL/RR*, vol. 2, no. 22, May 28, 1993, p. 46.

97. The detailed results of these polls are contained, respectively, in Tedstrom, "The Status of Soviet Cooperatives"; Jones and Moskoff, *Ko-ops*, p. 100; and *Izvestia*, March 3, 1990, *FBIS-SOV*, March 8, 1990, p. 76.

98. Poll of 801 residents in Moscow, *MN*, no. 20, May 27–June 3, 1990, p. 10.

99. Jones and Moskoff, *Ko-ops*, p. 100.

100. James Gibson et al., "Democratic Values and the Transformation of the Soviet Union," *Journal of Politics*, vol. 54, no. 2 (May 1992), p. 339.

101. *Ekonomika i zhizn*, no. 20 (May 1990), p. 9, reprinted in Jones and Moskoff, *Ko-ops*, p. 106.

102. Poll conducted by the All-Union Center for the Study of Public Opinion (VTsIOM) among 1,440 urban and rural residents in the Russian Federation, the Ukraine, Kazakhstan, and Kirgizia in May 1990, quoted in V. Kosmarskii et al., "Attitudes of the Population toward the Prospect of Making the Transition to a Market," *Soviet Review* (July–August 1991), p. 25.

103. See the same poll results cited in Jones and Moskoff, *Ko-ops*, p. 106.

104. Even scholars who have disputed the generalization about the prevalent Russian public hostility to a market economy acknowledge that lower-status groups in Russia were more likely to develop such hostility than higher-status groups. See Lynn Nelson et al., "Perspectives on Entrepreneurship and

Privatization in Russia: Policy and Public Opinion," *Slavic Review,* vol. 51, no. 2 (Summer 1992), pp. 271–286.

105. Poll of 922 Moscow residents, conducted by the Moscow Center for Political and Sociological Studies, *MN,* no. 2, January 8–14, 1990, p. 9.

106. *Argumenty i fakty,* no. 25 (June 1990), *FBIS-SOV,* July 26, 1990, p. 51.

107. See Slider et al., "Public Opinion on Privatization: Republic Differences," *Soviet Economy,* vol. 7, no. 3 (July–September 1991), p. 258.

108. For an excellent study on the criminalization of the private sector, see Jones and Moskoff, *Ko-ops,* pp. 78–93.

109. For a brief description of the participation by the *nomenklatura* in privatization, see Boris Rumer, "New Capitalists in the U.S.S.R.," *Challenge* (May–June 1991), pp. 19–22.

110. Tedstrom, "The Status of Soviet Cooperatives"; Plokker, "The Development of Individual and Cooperative Labor Activity in the Soviet Union," p. 415; Johnson and Kroll, "Managerial Strategies for Spontaneous Privatization," p. 312.

111. Original Soviet study cited in Jones and Moskoff, *Ko-ops,* p. 27.

112. Burawoy and Hendley, "Between *Perestroika* and Privatization," p. 381.

113. Filatotchev, Buck, and Wright, "Privatization and Buy-Outs in the USSR," p. 272.

114. *Izvestia,* December 22, 1987, *CDSP,* vol. 40, no. 51, January 18, 1988, p. 10.

115. Jones and Moskoff, *Ko-ops,* pp. xv and 8; Smith, *The New Russians,* pp. 175–261. John Tedstrom, "In Search of New Political and Economic Structures," *RL/RUSSR,* vol. 3, no. 42, October 18, 1991, p. 7.

116. Johnson and Kroll, "Managerial Strategies for Spontaneous Privatization," pp. 312–313.

117. Slider, "Embattled Entrepreneurs," p. 812, note 66.

118. Paul Gregory's study found that administrative staff in ministries and central institutions were least supportive of the private-sector activities (such as cooperatives and leasing). See Gregory, "The Impact of *Perestroika* on the Soviet Planned Economy: Results of a Survey of Moscow Economic Officials," *Soviet Studies,* vol. 43, no. 5 (1991), p. 870.

119. *Trud,* January 4, 1989, *FBIS-SOV,* January 6, 1989, p. 36.

120. *Izvestia,* March 3, 1990, *FBIS-SOV,* March 8, 1990, p. 76.

121. It was found that among people who received 80 rubles a month, only 8 percent supported cooperatives; among those who got 250 rubles a month, 20 percent voiced approval. And 24 percent of those with higher educations firmly supported cooperatives, while less than 10 percent of those with primary and incomplete secondary educations supported cooperatives. *Izvestia,* March 3, 1990, *FBIS-SOV,* March 8, 1990, p. 76.

122. Keith Bush, "Commonwealth of Independent States: Foreign Indebtedness," *RFE/RL/RR,* vol. 1, no. 2, January 10, 1992, p. 21.

123. *Sotsialisticheskaya industriya,* April 25, 1989, *FBIS-SOV,* May 2, 1989, p. 73.

124. *Washington Post National Weekly,* December 9–15, 1991, p. 20.

125. Andrei Vernikov, "New Entrants in Soviet Foreign Trade: Behavior Patterns and Regulation in the Transitional Period," *Soviet Studies,* vol. 43, no. 5 (1991), pp. 824–825; John Tedstrom, "Soviet Foreign Trade in 1990," *RL/RUSSR,* vol. 3, no. 15, April 12, 1991, p. 12.

126. Philip Hanson, "Joint Ventures Still Expanding despite Everything," *RL/RUSSR*, vol. 3, no. 32, August 9, 1991, p. 6; *Soviet Observer* (May 1991), p. 7.

127. *Soviet Observer* (May 1991), p. 7.

128. *Commersant*, March 11, 1991, p. 6.

129. *Izvestia*, April 3, 1990, *CDSP*, vol. 42, no. 15, May 16, 1990, pp. 28–29; *MN*, no. 51, December 24–31, 1989, pp. 8–9.

130. Tedstrom, "Recent Trends in the Soviet Economy," p. 13.

131. *Komsomolskaya pravda*, December 13, 1989, *FBIS-SOV*, December 15, 1989, p. 45.

132. *Pravitelstvennyy vestnik*, no. 44 (October 1990), *FBIS-SOV*, November 15, 1990, pp. 41–42.

133. *NYT*, April 23, 1992, A3.

134. Soltan Dzarasov, "What the USSR Wants from the West," *Business in the USSR* (May 1991), p. 2.

135. International Monetary Fund, *World Economic Outlook, 1991* (Washington, D.C., 1991), p. 29.

136. *Zhongguo shangye waijing tongji ziliao, 1952–1988 (Statistical Data of China's Commerce and Foreign Trade*, Beijing: Zhongguo Tongji Publishing Co., 1990), p. 545; *ZGTJNJ, 1991*, p. 630.

137. Zhongyang wenxian yanjiushi (The Office for Archive Research, the Central Committee of the CCP), *Chedi fouding wenhua dageming (Thoroughly Negate the Cultural Revolution*, Beijing: People's Publishing House, 1985), pp. 171–173.

138. John Scherer, ed., *USSR Facts and Figures Annual, 1987* (Gulf Breeze, Fla.: International Academic Press, 1987), p. 31.

139. Calculated from figures obtained from Stanley Rosen, "The Chinese Communist Party and Chinese Society: Popular Attitudes toward Party Membership and the Party's Image," *Australian Journal of Chinese Affairs*, no. 24 (July 1990), p. 55; Scherer, *USSR Facts and Figures Annual, 1987*, p. 31; *Guoji jingji he shehui tongji tiyao (Digest of International Economic and Social Statistics*, Beijing: Chinese Statistical Publishing House, 1985), p. 162.

140. Pollard, ed., *USSR Facts and Figures Annual, 1990*, p. 87.

141. Burawoy and Hendley, "Between *Perestroika* and Privatization," pp. 388–389.

142. Mary McAuley, "Politics, Economics, and Elite Realignment in Russia: A Regional Perspective," *Soviet Economy*, vol. 8, no. 1 (1992), pp. 68–76.

5.   The Self-Liberalization of China's Mass Media

1. Deng Xiaoping's December 25, 1980, speech, "Implement the Policy of Readjustment and Ensure Stability and Unity," *Chinese Press Almanac, 1984 (Zhongguo xinwen nianjiang)*, pp. 6–7. The four principles were "Marxism-Leninism-Mao Zedong thought, socialism, the leading role of the Communist Party, and the people's democratic dictatorship."

2. *Chinese Press Almanac, 1988*, pp. 30–31; *DL* (August 1987), pp. 8–9.

3. *PD*, October 23, 1990, p. 1. The number of newspapers was 2,340 at the end of 1988. *Outlook*, December 19, 1988, p. 4; *WJ*, July 27, 1991, p. 10.

4. *WJ*, December 19, 1991, p. 4; *PD*, December 19, 1991, p. 4.
5. *NF* (April 1988), pp. 9–10; *Outlook*, April 18, 1988, pp. 18–19.
6. *DL* (December 1988), pp. 18–21.
7. *Outlook*, March 28, 1989, pp. 16–17.
8. *DL* (May 1989), p. 38; (June 1989), pp. 36–37.
9. *DL* (November 1988), pp. 18–19.
10. *WJ*, April 1, 1993, p. 17.
11. *WJ*, November 13, 1991, p. 10.
12. *DL* (April 1989), pp. 12–13.
13. *NF* (December 1989), pp. 8–13.
14. "Ministry of Finance's Document on the Interim Regulations on Self-Responsibility for Budgeting for Cultural, Educational, Health, and Administrative Agencies," November 23, 1979, in *Collection of PRC Financial Laws and Regulations* (Beijing: Chinese Financial and Economic Publishing House, 1987), pp. 1–2; "The State Council's Announcement on Full Financial Self-Responsibility for the Publication of Periodicals," December 29, 1984, in *Collection of Chinese Laws on Economic Management*, vol. 2, ed. the Institute of Law, the Chinese Academy of Social Sciences (Changchun: Jilin People's Publishing House, 1985), pp. 1869–1870.
15. *WJ*, November 12, 1992, p. 16.
16. *Outlook*, August 7, 1989, pp. 34–35.
17. *Outlook*, January 2, 1989, p. 34.
18. *China Spring*, no. 68 (January 1989), p. 48.
19. *WJ*, May 3, 1993, A19.
20. *CD*, December 20, 1991, p. 4; *CD/BW*, August 5, 1991, p. 1.
21. *ZGTJNJ, 1991*, pp. 419–420.
22. *Outlook*, March 5, 1990, p. 10.
23. *Outlook*, January 2, 1989, p. 34.
24. Ibid., pp. 34–35.
25. These wholesale networks were "underground" because the government issued private book vendors permits to engage in retail, but not wholesale. *LW*, October 10, 1988, p. 28.
26. *Outlook*, August 7, 1989, pp. 34–35. *PD*, November 14, 1988, p. 4. *LW*, October 10, 1988, p. 28.
27. *PD*, November 6, 1992, p. 3.
28. *CD*, March 24, 1992, p. 4.
29. "Ministry of Finance's Document on the Interim Regulations on Self-Responsibility," pp. 1–2.
30. *CD*, March 24, 1992, p. 4.
31. *Outlook*, November 4, 1985, pp. 41–42; *New Observer* (1989), no. 2, pp. 21–23.
32. *Outlook*, November 4, 1985, p. 41.
33. *Outlook*, October 14, 1985, p. 31.
34. *Outlook*, July 11, 1989, pp. 5–7; August 14, 1989, pp. 8–9; *PD*, July 14, 1989, p. 4; *LW*, October 10, 1988, p. 28.
35. *WJ*, December 26, 1991, p. 11.
36. For example, *Qinggong Daobao (Light Industry Herald)* of Anhui had its li-

cense revoked in early 1993 when the government found that it had sold the license to a private firm that turned the paper into a tabloid devoted to violence and sex. Even *Jiangxi Ribao*, the organ of the Party in Jiangxi Province, sold the editorial rights of its weekend edition to a private book vendor, who filled it with racy stories and pornographic materials. *WJ*, May 15, 1993, A19.

37. *PD*, October 30, 1991, p. 4.
38. *Chinese Press Almanac, 1986*, pp. 127–128.
39. Ibid., pp. 121–126.
40. Data calculated from *Chinese Press Almanac*, various years.
41. *NF* (February 1989), pp. 8–9.
42. *NF* (January 1985), pp. 12–13.
43. *Chinese Press Almanac, 1988*, pp. 35–36; *NF* (October 1988), p. 25.
44. *Chinese Press Almanac, 1986*, pp. 121–126.
45. *New Observer* (1989), no. 2, pp. 21–23.
46. *WJ*, January 29, 1993, p. 16.
47. *WJ*, September 18, 1992, p. 16.
48. *WJ*, May 15, 1993, A19; *WJ*, September 18, 1992, p. 16.
49. *Outlook*, July 4, 1988, pp. 12–13; *New Observer* (May 1989), pp. 22–23; *LW*, August 21, 1989, pp. 31–32.
50. *NF* (December 1989), p. 8.
51. *LW*, December 16, 1991, p. 31.
52. *Outlook*, October 3, 1988, pp. 34–35; *Outlook*, March 20, 1989, pp. 35–36.
53. *WJ*, November 12, 1992, p. 16.
54. *CTW*, no. 66, April 4, 1993, pp. 77–79; *CTW*, no. 70, May 2, 1993, pp. 76–77; *WJ*, February 1, 1993, p. 15.
55. *ZGTJNJ*, 1991, p. 759.
56. *CTW*, no. 64, March 21, 1993, pp. 74–76.
57. *ZGTJNJ*, 1991, p. 634.
58. *Outlook*, August 28, 1989, p. 10.
59. "Detailed Rules concerning Foreign Enterprises," clause no. 88 in article 13, reprinted in *WJ*, December 20, 1990, p. 11. This rule ceased to be effective in early 1993, when a Hong Kong company became the first outside investor to form a joint venture in a Chengdu cable television system.
60. The Shanghai Municipal Statistics Bureau, *Shanghai Statistical Yearbook, 1989* (Beijing: The Chinese Statistical Publishing House, 1989), p. 402.
61. *Beijing Social and Economic Statistical Yearbook, 1990* (Beijing: The Chinese Statistical Publishing House, 1990), p. 602.
62. *PD*, June 12, 1992, p. 3; *Chinese Translators' Journal*, no. 1 (January 1989), pp. 2–3; *PD*, November 18, 1991, p. 4.
63. *Outlook*, September 29, 1988, p. 11.
64. *Outlook*, March 21, 1988, p. 14; *Outlook*, April 4, 1988, p. 32.
65. Yang Huiru et al., "The Impact of Western Intellectual Thinking on College Students Today," *Zhengming*, no. 1 (1991), pp. 77–79.
66. *WJ*, February 13, 1992, p. 11.
67. *WJ*, January 4, 1992, p. 11; *CD*, February 3, 1993, p. 2.
68. *LW*, August 28, 1989, pp. 32–33; *CD*, November 26, 1991, p. 4.
69. *WJ*, February 8, 1993, p. 32.

70. *Outlook,* August 28, 1989, pp. 10–11; *PD,* April 24, 1991, p. 4.
71. *WJ,* September 30, 1990, p. 11.
72. *CTW,* no. 50, December 13, 1992, p. 28; *CTW,* no. 52, December 27, 1992, pp. 66–67.
73. *WSJ,* May 10, 1993, A1; *NYT,* April 11, 1993, p. 12; *CTW,* no. 52, December 27, 1992, p. 67.
74. *CTW,* no. 52, December 27, 1992, p. 67.
75. Larry Diamond, "Beyond Authoritarianism and Totalitarianism: Strategies for Democratization," in *The New Democracies,* ed. Brad Roberts (Cambridge, Mass.: MIT Press, 1990), p. 242.
76. For a classic study of the impact of modernization on communist regimes' ability to control their societies, see Mark Field, ed., *Social Consequences of Modernization in Communist Societies* (Baltimore: Johns Hopkins University Press, 1976).
77. *WJ,* November 22, 1991, p. 11; *CD,* December 5, 1991, p. 2.
78. *ZGTJNJ, 1990,* p. 321.
79. *WJ,* May 5, 1993, A19.
80. In 1980, the percentage of people with radio receivers was 49 in the Soviet Union, 25 in Hungary, and 14 in Romania; the percentage of people with television receivers was 30 in the Soviet Union, 22 in Poland, and 18 in Bulgaria. George Schopflin, ed., *The Soviet Union and Eastern Europe* (New York: Facts on File Publications, 1986), p. 167.
81. *WJ,* February 27, 1993, p. 16.
82. *CTW,* no. 69, April 25, 1993, pp. 22–23.
83. *CTW,* no. 52, December 27, 1992, pp. 24–25.
84. *PD,* April 15, 1993, p. 3; *WJ,* November 12, 1992, p. 16; *WJ,* December 13, 1992, p. 14.
85. According to Liu Binyan, many former Rightists returned to *Zhongguo Qingnianbao* and transformed the paper into a proreform forum. Interview with Liu, November 1990.
86. *Chinese Press Almanac, 1986,* p. 89; *WEH,* February 27, 1989, p. 3.
87. *WEH,* February 27, 1989, p. 2.
88. *NF* (December 1989), p. 8.
89. The State Press and Publications Administration and the Research Office of the General Office of the Central Committee of the CCP, eds., *Saohuang Xinbian* (Beijing: Falu Publishing House, 1990).
90. *WJ,* September 21, 1991, p. 2.
91. *PD,* October 30, 1991, p. 4; *WJ,* December 19, 1991, p. 11.
92. *WJ,* January 28, 1993, p. 15.
93. *WJ,* November 12, 1991, p. 2.
94. *WJ,* October 16, 1991, p. 11.
95. *WJ,* August 1, 1991, p. 11.

6. The Liberal Takeover of the Soviet Mass Media under *Glasnost*

1. *Krasnaya zvezda,* February 14, 1987, quoted in Natalie Gross, "*Glasnost:* Roots and Practice," *Problems of Communism* (November–December 1987), p. 73.

2. Ritta Pittman, "Perestroika and Soviet Cultural Politics: The Case of Major Literary Journals," *Soviet Studies*, vol. 42, no. 1 (January 1990), pp. 111–132; Julia Wishnevsky, "Aleskandr Yakovlev and the Cultural 'Thaw,'" *RL/RUSSR*, vol. 31, no. 6, February 11, 1987.

3. Interview with V. Korotich, in *Le Monde*, November 4, 1987, *FBIS-SOV*, November 10, 1987, p. 71.

4. John Dunlop, "Soviet Cultural Politics," *Problems of Communism*, vol. 36, no. 6 (November–December 1987), pp. 36–39.

5. *Moscow Domestic Service*, May 4, 1990, *FBIS-SOV*, May 7, 1990, p. 53.

6. *Le Monde*, November 4, 1987, *FBIS-SOV*, November 10, 1987, p. 71; Hedrick Smith, *The New Russians* (New York: Random House, 1990), p. 105.

7. Smith, *The New Russians*, p. 103.

8. *Izvestia TsK KPSS*, no. 2 (1989), quoted in Viktor Yasmann, "*Glasnost* versus Freedom of Information: Political and Ideological Aspects," *RL/RUSSR*, vol. 1, no. 29, July 21, 1989, p. 2.

9. *Pravda*, January 4, 1987, *CDSP*, no. 1, February 4, 1987, pp. 1–3; Viktor Yasmann, "Drafting a Press Law: *Glasnost* as an Alternative," *RL/RUSSR*, vol. 31, no. 2, January 14, 1987, pp. 1–2.

10. *Kyodo*, April 4, 1986, *FBIS-SOV*, April 7, 1986, R2.

11. *MN*, no. 9, March 6–13, 1988, p. 9.

12. *Sovetskaya kultura*, March 22, 1988, *FBIS-SOV*, March 24, 1988, pp. 54–55.

13. *Pravda*, July 15, 1987, quoted in Natalie Gross, "*Glasnost*: Roots and Practice," p. 74.

14. For an excellent study on the political participation by the intelligentsia in the prereform Soviet Union, see Donna Bahry and Brian Silver, "Soviet Citizen Participation on the Eve of Democratization," *American Political Science Review*, vol. 84, no. 3 (September 1990), pp. 821–847.

15. Smith, *The New Russians*, p. 102.

16. These included the literary critics Nataliya Il'ina, Benedickt Sarnov, and Stanislav Rassadin. Julia Wishnevsky, *A Guide to Some Major Soviet Journals*, *RL/RUSSR*, supplement no. 2 (1988), pp. 4–5.

17. Wishnevsky, "Alexander Yakovlev and the Cultural 'Thaw,'" p. 2.

18. Quoted in Vera Tolz, "*Glasnost* and the Rewriting of Soviet History," *RL/RUSSR*, vol. 31, no. 21, May 27, 1987, p. 2.

19. Gorbachev eventually toned down the speech; Stalin was described as having made an "indisputable contribution to the struggle for socialism, to the defense of its gains, as well as [being responsible for] the gross political mistakes and the abuses committed by him and his circle." David Remnick, "Dead Souls," *New York Review of Books*, December 19, 1991, p. 73.

20. *Glasnost*, no. 7, February 14, 1991, *FBIS-SOV*, March 8, 1991, p. 56.

21. *FBIS-SOV*, July 7, 1988, p. 66.

22. *AFP*, March 23, 1987, *FBIS-SOV*, April 2, 1987, R15; Pittman, "Perestroika and Soviet Cultural Politics," pp. 111–132.

23. *Tanjug* (Belgrade), November 30, 1987, *FBIS-SOV*, December 2, 1987, p. 73.

24. *AFP*, August 14, 1987, *FBIS-SOV*, August 17, 1987, R5–6; *Pravda*, August 26, 1989, *FBIS-SOV*, August 31, 1989, pp. 64–66.

25. *MN*, no. 18, May 13–20, 1990, p. 11.

26. *MN*, no. 38, September 24–October 1, 1989, p. 8.

27. Vera Tolz, "Alternative Press in the USSR," *RL/RUSSR*, vol. 3, no. 21, May 24, 1991, pp. 7–8; Tolz, "Recent Developments in the Soviet and Baltic Media," *RL/RUSSR*, vol. 3, no. 23, June 7, 1991, p. 15.

28. *Pravda*, August 26, 1989, *FBIS-SOV*, August 31, 1989, pp. 64–65.

29. TASS, May 3, 1991, *FBIS-SOV*, May 6, 1991, p. 17.

30. Julia Wishnevsky, "A Rare Insight into Soviet Censorship," *RL/RUSSR*, vol. 2, no. 36, September 7, 1990, pp. 5–6. For a sample of letters-to-the-editor, see Christopher Cerf, Marina Albee, and Lev Gushchin, eds., *Small Fires: Letters from the Soviet People to Ogonyok Magazine, 1987–1990* (New York: Summit Books, 1990).

31. John Newhouse, "Chronicling the Chaos," *New Yorker*, December 31, 1990, p. 38.

32. Interview with Studs Terkel, *Nation*, July 30, 1990, p. 132.

33. *Le Monde*, July 11, 1989, *FBIS-SOV*, July 31, 1989, p. 97.

34. Julia Wishnevsky, "Korotich under Fire," *RL/RUSSR*, vol. 1, no. 5, February 3, 1989.

35. Quoted in Newhouse, "Chronicling the Chaos," p. 39.

36. Ibid.

37. *MN*, no. 48, November 27, 1988, p. 15.

38. *Commersant*, January 21, 1991, p. 1; Vera Tolz, "Soviet Central Media Coverage of Events in the Baltic Republics," *RL/RUSSR*, vol. 3, no. 5, February 1, 1991, pp. 8–9.

39. Dzintra Bugns, "People's Front of Latvia: The First Year," *RL/RUSSR*, vol. 1, no. 41, October 1, 1989, p. 25.

40. *Soyuz*, no. 48 (1990), p. 15, *FBIS-SOV*, December 10, 1990, p. 53.

41. For a brief summary of the changes that occurred during this phase in the Soviet film industry, see Richard Stites, *Russian Popular Culture: Entertainment and Society since 1900* (Cambridge: Cambridge University Press, 1992), pp. 184–192.

42. Julia Wishnevsky, "The Purge of 'TSN': A Ban on Information," *RL/RUSSR*, vol. 3, no. 4, April 5, 1991, p. 6; Smith, *The New Russians*, pp. 165–173.

43. Wishnevsky, "The Purge of 'TSN,'" pp. 5–9; *Govorit i pokazyvayet moskva*, April 10, 1985, *FBIS-SOV*, April 15, 1985, R3.

44. Wishnevsky, "The Purge of 'TSN,'" p. 6.

45. Smith, *The New Russians*, pp. 148–165.

46. Ibid., p. 161.

47. Tolz, "Alternative Press in the USSR," p. 9.

48. Julia Wishnevsky, "Censorship in These Days of *Glasnost*," *RL/RUSSR*, vol. 32, no. 46, November 16, 1988, p. 2.

49. Wishnevsky, "A Rare Insight into Soviet Censorship," p. 6.

50. Wishnevsky, "Censorship in These Days of *Glasnost*," pp. 4–5.

51. Vera Tolz, "New Restrictions on Activities of Soviet Journalists," *RL/RUSSR*, vol. 1, no. 12, March 24, 1989, p. 11.

52. Viktor Yasmann, "Drafting a Press Law," p. 2.

53. Viktor Yasmann, "Soviet Jurists Discuss Draft Press Law," *RL/RUSSR*, vol. 31, no. 23, June 10, 1987, pp. 1–6.

54. Quoted in Newhouse, "Chronicling the Chaos," p. 47.

55. Vera Tolz, "Controversy over Draft Law on the Press," *RL/RUSSR,* vol. 32, no. 51, December 21, 1988, pp. 1–7.
56. Julia Wishnevsky, "*Pravda* Editor in Trouble?" *RL/RUSSR,* vol. 1, no. 42, October 20, 1989, pp. 5–8.
57. Vera Tolz, "Adoption of the Press Law: A New Situation for the Soviet Media?" *RL/RUSSR,* vol. 1, no. 42, July 6, 1990, pp. 9–11.
58. *Commersant,* February 11, 1991, p. 12.
59. TASS, September 28, 1990, *FBIS-SOV,* October 2, 1990, p. 42.
60. Moscow Central Television, January 13, 1991; *Komsomolskaya Pravda,* January 12, 1991; AFP, January 12, 1991, *FBIS-SOV,* January 14, 1991, pp. 28–29. Yeltsin was said to have provided Interfax with office space and equipment. Vera Tolz, "Recent Attempt to Curb *Glasnost,*" *RL/RUSSR,* vol. 3, no. 9, March 1, 1991, note 13.
61. *Pravda,* June 5, 1990, *FBIS-SOV,* June 13, 1990, pp. 102–103.
62. *Sovetskaya litva,* February 18, 1990, *FBIS-SOV,* April 12, 1990, p. 95.
63. *Moscow Domestic Service,* May 10, 1990, *FBIS-SOV,* May 11, 1990, p. 63.
64. *Pravda,* May 5, 1991, *FBIS-SOV,* May 9, 1991, p. 20.
65. *Trud,* January 14, 1992, *CDSP,* vol. 44, no. 4, February 26, 1992, p. 13.
66. *Rabochaya tribuna,* January 31, 1991, *FBIS-SOV,* February 15, 1991, p. 50.
67. Tolz, "Recent Developments in the Soviet and Baltic Media," p. 14.
68. *MN,* no. 4, January 27–February 3, 1991, p. 6.
69. *Commersant,* February 18, 1991, p. 12.
70. John Tedstrom, "New Regulations for Soviet Cooperatives," *RL/RUSSR,* vol. 1, no. 5, February 3, 1989, pp. 31–32. Viktor Yasmann, "Independent Radio and Television in the Soviet Union," *RL/RUSSR,* vol. 1, no. 51, December 22, 1989, p. 7.
71. *Izvestia,* March 18, 1990, *CDSP,* vol. 42, no. 12, April 25, 1990, p. 34; TASS, February 8, 1989, *FBIS-SOV,* February 9, 1989, p. 80. The figure for the total number of books printed in the USSR annually, given by *Izvestia,* was about 300 million copies; this figure appeared to be too low. The TASS figure was 2 billion copies (including pamphlets), which appeared to be more accurate.
72. Tolz, "Recent Attempts to Curb *Glasnost,*" pp. 1–2.
73. Yasmann, "Independent Radio and Television in the Soviet Union," p. 7.
74. Tolz, "Recent Attempts to Curb *Glasnost,*" pp. 2–3.
75. TASS, September 14, 1990, *FBIS-SOV,* September 20, 1990, p. 61.
76. Tolz, "Recent Developments in the Soviet and Baltic Media," p. 16.
77. Quoted in Newhouse, "Chronicling the Chaos," p. 48.
78. *Izvestia,* July 20, 1990, *FBIS-SOV,* June 27, 1990, p. 71.
79. *Trud,* June 9, 1990, *FBIS-SOV,* June 27, 1989, p. 63.
80. *Izvestia,* May 21, 1990; *Literaturnaya gazeta,* no. 20, May 16, 1990, *CDSP,* vol. 42, no. 20, June 20, 1990, p. 31.
81. *MN,* no. 30 (1990), p. 6.
82. Pavel Astakhov, "The Independent Press," *Business in the USSR* (February 1991), p. 99.
83. *Commersant,* January 28, 1991, p. 7.
84. Tolz, "Alternative Press in the USSR," *RL/RUSSR,* vol. 3, no. 21, May 24, 1991, p. 10.

85. Ibid.
86. *MN*, no. 31, August 4–11, 1991, p. 5.
87. *MN*, no. 48, December 9–16, 1990, p. 1. *Moscow News* itself was an exception, with its 1991 circulation estimated at 5 million.
88. *NYT*, February 20, 1992, A6.
89. Interview with P. K. Luchinsky, *Pravda*, May 5, 1991, *FBIS-SOV*, May 9, 1991, p. 20.
90. Tolz, "Recent Developments in the Soviet and Baltic Media," p. 15.
91. *Trud*, January 14, 1992, *CDSP*, vol. 44, no. 4, February 26, 1992, p. 13.
92. For an eyewitness account of the anticoup efforts by the Soviet journalists, see Iain Elliot, "Three Days in August: On-the-Spot Impressions," *RL/RUSSR*, vol. 3, no. 36, September 6, 1991, pp. 63–67.
93. Elliot, "Three Days in August: On-the-Spot Impressions."
94. *World Press Review* (October 1991), p. 32.
95. *WSJ*, March 9, 1992, A6.
96. *Moskovskie novosti*, January 24, 1993, *CDSP*, vol. 45, no. 3, February 17, 1993, p. 31.
97. *MN*, no. 47, November 24–December 1, 1991, p. 3.
98. *NYT*, January 26, 1993, A6; *Commersant*, December 2, 1991, p. 2; *Moskovskie novosti*, January 24, 1993, *CDSP*, vol. 65, no. 3, February 17, 1993, p. 31.
99. *NYT*, March 22, 1992, p. 6.
100. *Kuranty*, April 14, 1992, *CDSP*, vol. 44, no. 15, May 13, 1992, p. 12.
101. *Trud*, January 14, 1992, *CDSP*, vol. 44, no. 4, February 26, 1992, p. 13.
102. *Commersant*, March 9, 1992, p. 6; *NYT*, January 26, 1993, A6.
103. For an excellent summary of the changes in the mass media after the collapse of communist rule in Eastern Europe and the former Soviet Union, see a special issue on the topic from *RFE/RL/RR*, vol. 1, no. 39, October 2, 1992.
104. *WSJ*, March 9, 1992, A6.
105. Ibid.
106. *Rossiskaya gazeta*, February 22, 1992, reprinted in *CDSP*, vol. 64, no. 7, March 18, 1992, p. 9.
107. *Izvestia*, March 20, 1992, *CDSP*, vol. 44, no. 12, April 22, 1992, p. 9.
108. *NYT*, January 26, 1993, A6.
109. *Nezavisimaya gazeta*, February 22, 1992, *CDSP*, vol. 44, no. 8, March 25, 1992, p. 26.
110. *Megapolis-Express*, March 25, 1992, *CDSP*, vol. 44, no. 12, April 22, 1992, p. 10.
111. *MN*, no. 46, November 17–24, 1991, p. 2.
112. Vera Tolz, "The Plight of the Russian Media," *RFE/RL/RR*, vol. 1, no. 9, February 28, 1992, pp. 55–56.
113. Itar-Tass, November 24, 1992, *FBIS-SOV*, November 25, 1992, p. 14.
114. Julia Wishnevsky, "Media Still Far from Free," *RFE/RL/RR*, vol. 2, no. 20, May 14, 1993, pp. 89–90.
115. *Rossiskaya gazeta*, December 30, 1992, *FBIS-SOV*, December 30, 1992, p. 21; Wishnevsky, "Media Still Far from Free," p. 88.
116. Wishnevsky, "Media Still Far from Free," p. 88.

117. *WSJ*, March 29, 1993, A8.
118. Mark Rhodes, "Roundup: How Russians View Their Media," *RFE/RL/RR*, vol. 1, no. 31, July 31, 1992, p. 71.
119. Mark Rhodes, "Declining Influence of the Russian Media," *RFE/RL/RR*, vol. 2, no. 17, April 23, 1993, pp. 50–51.
120. *Sovetskaya rossiya*, August 11, 1988, *FBIS-SOV*, August 16, 1988, p. 61.

Conclusion

1. Samuel Huntington and Joan Nelson identified similar options for reformers in developing countries. See Huntington and Nelson, *No Easy Choice: Political Participation in Developing Countries* (Cambridge, Mass.: Harvard University Press, 1976), p. 33.
2. *RFE/RL/RR*, vol. 2, no. 24, June 11, 1993, p. 54; *Washington Post*, December 13, 1993, A16.
3. See transcripts of Yeltsin's press conference during his visit to Beijing in December 1992, Interfax, December 21, 1992, *FBIS-SOV*, December 22, 1992, p. 6; Jim Rohwer, "The Titan Stirs," *Economist*, November 28, 1992, pp. 1–18.

Acknowledgments

In writing *From Reform to Revolution* I have accumulated debts to many people. I am most grateful to my dissertation committee at Harvard University: Roderick MacFarquhar, Samuel P. Huntington, and Jorge Dominguez provided invaluable intellectual inspiration and guidance during 1990–1991, when the first draft of the book was written. The intellectual influence of Samuel Huntington was especially strong in shaping many of the theoretical arguments of the book.

Edwin Winkler, Lynn White III, Juliet Johnson, and Ezra Vogel also offered helpful comments on earlier drafts of some of the chapters. My dear friend for many years, Matthew Grace, helped polish Chapters 3–5 and taught me how to write better prose. Iraida Alvarez provided indispensable research assistance during 1992–1993 at Princeton University.

I am also grateful for the support given by Davidson College in the summer of 1992, when I undertook the first major revision of the study. I especially wish to thank Dean Robert Williams for his encouragement.

I am thankful to Aida Donald and Elizabeth Suttell of Harvard University Press for their assistance, and to Christine Thorsteinsson for her editorial help.

Part of Chapter 2 contains materials previously published in "Societal Takeover in China and the USSR," *Journal of Democracy,* vol. 3, no. 1 (1992); I wish to thank the Johns Hopkins University Press for permission to use the materials.

The greatest debt I have incurred is to my wife, Meizhou Wang. This book could not have been written without her enormous support and personal sacrifice.